THE
GOLDEN ASS
OF APULEIUS

A C. G. JUNG FOUNDATION BOOK

The C. G. Jung Foundation for Analytical Psychology is dedicated to helping men and women grow in conscious awareness of the psychological realities in themselves and society, find healing and meaning in their lives and greater depth in their relationships, and live in response to their discovered sense of purpose. It welcomes the public to attend its lectures, seminars, films, symposia, and workshops and offers a wide selection of books for sale through its bookstore. The Foundation also publishes *Quadrant,* a semiannual journal, and books on Analytical Psychology and related subjects. For information about Foundation programs or membership,
please write to the C. G. Jung Foundation,
28 East 39th Street, New York, NY 10016.

The
Golden Ass
of Apuleius

THE LIBERATION OF
THE FEMININE
IN MAN

MARIE-LOUISE
VON FRANZ

Revised Edition

SHAMBHALA
Boston & London
1992

SHAMBHALA PUBLICATIONS, INC.
Horticultural Hall
300 Massachusetts Avenue
Boston, Massachusetts 02115
www.shambhala.com

Printed in the United States of America

Distributed in the United States by Random House, Inc.,
and in Canada by Random House of Canada Ltd

LIBRARY OF CONGRESS CATALOGING-IN-PUBLICATION DATA

Franz, Marie-Louise von, 1915–
    The golden ass of Apuleius: the liberation of the feminine in man /
    Marie-Louise von Franz.—Rev. ed.
        p.   cm.
    "A C. G. Jung Foundation book."
    ISBN 1-57062-611-1
    1. Apuleius. Metamorphoses.   2. Apuleius—Knowledge—Psychology.
    3. Femininity (Psychology) in literature.   4. Archetype (Psychology) in
    literature.   5. Metamorphosis in literature.   6. Sex role in literature.
    7. Men in literature.   I. Title.
    PA6217.F7   1990   89-43309
    873'.01—dc20   CIP
    BVG 01

CONTENTS

PREFACE TO THE
REVISED EDITION

This book is neither a historical nor a literary essay. It represents an attempt to elucidate and illustrate the problem of what C. G. Jung called the anima: that is, the feminine aspect of a man's psyche. The book originated in a series of lectures I gave at the C. G. Jung Institute in Zurich in 1966. Instead of using case material, I chose this novel of an ancient author because it illustrated the anima problem in all its depth and in a way which is still valid for modern man.

The text of this book has almost suffered the fate of Lucius, the hero of Apuleius's story. In the various former editions, well-meaning editors improved on the style so much that the meaning that I wanted to express got more and more obfuscated and even partly distorted. In this revised edition I have tried to restore the original text and enlarge it with some new passages. I want to express my thanks to Dr. Manolis Kennedy for having translated the additions made in the German edition and also to Miss Deirdre Bischofberger for the difficult typing. My greatest gratitude, however, goes to Dr. Vivienne Mackrell, without whose daily support and valued suggestions I could not have fulfilled my work.

THE
GOLDEN ASS
OF APULEIUS

INTRODUCTION

This celebrated novel by Apuleius of Madaura[1] has always been the object of contradictory evaluations. There are, we think, many different reasons for this: some are inherent in the composition and the sources of the work itself, while others come from the personality of the author.

This Latin text from the second century A.D. has baffled commentators, for it seems to have been written according to two plans. It tells one main story, that of Lucius and his transformations, interspersed with a number of tales which, from a purely rational and superficial point of view, do not appear to have much in common with the adventures of the hero. What we know of the novel's background explains and confirms this impression of duality, for it is not an entirely personal creation. The author was inspired by a lost text attributed to Lucius of Patrai, and the text itself was taken from a destroyed original Greek text that had also served as a model for *The Ass,* a novel written by a pseudo-Lucian. There was thus a collection of novels by various authors which later disappeared and which are thought to have been in the style of Boccaccio's *Decameron* or Chaucer's *Canterbury Tales.* All these earlier collections contained neither the tale of Amor and Psyche nor the initiation into the Isis mysteries that are so important in Apuleius's book.[2] Apuleius has not only added two significant passages but has probably also transformed, at least partially, the original stories to adapt them to their new context. In spite of using many older stories, Apuleius has actually created a completely new book with a completely new inner message.

From a literary standpoint, one will notice that the work is complicated by its affected style and its many plays on words. Knowing nothing of its cultural background, one would think its language to be that of a neurotic, but it simply corresponds to the so-called Milesian style, which Apuleius probably acquired in the course of his studies.[3] In its content the book shows certain Don Quixotish characteristics, with an admixture of occultism. The composition has often been criticized, since the author, instead of taking the trouble to introduce an incidental story logically, generally is content with something like, "This reminds me of a juicy story. . . ." This sort of loose composition gives one the impression of a certain *abaissement du niveau mental*.[4] It is possible that Apuleius, being a successful writer and lecturer, composed the novel in great haste and that his unconscious had therefore a hand in composing the story, in other words, that he followed a train of associations, a chain of creative fantasies whose meaning goes much deeper than even he himself knew.[5] This seems to me to explain in part the conscious-unconscious duality of the composition.

This novel, as I have said, has had a considerable amount of commentary, ranging from extreme admiration to complete scorn. According to some authors, Apuleius does little more than compile a poor collection of anecdotes, already known for the most part, while the whole of the work seems to be no more than satire or frivolous amusement. It is to his credit that Karl Kerényi, who dedicated the major part of his study to the story of Amor and Psyche,[6] recognized its value and religious depth. After Kerényi, Reinhold Merkelbach realized for the first time that the book as a whole has a deep religious meaning which increasingly reveals itself toward the end.[7] Merkelbach, however, did not analyze the book in its entirety. One needs the key of Jungian psychology and knowledge of the unconscious in order to follow the inner process of psychic development which the author describes in his book. It then reveals itself to be a completely coherent whole.

In some older translations, a good number of the work's erotic anecdotes are omitted. Some modern versions, on the other hand, have preserved the sexual passages but have suppressed the initiation mysteries, considering them to be a useless addition that does not correspond to the spirit of the rest of the work. Erudite authors have even attempted to prove that the last book, the eleventh, the initiation into the Isis mysteries, had been added perhaps by another author or by Apuleius himself in a later part of his life.[8]

There we touch on the most difficult problem of the proximity of sexual passion and its accompanying spiritual, religious experience. On the one hand, many differentiated religions stress the contrast of sexuality and spirituality, as the existence of many ascetic and monastic institutions proves. On the other hand, however, the orgiastic character of numerous religious rituals proves that the deepest root of sexuality and religious ecstasy seems to be one. It is also well known that many Christian saints lived a riotous life before their conversion. Apuleius's work contains both poles of these opposites and sheds new light on this fundamental problem.[9]

Another source of difficulty which troubles most commentators is that, ignoring the psychology of the unconscious, they suppose that Apuleius consciously introduced all the symbolic allusions present in the novel. This, as I said earlier, does not seem probable. I am convinced that Apuleius intentionally slipped in many symbolic ideas, but that others flowed unconsciously from his pen. Where Apuleius consciously placed certain symbolic motifs in his story, one could be justified in treating them allegorically, in the Platonic sense of the term: as a profound philosophical significance hidden beneath the symbolic image.[10] In support of this thesis, Merkelbach remarked that Apuleius attributed significant names to almost all of his characters. Similarly, it was certainly by design that he chose to transform Lucius into an ass, for Seth, the enemy of Isis and Osiris, was frequently represented in this animal form. To live the life of an ass thus signifies, as Merkelbach emphasizes, enduring "a life without Isis." But from the fact that certain symbolic elements have been consciously introduced in his story, one need not deduce that Apuleius wrote this novel without the inspiration of the unconscious. The contribution of the unconscious to this work is all the more probable since we know that he experienced a profound religious conversion. As the word indicates, conversion signifies a sudden and radical change of personality, as was the case with Saint Paul and Saint Augustine.[11] Such changes are abrupt only in appearance, and thanks to depth psychology, we can watch their preparation in the unconscious. It is a common occurrence in analytical practice to see the appearance in dreams of symbolic themes tending toward a psychic development often not realized for several months, or even years. In certain cases of neurotic psychic dissociation, it is common for a subject to lead two lives: the one conscious, on the surface, and another which is secretly developed on a deeper unconscious level. Conversion corresponds to the moment at which the two unite.

Jung thought very highly of *The Golden Ass* and several times suggested that I look at it more closely. I must say that at first I did not know how to approach it. I understood from the outset that all parts of the book were absolutely essential and inseparable and that, thanks to the key of Jungian psychology, a coherent interpretation was possible. But somehow I did not know how to get at it, until at last I discovered a very simple trick—though perhaps it is a bit more than a trick. I took a pencil to try to find out the composition of the book. I first wrote out what the hero, Lucius, experienced in the "I" form, that is, his experience of being changed into an ass and all his unfortunate adventures until he is redeemed. I cut out the inserted stories for the moment so as to get one coherent line. Then I made the following discovery: one can make a dividing line, and above the line write all of the story that happened to Lucius, and below the line all the inserted tales. Between these two classifications I drew a zigzag line, the actual thread of the story. In this way I discovered a consecutive

Adventures of Lucius—the Ass

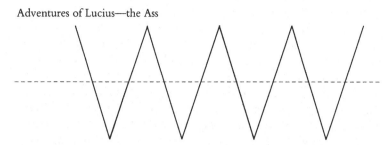

Inserted stories and descriptions

line going through as well. Above the line is the story of Lucius as the ass, but underneath something else is happening, as shown in the diagram.

I made a second conjecture and asked myself why one should not treat the inserted stories like dreams of Lucius. We have a day life, with all sorts of fortune and misfortune, and at night we are told a story; the problem is to see how the two connect. So why should one not treat the stories here as if they were dreams within the story?

From the point of view of personal psychology, Lucius is that type of man who suffers from a negative mother complex,[12] but to a certain degree, the positive aspect of the complex also appears in the story, because the opposites are always together. Apuleius himself had a positive relationship with his mother. We know, in fact, that in real life he married a woman about twenty years his elder, with whom he lived happily until his death, while the novel throughout expresses the other face of the problem: the dark side of the mother complex.

As Jung has shown, the mother sometimes symbolizes, on a deeper level, the entire unconscious of man. When she thus appears at the end of the novel in the archetypal form of the great mother goddess Isis, she is the personification of an interior cosmos that surpasses the limits of the conscious personality: the world that Jung has called "the reality of psyche." We will see that on this deeper level Apuleius gives form to a deep process of evolution of historical dimension:

the coming back of the feminine principle into the patriarchal Western world. This slow comeback of the feminine principle[13] intermittently surfaced in the Middle Ages, but it is only today that it seems to have broken through into the collective consciousness. Courtly love provided an opportunity, and there it broke through partly, and with it the symbolism of the Grail, but it all came as a tremendous problem. For these chevaliers were not capable of having only courtly, platonic love for their ladies, just letting themselves be killed, or half-killed, in tournaments, and then getting only a little rose emblem on their heads as a reward. Normally they asked for, and usually got, the whole reward. At that time, however, there were no contraceptives, and as this was happening in aristocratic families there was the tremendous problem of the bastard. That created an impossible sociological situation, and the Church saw its chance, condemned sexual courtly love, and urged the worship of the Virgin Mary. So more and more of the chevaliers adopted the Virgin Mary as the *dame du coeur* for whom they fought, because that involved no danger. But, as Jung points out so clearly, at that moment began the witch persecutions! For the anima problem cannot be solved on just an impersonal level; it cannot be solved by a principle. Whatever is decided sociologically, collectively, can only be wrong. If there is a solution it can only be unique, from individual to individual, from one woman to one man. Eros is in its essence only meaningful if it is completely, uniquely individual. In courtly love the move was toward bringing the impossible together through the uniqueness of the personality. But the collective broke in, and the collective needed principles, so there was another failure, which is why we are still in the same soup. If we read it with this in mind, *The Golden Ass* is *the* modern description of the development of a man's anima or feminine unconscious personality. Today there is much discussion of the liberation of women, but it is sometimes overlooked that this can only succeed if there is a change in men as well. Just as women have to overcome the patriarchal tyrant in their own souls, men have to liberate and differentiate their inner femininity. Only then will a better relationship of the sexes be possible.

I
The
Life and
Times of Apuleius

Before we go more closely into the content of *The Golden Ass,* let us bring to mind what we know of the life of the author, Apuleius. Very little is historically established and can be treated as actual fact, while the greater part of the biography, handed down to us, remains legendary.[1] Apuleius was born about A.D. 124/125 in Madaura, a little town which still exists in Algeria, as the son of a highly placed Roman official. From a description of his features, which says that he was blond and had fair skin, one might conjecture that he possibly had some German blood through some invaders of North Africa. He lived in Madaura until the height of his career in the middle of the second century A.D. At the time of his birth, Saint Paul's epistles had already been written, but probably not all of the gospels. Christianity was known to him just as one of the many queer local sects which existed in so many variations in the Roman Empire at that time. He certainly was not touched in any closer way by Christian teaching.[2] On his mother's side he claimed relationship with Plutarch, the great Neoplatonic philosopher, but some say this is a legend, or that he made his claim because he was a great admirer and adherent of Plutarch and of the Neoplatonic school. In one of his philosophical writings he confesses to this, but by that time philosophy was no longer purely Platonic, but a mixture including Pythagorean, Stoic, and other elements. He was a brilliant intellectual and very gifted writer in many fields, and, as was the fashion at that time for the leading intellectual people in the Roman Empire and the style of the Sophists, he endeavored to be great in all fields of knowledge and so wrote on natural science, philosophy, poetry, novels, and drama. He also was a brilliant lawyer. Having such manifold ways of self-expression was the ideal of the intellectual man of that time, and in part it accounts for the tremendous variety of styles which we meet in the story, from the dramatic to the simple and naive, to extreme mannerisms, and from the vulgar to the highest spiritual elation. Probably *The Golden Ass* was written about A.D. 170 in the later part of Apuleius's life.

The only biographical details we have of him are through a famous lawsuit he got into in A.D. 158. By this we learn that he married very late. The only love poems of his which have been preserved are homoerotic love poems addressed to young boys. He probably had, like most Romans at that time, a certain bisexual trend, if he was not in his early youth completely homosexual. On a trip in Oea in Tripoli, Apuleius fell ill when with a friend, Ponticianus, with whom he had studied, and this friend introduced him to a rich widow. At that time if one fell ill on a trip it was not so simple. One could not just go to the nearest doctor or hospital, so Ponticianus dragged him to the house of this rich widow with the name Aemilia Pudentilla, and they fell in love with each other and married. She was about fifty and he probably thirty years old.

This woman had been widowed for fourteen years, and her former husband's father had constantly pestered her to marry a certain other man, but she had remained single for all that time. Then Apuleius turned up and was ill in her house and she nursed him; the romance took place and he married her. That annoyed some members of her family who had planned what was to happen to her fortune after her death. Together with the second son of the first marriage (I am skipping details because we are not sure of their authenticity) these family members worked up an accusation that he had used magic to win the lady. He obviously, as we will see from the story, had a huge mother complex, so to fall for a slightly elderly but still beautiful and rich lady was not entirely unnatural. In the Roman Empire the use of magic entailed capital punishment. So Apuleius was in great danger because the accusation was not all that ungrounded. He was passionately interested in what we would now call parapsychological phenomena, so he could not deny that he was absolutely steeped in and well versed in all the current knowledge on magic. It would not be possible for him to defend himself against those charges very well. We still have his *Apologia*,[3] his court defense, in which he relied more on eloquent, scornful, aggressive attack in defending the purity of his motives in the marriage, and elegantly evaded the most dangerous point of magic. Thanks to his brilliant self-defense, he won his case. That episode gives us a small amount of information as to his private life. He had no children, but it seems to have been a very happy marriage. His wife became his intellectual collaborator, even writing parts of his many speeches and sermons and going around with him, and also lecturing herself. He treated his stepsons, his wife's sons by her first marriage, very generously, and even before his accusation had arranged that they should get the mother's money. This was a major point in his defense, for he could prove in court that without any foreknowledge of a coming accusation, he had never tried to get her fortune into his own hands.

In later times he held several official posts in the Roman religious administration, and for a while was Aesculapius's priest—as *sacerdos provinciae*—in Carthage. These posts were purely administrative at that time. They were well paid but had very little to do with what we, from a Jungian standpoint, would call religion. He was very much admired as a successful lecturer and got many awards. Later he retired once more to Rome and practiced there as a lawyer. His initiation into the cult of Isis, of which he wrote at the end of his life, is also in my view an absolutely authentic bit of autobiography.[4]

When I first read this novel I was put off by the mannerisms, the joking, the irony, the too-flowery style. If we ask ourselves what this kind of writing betrays psychologically, we would have to say that it is the typical language of a split personality. Whenever somebody is split, cut off from his primitive, naive deeper emotions, he lacks the possibility of simple self-expression. It is replaced by all sorts of artificial formulations.

We also have to know that Apuleius was in a situation which we still can observe in modern Europeans. He was a member of a Roman family which settled in North Africa and which in the second generation shows certain typical defects that we now express by saying that those people have "gone native." If people of white civilizations go to such countries, where the primitive modes of life and behavior are better preserved within their natural frame than with us, then the instinctual layer of the personality, and the original primitive impulses, are reinforced. If this is not observed and dealt with consciously, a split personality develops. One can observe this for instance in British people who have lived a long time in Africa. They have a wonderful way of not being disturbed in their own habits, and even when in the bush they will change for the evening into a smoking jacket and *décolleté,* and read home newspapers while surrounded by mosquitoes, snakes, and panthers. But it does not help, for the "native mentality" gets into the white people who go to Africa, and if you visit such families, you will find that they have the style of the white man as far as their way of living is concerned, but that little African traits come in negatively: the crockery is chipped, the curtains are not clean, everything becomes a bit sloppy.

This is really a symptom of something which is deeper, for it indicates a slight *abaissement du niveau mental* and a reinforcement of the primitive layer of the personality. If, on the contrary, the culture of the primitive people was accepted and studied consciously, it would be for the white settler a great enrichment. For the white man who lives in such conditions, it is a task to get again into tune with the primitive man within himself, but he has to do it consciously. This is something which happened also to pure-blood Romans in the second generation after they had invaded North African countries.

Apuleius demonstrated this even more than certain other Romans of the time, because, as we shall see, he had an African unconscious and a Roman consciousness. Lucius's initiation at the end of the book is the positive breakthrough of African spirituality. In a part of himself, Apuleius lived in North Africa, mainly Egypt, which had the highest form of African civilization at the time. In another part of himself, he was an intellectual Roman philosopher. As an African person he would have been able to express his emotions freely, but as a Roman intellectual he could not admit them. As soon as a person does not, or cannot, express strong emotions, he loses his simplicity of self-expression, because emotion is the great simplifier and unifier of expression. This explains Apuleius's flowery style, which gives one the feeling that he is not touched by his subject. Actually he is, but he tries to keep away from it. His attitude is ambivalent, as if he were touched somewhere but then tried consciously to hover ironically above it.

Here one could ask oneself whether there is a parallel between the attitude of a man of the second century A.D. and of a man of today. We do have such analogies, especially marked in papers and articles on parapsychology, magic, and occult matters, where people display just this split attitude of being fascinated or touched somewhere by the irrational, but at the same time—partly to show off their own enlightenment, and partly because they are afraid—acting scornfully superior to the material and implying that of course the writer doesn't believe it!

To my great amazement, I have also met in Europe primitive people who are deeply steeped in magic, believing in it one hundred percent, believing in ghosts and seeing and talking to them, and who also have the same split attitude. In my family we had a maid who came from a very primitive Bavarian peasant family, and who was psychic and could talk to ghosts. Three weeks of the month she talked to ghosts and exorcised them, and did all sorts of things with them. But then, suddenly, she would feel that this was going too far and she would actually say, "You know, ghosts do not exist; that's all junk." The next day she would talk to them again. I was amazed when I discovered this in my childhood, until I learned that the Siberian shamans who have to cope in particular with parapsychological phenomena and have the living experience of such occult matters, and therefore know more of the subject than anyone else, do the same thing among their colleagues. When they meet together they make fun of it all as though it were nothing but trickery and cheating.

There are therefore two reactions: the one of the shaman is fear, because such material is dangerous and uncanny, and there is a kind of effort to push it away so that the ego may be preserved to keep one's head above water; the other attitude is specifically that of the civilized man and is a split reaction of curiosity, attraction, and fascination. It will be shown that Apuleius had the same problem. He was completely fascinated by the occult parapsychological phenomena on the one side, and on the other he had a scornful reaction which we can either interpret as intellectual distance-keeping or as some understandable fear.

If we go deeper into what is happening behind the screen of the time in which Apuleius had the bad luck to be born, we can see that it was an age which in many ways resembled our own. The Roman Empire was outwardly, politically, still at the height of its power, but the original religious impulse, the whole moral setup of the Empire, was already completely decayed.[5] To use drastic language, Apuleius was really born into the decaying corpse of a dying civilization, as far as spiritual values are concerned. Within the decaying form, in the most unexpected corner, the process of renewal had already taken place and somewhere where nobody had ever expected it—Nazareth—and it was already slowly spreading surreptitiously and subterraneanly among the simple people, mainly in the circles of the slaves.

If you want to get an impression of what the cultured layers, the privileged, educated people in the Roman Empire, thought about Christianity at the time, one must read the letter which Pliny wrote to the Emperor Trajanus in A.D. 119, which is the most revealing document that we have of the period.[6] When Pliny became administrator of Bithynia, there was submitted to him anonymously a list of people who allegedly belonged to a sect of Christians accused of being dangerous to the security of the state. He wrote to Trajanus that he had picked the people up and, as Roman citizens could not be tortured, he had tortured two slave women who belonged to the sect. But, he said, he could not get any more out of them than a *prava superstitio* (distorted superstition). These people met on Sundays, a day which they called the Lord's Day. They sang certain songs and said certain prayers together and afterward dined. Because that could be the hatching place of political plotting, he forbade the Sunday dinner parties, but otherwise dismissed this "distorted crazy crowd." The investigation, however, had the desired results, for the meat market improved again. What the cattle dealers and butchers had complained of was that no more animals were being bought for sacrifice, but now the market had recovered!

The words *prava superstitio*—"distorted superstition"—indicate how the educated man of the time felt about this new subterranean movement and shows the principal line of interest among people who were looking seriously for religious consolation. What flourished were the Mithraic, Dionysian, Sarapis, and Isis mysteries, in which people found some inner fulfillment. Yet only a smaller part of the population were initiated in such secret mystery cults. The greater part did not believe anything any longer. They adhered to some kind of nihilistic or rational philosophy, and the religious interests of the lower layers of the population regressed into the original level of magic and superstition, astrology, soothsaying, palmistry, and other archaic connections with the unconscious.

Apuleius first went to school in Carthage and then to Athens where he studied philosophy and rhetoric and became one of Plutarch's adherents. He endeavored to obtain admission to as many mystery cults as possible and through his family background was able to get introductions to them. He was probably initiated into the Eleusinian mysteries; he went to the cave of Trophonius, and later traveled in Asia Minor in search of other mystery cults—probably Mithraic.

Of Apuleius's works, only his *Apologia,* a few philosophical essays, and this novel have been preserved completely.[7] On account of its pornographic episodes, The Golden Ass was the favorite reading of all the poor little monks and novices in monasteries throughout the Middle Ages. They copied it out and got all their forbidden information from it and, owing to this habit, the book was fortunately preserved until today.

In order to come closer to the content of the novel, we must now look briefly at the philosophical ideas of the author, especially insofar as they relate to his theory of the human soul. As a parallel to Plutarch's De Genio Socratis, Apuleius brought out his own ideas under the title De Deo Socratis. In this writing about the daimon of Socrates[8] he develops a highly interesting theory with the following essence: the Olympic gods in whom people were supposed to believe at that time, he says, were too remote to bother about human beings in an emotional way. Zeus occasionally looked down, so to speak, and if things were too bad he sent a thunderbolt, but otherwise the gods did not concern themselves in any emotional way with human affairs. Man could not, therefore, communicate with the Olympic gods about his little sorrows and what one might call his emotions and feelings. Such intermediary traffic was made by the daimones, the demons, in the positive sense of the word. Much later, these daimones were the archetypal models for what in Christianity became the angels. They brought the prayers of human beings up to the Olympic gods, and intervened to and fro as messengers.

In contrast to the Olympic gods, the daimones could be emotionally touched. They could show pity or anger, and were, so to speak, concerned with human affairs and could be influenced. Using magic or prayer one could have a positive or negative impact upon them. But besides that, each individual had his idios daimon—his own specific daimon. I do not say demon, for this evokes negative associations—something which would be wrong in our context, since we are dealing with a later period of time—but rather daimon, the Greek word which Apuleius translates quite adequately in Latin as "genius." From the Jungian point of view, one could say that it is the preconscious form of individuality—a preconscious ego *and* a preconscious self—and the nucleus of the whole personality. In Rome on one's birthday, one brought a sacrifice to his own genius, so that it might bring another good year. The genius made one *genialis*—sparkling with spirit and life. Naturally, the root of the word has also to do with *genus*—sex—so it made a man or a woman sexually potent, capable of functioning, spiritually fertile. It made one witty, put one into a good mood, made one emanate vitality and feel happily alive in all fields—creatively genial. Our specific use of the word *genius* is very restricted. As for women, they are endowed with a feminine psychic nucleus, a *juno* instead of a genius.[9]

If one cultivated his own daimon, the genius-juno, by leading the right kind of life morally and religiously, then, according to Apuleius, one developed it, after death, into the positive figure which he calls a *lar*. The lares, like the Roman penates, are the household gods. In a Roman house the memory of somebody who had died was still worshipped. The son poured out wine for the lares, who inhabited those little statues of household gods generally kept on the hearth, and who also personified the spirit of the dead. They were supposed to increase the fertility of the family and to protect the house from damage by fire or water. They watched over the descendants in a place as protective ancestral spirits. If one neglected one's *idios daimon,* according to Apuleius, one became after death a *larva,* a ghost, an evil spirit. Since they brought possession and illness, these spirits had to be exorcised.

In such beliefs the oldest archetypal ideas of mankind were still preserved. The idea of the ancestral spirit becoming the household spirit is, for instance, found among many African tribes who keep the skulls of their ancestors in the hut as a kind of protective spirit. The idea that one's conduct in life determined whether one became a positive or a negative ghost after death is more particularly Roman, though it exists also with certain primitive tribes. In western Nigeria they have the same ideas but say that the positive or negative behavior of an ancestral ghost depends on whether the person has behaved well according to their standards during life, so that a good man becomes a good ghost and a bad man a bad ghost. But this is complicated by certain taboo problems. For instance, if a cat or some other unclean animal jumps over a good man's corpse before he is buried, the man might also become an evil ghost. According to Apuleius, however, it only depends on the religious and moral conduct of the person as to whether the daimon becomes a lar or a larva. He says that certain outstanding religious personalities such as Socrates and Aesculapius cultivated their inner daimon to such an extent during their lifetime that it became an actual part of them. Socrates, for instance, during his lifetime had such an intimate connection with his greater personality, that part which after his death would remain as his "soul." Outstanding religious personalities developed their daimon to something higher than the average person did. They charged or loaded up the potential of their unconscious greater personality to such an extent that after death their daimon became a kind of collective or local god. Not only did the few descendants pray to that lar in ancestral worship, but many other people prayed or turned to it for help as well, so that lares became protective spirits of whole communities.

There are innumerable parallels to this. Thus, one still sees today in Egypt those beautiful little tombs of the sheiks all over the place. Exceptionally pious men were not buried in the common cemetery, but had little funeral chapels in the desert where others besides their relatives could go to pray. The worship of the lares, as it was practiced in Rome, was also the germ, the beginning of the cult of the "saints" in the Catholic Church, for this has its roots in part in this worship of the postmortal genius of an outstanding religious personality. In the Catholic Church it began with the tombs of the martyrs and later developed into what we now would call the cult of the saint. This did not become part of the dogma until the eleventh and twelfth centuries.

It is important to look more closely at this theory of Apuleius because, apart from few exceptions, it has not been examined seriously until now: in literary works his writings are simply referred to in a cursory way as a repetition of Neoplatonic or Plutarchian ideas. It seems to me that the way he represents it means more than that. To my mind it is not only a creed or theory, but was what he *really* believed in consciousness. If one reads it with the key of psychology, it gives a very meaningful picture. One could say that the daimon represented a man's greater inner Self. Jung describes the "Self" as the conscious and unconscious totality of the psyche—a kind of nucleus or core which centrally regulates the psychic processes, and which is in no way identical with the conscious ego. The Hindus, like some of our Western mystics, have, among other things, sought direct experience with this core and have recognized in it an inner reality; more frequently, however, it was projected onto an outer figure or a protective daimon. At the end of *The Golden Ass,* this daimon or symbol of the Self appears in the form of the god Osiris; before that he has been already embodied through the god Eros. Osiris was for the Egyptians a collective god, but one assumed that he also lived in every individual human being and that he represented the soul which survived after death. According to Plutarch, Osiris is a daimon. In all older civilizations the unconscious is seen as an outer being, whether it is in the form of an invisible spirit which accompanies us or is projected onto a talisman or medicine bag or any other such object. The Gnostics called this spirit a *prosphyes psyche,* an additional soul. However, it is especially in the mystery cults of late antiquity that one began gradually to recognize more and more clearly that one is dealing with an inner element of the individual of a purely psychic, but not subjective, nature. Apuleius was one of the first who experienced this deeply.

2
The Two Companions and the Tale of Aristomenes

At the beginning of the book, the hero, a young man named Lucius, decides to go to Thessaly, from which place his mother's family is said to have come. He is riding a white horse and is going there with the intention of investigating witchcraft, Thessaly being in the whole antique tradition *the* place where the great witches lived and where black magic and occult phenomena took place. On the way he meets two people who are engaged in a heated discussion about a story which Aristomenes, a cheese and honey merchant, is telling. This is the first inserted story, together with the strange events the merchant experiences with his companion, Socrates. Aristomenes' other companion seems a hardboiled rationalist who rejects the superstitious old wives' nonsense Aristomenes is relating. Our hero, Lucius, who joins in the discussion, asks to have the story repeated and takes a third standpoint. Aristomenes believes it, having actually experienced it; the counterpart scoffs at it with rational arguments; and Lucius enjoys it aesthetically just as an amusing story, evading whether it is true or not.

Apuleius has all three aspects of these personalities. He is the primitive man who believes and experiences such things in a naive form, but by philosophical training he is a rationalist and so also says it is all nonsense. Then, for the moment, too, Lucius probably represents more or less his original conscious attitude that whatever it is, it's very enjoyable (which is also a way of keeping out of it a bit).

Lucius has a meaningful name. It comes from the verb *lucere,* "to shine," and from *lux,* "light" (which fits well with Photis, his female friend, whom we meet later and whose name is derived from the Greek word *phos,* which means "light"). Lucius thus represents the principle of consciousness or the possibility of becoming conscious through lived life experience.

We will see, in fact, throughout the story, that names are used in an intentional way. The name *Aristomenes*—the best, the most valiant man—is naturally ironic because the man in the story does not behave at all like a hero. But it is also not by chance that such a very positive name is given to the man who believes in supernatural phenomena. The book is written in the first person and the hero calls himself Lucius,[1] "the light one." And this introduces us to the ticklish problem of the relationship between the hero in the novel and the author. What relationship had Goethe to Faust? Naive people who jump to conclusions assume that the hero represents the author's ego complex, and more or less the author himself: Goethe would then be Faust, his shadow[2] would be Wagner, and Mephisto would be his unrealized Self. That is true in a way, and in a way it is not. The hero of a novel or a story represents only a part of the author's conscious personality. Whatever Goethe was, he was not an abstract scientist lost in academic dust, which is where Faust begins. Thus Faust could represent only a part of Goethe, but not his whole ego. And so it is with Apuleius-Lucius. Lucius probably represents an extraverted youthful aspect of the author's ego, which lets itself get involved in an adventure in search of the truth.

So, in the beginning of the novel, Lucius is on his way to his mother's native land, Thessaly. He is a cheerful, lighthearted young man, normally interested in women, and rather the Don Juan type. He is intellectually curious about magic, but not deeply so. We know that Apuleius was a philosopher, that he wanted to be initiated into religious mysteries, that he had a mother complex, and was an intellectual, spiritual personality. Therefore, Lucius cannot represent his shadow but rather is his young extraverted side, that part in him which looks for life. With our ego we can split off an imaginary part of ourselves. We do it when daydreaming, when we say, for instance, "If I had my holiday now I would go to Greece and Istanbul." You cannot call that your shadow, for you have used a conscious part of your ego to imagine something which you cannot do at the moment. Usually introverts put the extraverted part into such fantasies. An elderly man will imagine all that he would do as a young man. He imagines a personality which personifies certain parts of the ego complex, for the younger man in him wants to throw himself into life. Apuleius has been parked in his mother's lap and stayed there, and his wish for adventure has not been lived, and probably that is what he has put into Lucius. So, filled with the spirit of adventure, riding on the hero's white horse like the sun god, not carried by the chthonic, but by the light forces, Lucius is going to the land of the "mothers." Like Faust, he goes where his mother complex is projected, to where he feels hidden things are taking place. He is fascinated by black magic and the chthonic side of reality which he has ignored until now.

Within the intellectual who cuts himself off from the immediacy of life experience through his intellectual theories, as Apuleius did, there remains a kind of hunch or idea that certain things can only be made conscious through being suffered or lived, and not by intellectual philosophical views alone. Hence, Lucius also represents an aspect of the Self[3] of Apuleius, the most essential nucleus of his personality, which will lead the author to a state of higher consciousness through life experience. He represents a preconscious form of his future ego, everything which for the time being is no more than a fantasy image in him, which he would like to realize. Generally such a figure of imagination expresses a wish, a naive hero fantasy, for almost all of us wish to be more brave and noble than we really are. I would therefore interpret Lucius as this aspect of the writer Apuleius: a model for his ego, which acts in the "right" way in order to acquire a higher state of consciousness and at the same time lives all the things Apuleius would have liked to have lived and never did to such an extent.

Lucius has throughout the story only one main motif: he wants to experience the mysteries of the dark side of the feminine principle, of witchcraft, magic, and ghosts. That this is his main purpose shows that Apuleius probably had an enormous mother complex which took the form the mother complex often takes, that of being threatened by an overwhelming power, namely the archetypal feminine principle. If a man is too much impressed by the figure of his mother, whether by her fault or by his own disposition, she interferes with his contact with reality, with women, usually inhibiting or eating up his chthonic sexual personality. He may, being oversensitive, not have a strong enough masculine brutality to escape the mother and fight his way to freedom. Instead he escapes into the intellect where generally she cannot follow. In poetry or complicated philosophical systems, for example, he builds up a masculine world in which he can live his own life freely with masculine friends. I call this the escape from the mother into the stratosphere: one leaves the earth, takes an airplane and goes twelve thousand meters above the earth, where the old lady cannot reach, and one feels a man and free, but this has naturally some disadvantages. This is a very widespread type of young man who has a form of the *puer aeternus*[4] problem, namely, as soon as he wants to touch the earth, either to have sex, or to get married, or to do anything that means descending to the earth again, there the old lady stands, awaiting him at the airport, and he still has to fight her. This is not as negative as it looks because at least in this excursion into the intellectual world where the mother has no say, he has acquired a certain amount of freedom, courage, insight, and so on, which later might enable him to come down and conquer his mother complex on the level of reality. So this detour is not a waste of time and nonsense, for if a man knows how to return at a certain moment it can be a good thing.

From the little bit of data we have of Apuleius's life he seems to have been one of these men who evaded for a long time an ultimate fight with his mother to free his masculinity. By escaping into homosexuality and into an intellectual way of living, in a way eliminating the feminine principle, the man of concrete enterprise in him did not get into life, did not fight the fight against the mother principle. In his novel Apuleius tries now to compensate for what was lacking. Lucius is now the man in him, that part which, at least in anticipation, goes right through the real fight with the mother complex in all its positive and negative aspects. In this way Apuleius created a figure of a man who is now penetrating, not with the intellect but in actual reality, the realm of the dark mother and the emasculating tricks she plays on him; he is bringing into reality that part of his personality which had been left out of his life. Unfortunately we do not know exactly when he wrote the story, but most probably after his marriage. Consciously he must have been a man who feared the irrational, chthonic aspect of the feminine principle, because as we know he married an intellectual woman who became a cowriter and colecturer with him. Men who are sensitive in their feelings are often frightened of the elementary unconscious primitivity within themselves, and in women, and therefore are happy if they can find a woman to share some of their intellectual interests, because that protects them a bit against the chthonic underworld. Judging by the woman he married, Apuleius must have been such a man with a strong spiritual leaning and a certain fear of the chthonic feminine principle. This was compensated by a fascination for this dark world into which now Lucius, his fantasy hero, penetrates.

Lucius, however, takes over an attitude from Apuleius: he wants to explore this whole darkness without committing himself. This feature which Lucius displays in the very first scene is his main problem: his absolute determination not to commit himself personally to his adventures, which is naturally wrong. Either one keeps out of it, but then one does not experience anything, or one studies it honestly and then one gets involved. One cannot study anything without getting involved inwardly. That is the case even in science. The effect of this story, toward which Lucius keeps an aestheticizing literary attitude, does not help. One sees so clearly what always happens—it just creeps up on him from behind.

On the road Lucius relaxes and lets his horse feed. Then he meets two men, one of whom is Aristomenes, the traveling merchant of honey and cheese who has just joined up with another commercial man going the same way. One must imagine what traveling meant when there were neither trains nor police. Robbers could steal all your possessions and you could be sold as a slave at the next market and not be able to protect yourself. Even Plato once had to be bought back by his friends from the slave market. Traveling was therefore very dangerous. What helped was a widespread belief that travelers were under the protection of Zeus and Hermes and that murdering them would bring bad luck to the murderer. In such conditions travelers liked to join up to defend themselves together in case of need. In this way Lucius joins the two men and finds them in the middle of a fierce discussion. Aristomenes tells his companion what had happened to him and the latter refuses to believe it. The man who believes in miracles and witchcraft is for very real reasons the traveling salesman in cheese and honey, for these form a sacred food in many mystery cults, especially in those of the Great Mother in the Dionysian, Eleusinian, and Orphic mysteries. For you either drank milk and honey at sunrise or had your tongue smeared with a little honey, which meant that you were inspired.[5] Poets were thought to have eaten honey, the divine food of the gods, which made you perfect and gave you a subtle spirit. Cheese is solidified milk and has also to do with the mother cult. In ancient times people would know about such things, and a honey and cheese merchant would believe in magic. The merchant tells his story, the one which the other man did not want to believe, and that is the first "inserted" story in the book. For reasons which I presented in the introduction, we should interpret the story as a dream, as an inspiration of the unconscious.

The cheese and honey merchant goes to the market and finds an old man in rags, without money and in a sadly di-

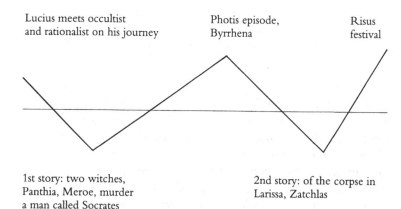

Lucius meets occultist and rationalist on his journey

Photis episode, Byrrhena

Risus festival

1st story: two witches, Panthia, Meroe, murder a man called Socrates

2nd story: of the corpse in Larissa, Zatchlas

lapidated state. It is his old friend, Socrates. He says to him, "Alas, my Socrates, what meaneth this? How fareth it with thee? What crime has thou committed?" He tells Socrates that there is lamentation and weeping for him at home and that his wife has been forced to take a new husband. He discovers that Socrates, on his travels as a merchant, had been set upon by robbers, but escaped with his life. He was allowed to go free, for he was too old to be a slave, and so went to the house of an old woman who sold wine and who was called Meroe.

The name Meroe is generally associated with the Latin *merum,* meaning wine unmixed with water. A man who drank wine without water was a drunkard, and therefore this old woman is an innkeeper and herself likes the bottle a lot. *Meroe* is also the actual name of an island in the upper Nile, very little known at that time, which was said to be a magic place like Thule, or the Celtic Avalon, the faraway fairy-tale island. Perhaps this association was also somewhere in Apuleius's mind, more so since one met there Pan and Isis.[6] The old innkeeper is sex-mad, as only an old woman can be, and she takes possession of poor old Socrates, who has to serve her day and night. He tries to get away from her but discovers that she is a very powerful witch. He says:

Verily, she is a magician, a witch! She hath power to bring down the sky, to beare up the earth, to turne the waters into hills, and the hills into running waters, to lift up the terrestrial spirits into the aire, and to pull the gods out of the heavens, to extinguish the planets and to lighten even Tartarus, and the deepe darkness of hell.[7]

That is the classic description of a witch in antiquity;[8] but what is interesting is her bringing together of the opposites: heaven and earth, waters and mountains. Terrestrial spirits are lifted into the air and gods are pulled down from heaven; planets are extinguished and the deep darkness of hell is illuminated. This witch interferes with the play of opposites; she is powerful as only a great goddess can be. All her lovers have to stay with her as long as she wants. She either castrates her lovers or, like Circe, turns them into animals. She does all that the "Great Mother" in her terrible form does to man in all myths.

Aristomenes now wants to help Socrates escape the witch. He takes him to the baths and then to an inn to eat and sleep. They have two beds in their room. Socrates at once falls asleep. Aristomenes bars fast the door and puts his bed against it, but is too frightened to sleep. And at midnight the door opens, in spite of his precautions, and his bed is turned over with him lying under it "like a snail in his shell." He recognizes the two women who walk in: one is Meroe, the other Panthia, her sister (*Panthia* means "all-powerful goddess"). After some vulgar but typical witch talk, they consider what they will do to Aristomenes, but say that first they will deal with Socrates. Then Meroe takes a knife and plunges it into Socrates' throat, and afterward pulls out his heart. But the wide wound in the throat they fill up with a sponge, and they stop the bleeding with a magic spell. Then they turn to Aristomenes and, turning over his bed, urinate on his face and then walk out of the room. When he has recovered from the shock, Aristomenes realizes that everybody will accuse him of having murdered Socrates, and that he will not be able to prove his innocence. That was why the witches did not kill him but said he would regret it if he resisted them. In his despair he tries to hang himself, but the rope, being old and rotten, breaks in the middle and he falls, tumbling down upon Socrates. Socrates wakes and curses him, so Aristomenes discovers that he is not dead. Early in the morning they depart and Socrates seems to be all right, but after breakfast he is thirsty and goes to the river to drink and the sponge falls out. This time he really dies, and Aristomenes is again faced with the same situation. So, after he has buried the body, he disappears as fast as he can. Here ends the story.

One could say that to give such an honorable name as Socrates to a poor old wretch as this old man who has fallen into the clutches of an old nymphomaniac witch was simply a joke. However, if we are not satisfied with that explanation and ask, "Why Socrates?" then at once we get into deep waters. As is known, it was the endeavor of the famous Socrates (or how he appears in the Platonic dialogues) to be *apathes,* which means not to have and not to display strong emotions. To have absolute emotional detachment was one of the main aims in Socrates' search for wisdom. He displayed this *apatheia* in a complete form at the end of his life when, in prison, he drank hemlock at his execution. By this time what had happened to him is what happens, amusingly enough, to every man who represses his emotions and with them his anima, his feminine element.[9] He had a wife, Xanthippe, the most emotional lady you can imagine, because if the husband does not have the emotion, it is generally the wife who has to have it, or the children. In this case it was the wife. We have, in Xanthippe, an archetypal model figure of the overemotional woman who moves from one noisy scene to another. Since, as a woman, I identify myself with the woman of the story, I must honestly admit that I would have made even worse scenes with Socrates. We know that Xanthippe went to prison to say goodbye to him and, in spite of his having been such a damn rotten husband, she showed some feeling and, according to the records, said, "Oh, Socrates, we are seeing each other for the last time!" He did not even speak to her but said to a slave, "Take her home." You can excuse it all and say it was the trend of the time, that for a man to detach himself from his primitive emotionality and build up a mental attitude of *apatheia,* of philosophical detachment from life, was at that time a great cultural achievement. We know that this development toward building up a superior consciousness, detaching from primitive animal involvement and emotionality, and constant *abaissement du niveau mental* and its shifting mentality, was a cultural necessity. But we must also add that here we are dealing with a rejection of the anima by men, which among other things led to the homosexual development of the Platonic-Socratic circle. There was in that time a rejection of the anima as well as of the positive value of emotions and of the feminine sensibility.

Folk tradition picked this up and spun out the figure of a Xanthippe who made continuous scenes in her desperate efforts to uphold the rights of emotion, of primitive warm feeling and involvement. The feminine principle, except in its sublime Diotima form, was not recognized by the school of Greek philosophy. The woman, as she is in reality, and not only in her sublime anima aspect, was not seen but was brushed aside as inferior. The famous discussion of Alcibiades with Socrates is an illustration: "How can you stand those scenes made by Xanthippe?" To which Socrates replies, "Oh, they do not disturb me any more than the cackling of the ducks and geese on your farm." Alcibiades answers, "Oh, well, but the ducks and geese on my farm lay eggs, they are at least useful." Socrates replies, "Well, Xanthippe gave me sons." With such an attitude one can expect that the feminine principle would become negative and destructive. This is revealed in our present story of Panthia, the "all-goddess," and of Meroe, the "wine goddess," who embody negative feeling and sex-possession and who completely overrun Socrates. The choice of the names points to an abysmal problem of the time, a problem which only centuries later shifted into consciousness and which in a certain way today has still not been solved.

As we know, in Greek philosophy the main society of the polis consisted of male groups such as the Platonic, Neoplatonic, and Stoic philosophical schools. These were patriarchal, not recognizing either the feminine element or the feminine aspect of Eros, nor, consequently, the anima. In later antiquity, however, a reinstatement of the feminine archetype began. As the next step one might then have expected either a regression to matriarchy or an attempt to develop the feminine aspect, but instead, the whole civilization broke down and was once more conquered by a patriarchal movement, the Judeo-Christian religion, which again reinforced the patriarchal trend. Early Christian theology assimilated much of Greek philosophy and its way of thinking; in their rejection of the feminine they were akin.

The whole sex morality of the Catholic Church, for instance, is not based on the Gospels. Squeeze the Gospels as much as you like, but you will not get the rules for sex which the Catholic Church has set up. Greek traditions and theological Gnostic and other traditions of the time were the main influence. The way the Church coped with the feminine, with sex, and so on—*grosso modo*—was partly due to the Jewish patriarchy, which continued into Christianity, and was partly also influenced by these Greek trends. That is a sketch in black and white, but there are naturally many shades. The return of the feminine, however, the reintegration of the feminine which began so hopefully, is the quintessence of Apuleius's book, but it was nipped in the bud and was repressed by the new patriarchal development which Christianity represented. It was as if the time had not yet come, as if still more patriarchal conditions, more development of the Logos principle and depreciation of the irrational had to be achieved before there could be an integration of the feminine principle and of the feminine goddess.

The Mediterranean civilization into which the Greeks immigrated was, not sociologically but mostly religiously, a matriarchal civilization. The Greeks broke into this older civilization with their strong patriarchal tradition. The classic Greek civilization is characterized by the antagonism of these two traditions and by the effort to bring together something which (according to the excellent formulation of the philologist Charles Seltmann)[10] is expressed symbolically through the unhappy marriage between Zeus and Hera. It is not by chance that the highest god of the Greek religion had a very quarrelsome marriage! Zeus and Hera were always together, but they fought from morning till night and, as most couples do in such cases, pulled their children into the conflict. In a way, that mirrors one of the deepest conflicts of the Greek soul. This underlying conflict probably gave dynamism to Greek civilization and is partly responsible for the birth of the scientific mind and the mental development to which we still hold nowadays. But on the other side it also set the stage for a conflict from which we are still suffering.

In the time of Apuleius impulses appeared which strove to bring to light the feminine. We will find them later in Psyche's fate, with the Isis initiation, and in several other inserted episodes. They appear not only in this novel but also, for instance, in the beautiful story of Dido and Aeneas in Virgil: in it, Venus, by helping Dido, tries to bring up the feminine principle. But in order to realize a political plot, Venus cuts the love relation apart, which then results in the suicide of Dido. Because the gods decide that Rome has to be founded, Aeneas cannot stay forever in the happy land of Carthage: the love affair which the gods themselves have arranged cannot go on. The destroyed feminine roams about as the ghost of an unredeemed suicide, as in the beautiful scene where Aeneas goes in the underworld and sees Dido there from far away. She turns away, still deeply resentful. The problem therefore does not appear only in our novel, but in many documents; and it always ends tragically.

When the Christian civilization spread into the world of antiquity, the feminine principle was once again pushed into the background. In the third century A.D. there followed an attempt toward the recognition of a goddess-mother, especially in Ephesus, where the cult of the Virgin Mary had reached its zenith. This movement reinforced itself in the Middle Ages, when the men devoted themselves to courtly love, which was then itself transformed into the worship of the Virgin Mary. But this cult, in contrast to courtly love, accepted the feminine principle only in a sublimated purified form. This engendered a countermovement, completely negative, in the form of witch persecution. The last witch in Switzerland was burnt only about two hundred years ago—we are always a bit behind. So this conflict is still going on today and we see that the story of Apuleius still concerns itself with one of the most important problems of the modern soul.

The first inserted story tells of two drunken, chthonian, destructive feminine beings, who ruin an idiotic old fellow named Socrates. It plays a completely complementary role to the reports which we possess of the philosopher Socrates, and thus corresponds completely to the psychological laws of compensation. The opposites are separated in such a way that no solution is possible anymore; they appear in a very grotesque but psychologically very characteristic form. There one can already see that this inserted story, according to my hypothesis, is understandable, if one takes it as a "dream." Indeed, the whole scene could be the typical complementary dream of a Neoplatonic philosopher: a drunken witch destroys Socrates because he behaves toward women like an idiot.

The miserable Socrates, naked, later betrayed and killed by the witches, embodies also an unconscious aspect of Apuleius himself: by avoiding his own emotional side, he becomes a victim of the witches. But, though the witches in the story of Aristomenes are nothing else but ugly, stingy old women, their names tell us that at the same time they are goddesses. Socrates is therefore actually murdered by goddesses. It is not just human dirt which overcomes him but the feminine principle itself in its destructive form, the same which later appears with the characteristics of Isis. This agrees with a very deep general psychological truth: the divine is often met first in its pathological and morbid form. *Here* is the divine experience, and that is what makes it difficult to accept. A Freudian would have enlightened Lucius-Apuleius about his Oedipus complex and probably gotten him away from elderly women. But then he would have never met the goddess Isis. This is the reason why the neurotic person often clings to his sickness; deeply he himself suspects that it is exactly there that his "god" is. But on the contrary, it also becomes evident that the highest value cannot be integrated in this low form; if one assimilates it at that level nothing will be accomplished but a falling back into the dirt and chaos.

Lucius finds the story very interesting, and thanks the traveling merchant for it, and when they come to the city of Hypate the three part company. Lucius has been given the address of a very rich and very stingy old man called Milo. He has a wife called Pamphile, the "all-loving" (*pan* = "all," *phileo* = "to love"). This woman, like Meroe, pursues all men for sexual pleasure but seems also to afford a good opportunity for Lucius to study witchcraft. In addition, there is in the house a young, attractive maid, Photis. This good-looking kitchen maid literally illuminates the darkness of the house. With her, the first image of the anima, the positive feminine element, emerges for Lucius; for the time being, however, it is experienced as simple sexual attraction.

3
Lucius Meets Byrrhena, Photis, and Goatskins

L ucius wakes up the next morning anxious to see some of the marvelous things to be found in Thessaly, where by common report sorceries and enchantments are often practiced. He remembers Aristomenes' story about the city, and everything in it seems to be transformed:

> Neither was there anything which I saw there that I did not believe to be the same which it was indeed, but everything seemed unto me to be transformed into other shapes by the wicked power of enchantment, in so much that I thought the stones against which I might stumble were indurate and turned from men into that figure, and that the birds which I heard chirping, and the trees without the walls of the city, and the running waters were changed from men into such feathers and leaves and fountains. And further I thought that the statues and images would by and by move, and that the walls would talk, and the kine and other brute beasts would speak and tell strange news, and that immediately I should hear some oracle from the heaven and from the ray of the sun.[1]

"Vexed with desire," Lucius "unawares" comes to the market-place.

It is obvious that Aristomenes' tale, which consciously Lucius had not taken very seriously, has touched him somewhere. Unconsciously something was constellated in him, for these ideas about the city of Hypate are a classical description of an *abaissement du niveau mental:* nothing seems quite real. He is in a dream world, and the outer and inner worlds begin to be close to each other. One knows this state from one's own experience, when one feels bewitched or enchanted. Autobiographies of schizophrenic people give classic descriptions in which suddenly reality is removed or different. It is both a normal and an abnormal state, which means that the unconscious is close to the conscious. There is also the motif of the transformation of men. Everything is in preparation for what is to happen to Lucius later when he is transformed into an ass.

We only know that a condition of strong emotional excitement brings about an *abaissement du niveau mental.* The range of consciousness is narrowed to a very small area, and in those moments synchronistic events occur. In some cases the experience becomes frightening. For instance, in an outbreak of psychosis, when people are just at the snapping point, strange things happen from morning till night. They ring up their analyst and say that it is absolutely terrible, that they cannot take a step or do a thing, for everything is synchronistic. Actually, what they do not see is that they have fallen into the collective unconscious where they are identical with their whole surroundings, so everything that happens around them is themselves. They are already, so to speak, spread into it, into the *unus mundus,* where everything that happens concerns them, and they begin to experience that, but this can happen also to normal people whenever they are tremendously emotionally involved. That is why Jung said he observed synchronistic phenomena only when an archetype was constellated, because that is where one gets involved with the deeper layers of the personality. When one is really involved, really gripped, the whole thing begins to play on those lines. The same thing happens when people do creative research, because there again they are involved with something deeper and more important than themselves and their little problems. They are generally involved in some way in an archetypal constellation, and the whole thing begins to act up. What this suggests is that the psychic and the physical energy interact somewhere, or are somewhere transformable into each other, so that there is a lowering of consciousness and a charging up of the intensity of the unconscious.

Lucius is rather dismayed to find that his host, Milo, is an old, stingy, narrow-minded bourgeois, and Pamphile obviously such an uncanny witch. But in the same house he also has discovered Photis, with whom a normal, youthful contact is at once established. Contrary to the fact that his relationship to Photis takes the normal course for a young Roman man of that time, and of youth in general, this relationship proves later to be actually strangely unfeeling. After Lucius has been turned into an ass, and the robbers have broken into the house of Milo and Pamphile, he never bothers to ask himself what became of Photis. He worries about his money and about his horse, but not about her, which shows a rather amazing lack of feeling. After all, he has had a very nice time with this beautiful girl, and she has very generously offered him her love, as he also has made her happy. We know from other stories and from the sociological insight they allow that Photis, after her captivity by the robbers, could not expect a nice life. The robbers would either kill her or make her a slave, and what it meant to be a slave we learn later throughout the book. But Lucius never asks a question about her, which shows clearly that he does not react quite as he should. In modern terms we would say that he has a feeling deficiency, which is very elegantly covered up by the love scene.

We know that Lucius gets turned into an ass *by mistake,* for he really wants to turn into a bird, or a winged being, but Photis uses the wrong box of ointment. This must be an unconscious revenge on her part! She probably feels that something is lacking, that he does not care for her in the most simple human way. She plays another trick on him when she is supposed to secretly obtain Pamphile's lover's hair from the hairdresser. The hairdresser catches her and takes it from her. So on her way home when she sees a man shearing goatskins in order to make them into bags, she grabs a bunch of them as a substitute. Thus when Pamphile performs her magic rites with these instead of with the hair of her lover, there comes to the gates—not the lover—but only goatskins. Lucius attacks them bravely in the night, since, in the darkness, he believes that they are robbers intent on entering the house, and thus is ridiculed in front of everyone in the city.

So twice Photis makes, absolutely involuntarily—with her left hand, so to speak—a little mistake which gets Lucius into trouble. If a woman does that, then she is not happy. Somewhere Photis is not satisfied with her lover, otherwise she would not play those two involuntary tricks. Obviously, something is not right between the two. He is cold, and she takes her revenge by playing these little witch tricks. She is somewhere a bit on the side of the witch, her mistress, so she too is cold somewhere. When a woman plays witch's tricks it means she does not love; there is a little left-handed calculation which happens behind her back. So, despite this first positive scene, where one has the feeling that Lucius gets into the secrets of life and is happy, and that by a love affair with Photis he can protect himself against the tricks of Pamphile, there is something wrong in a subtle way. Perhaps with that is also connected the *abaissement du niveau mental* which befalls him after his first visit to the house of Milo and Pamphile.

Invasions of the unconscious such as are described at the beginning of the chapter always come when one fails to have a normal reaction in some area. An intermittent lack of normal reaction in consciousness makes a hole where the unconscious breaks through. If one does not want to be invaded by the unconscious, one must pick up all the little details, such as laziness, feeling mistakes, and omissions of adaption to reality, because though they look absolutely unimportant they are the open door for invasion. As Jung said once in a seminar: *concupiscentia,* uncontrolled desire, is the open door to psychosis. And in cases I have seen of psychosis, this was so. So these little omissions are very dangerous, which is why I am pointing out something which the reader may scarcely notice: this secret unsatisfactory human relationship between Lucius and Photis, which then leads to Lucius's sinking slowly into the unconscious and into daydreaming, so that he is not quite sure what reality is any longer.

In the marketplace, "by chance," he meets Byrrhena, who is his mother's sister. She was not a real sister, but was taken into the house and educated with his mother, and therefore he calls her "Aunt." It seems strange that he did not go to stay at her house, instead of Milo's. They happen to meet, and she invites him to her house, a very pompous building. There is a description of an impressive bas-relief in its atrium representing the mother goddess Diana, about to take her bath in the woods, and of Actaeon, who tried to get a glimpse of her but was turned into a stag and torn to pieces by his own hounds. The moment when the dogs are preparing to tear the stag to pieces is the scene represented in the bas-relief. In this description given by Apuleius-Lucius we recognize the typical features of Hellenistic art with its sentimental and realistic traits. This bas-relief represents a very meaningful motif,[2] so that one can treat its content like an inserted story. For it anticipates in a symbolic form the whole future fate of Lucius: for he too sinned against the law of chastity in his affair with Photis, and he too is torn by the dark passions of the underworld and will be transformed into an animal—an ass instead of a stag. At an early stage of the story his own problem is brought right before his eyes in this bas-relief.

Artemis, and her Latin analogy, Diana, were the goddesses who unite within themselves a number of opposites. Artemis protected the chastity of boys and girls, and delighted in wild beasts. She was also the goddess of childbirth and the chthonic mother and the virgin. On the other hand, like Apollo, her brother, she was the goddess of death, for she could send out invisible arrows which bring death. Later she became connected with the moon and was goddess of the underworld (as Hecate), for in late antiquity the various types of gods and goddesses were syncretized and merged.

The late Judeo-Christian idea that we have the only true religion, and that all other religions are dark superstitious nonsense, did not exist in antiquity. The Romans conquering another country would ask the name of the main father god and mother goddess, and would say that these corresponded to their Jupiter, or Diana, or Ceres. It was discovered that everywhere there were the same types of gods, the father power and the fertility mother power, so they gave them mixed names or the name of their own god. Thus there grew up a kind of tolerant attitude, with the result that in every country there was a wonderful mixture of gods, and prayers started: "O thou mother goddess whom the Egyptians call Isis and whom the Greeks call Demeter. . . ." In other words, the same divine power was worshipped under different names in different countries. In this sense Artemis indeed represents the whole mother world.

The mother goddess in our artistic bas-relief takes a bath, and a mortal man, Actaeon, who with his sexual curiosity wants to see her bathe naked, is torn to pieces by his own dogs—the dark powers of the underworld. The multitude of dogs would stand for the dissociating aspect of animal passion. This motif is really a very deep one, for if a man transcends his human level—either goes above it into the realm of the gods or goes below it into the realm of the animals—it is the same thing. By becoming a stag he becomes what he wanted to be; he becomes divine and the object of interest to Artemis, for the stag is what she hunts. He becomes a divinity, and then he suffers the fate of the youthful lover-god of the great mother goddess, that is, he is dismembered. So we can say that the picture which Lucius meets at the entrance of the house of Byrrhena anticipates his whole problem: it says to him, "You are entering the realm of the great goddess and the realm of animal life; you will have to pay in the classical form."

Again something is lacking, for Lucius only enjoys this beautiful piece of art aesthetically and does not read the message. Also, it is only a sculpture, a bas-relief, not a living representation. If, in a modern dream, someone dreams of a picture or of a sculpture, this means that what is represented by it is not alive for them. They see it intellectually or aesthetically, but are not touched by it. So we can say that Lucius here sees what is going to happen and what a tremendous problem he is breaking into, but it is not yet alive for him. He just thinks it is a very elegant representation. That is typical for the man who has a mother complex, which above all things cuts a man off from immediate touch with reality. One could also describe the circumstances with an ugly analogy: such men walk about in a transparent plastic sack and only look out of it. There is no immediate friction with reality, no real touch with life, and that is the secret witchcraft power with which the mother complex affects a man. He is always somewhere cut off. Aestheticism and intellectualism are two well-known ways of having this plastic insulating layer between oneself and reality, preventing immediate experience and, through that, immediate suffering and becoming conscious. If, as an analyst, you have to cut this bag open and take him out of that artificial uterus, he generally wails in despair, because then begins his meeting with hot and cold reality, and all sorts of other sufferings from which he has hitherto been nicely protected.

Lucius is still only looking at things without getting the immediate impact of what is happening. He also does not, for instance, ask himself why he stumbles in his mother's sister's house on such a representation of a man whose interest in the great mother goddess gets him torn to pieces. He thinks of it as a beautiful piece of art which he describes in a literary manner. Aunt Byrrhena is obviously a counterpole to Pamphile and Milo, a real lady. She warns him immediately that he should not live in Milo's rather dubious house, but should stay with her. But she, too, is a mother figure. She, too, wishes to grab and imprison him in her house; so it is one aspect of the mother complex against the other. Byrrhena is respectable, educated, correct, so she is seemingly a positive mother, but with the negative implication that she would prevent Lucius from getting into mischief, and through that also into life. If Lucius had left Pamphile and had stayed with Byrrhena, the whole novel would not have happened! Hence the advice of Byrrhena is not right, though she looks like the wise woman who warns him not to fall into the trap. Thank God, she did not win out. It is also typical that she had only a stone bas-relief in her house, which means that though she has the right wisdom, it is not alive. So Lucius is really between the devil and the deep blue sea: bourgeois wisdom recommends him not to step into all sorts of dubious dirty affairs, but then he would never come out of the plastic sack, would be respectable but not alive. Fortunately Lucius does not follow this advice and steps into Milo's house, where he meets Photis in the kitchen preparing polenta. A relationship develops between the two. Photis conquers Lucius or Lucius, Photis. The fact that there is no warm feeling in it becomes obvious only later.

The next inserted tale is told by Milo about Diophanes, a fortune-teller who is advising a merchant about a journey the merchant intends to take, when suddenly Diophanes' brother appears and relates to Diophanes, within earshot of the bystanders, the considerable misfortune he has suffered on his latest journey, nearly losing his life. The people laugh, the merchant takes back his money, and Diophanes is shown up to be a cheat.

Naturally, people are wrong in saying that if a soothsayer cannot foresee for himself and protect his family and himself from misfortune, he is of no use. We know that the capacity for telepathy does not function at will, and therefore even someone who has such gifts cannot always save himself from falling into traps. It is the great crux in the investigation of these things.

Something which happened here in Zurich very much impressed me. There was for a long time at the theater a man named Sabrenno who cheated sometimes. Once some people I know put him on the spot and asked him why he did card tricks and cheated in all sorts of ways, and he gave a very meaningful explanation. He said that actually, he never knew, when he went to give a performance in the evening, whether or not he would be in the mood to function. Sometimes his capacities were available and he could do all the guesswork through the unconscious, and at other times he could not, and therefore he had prepared and learned a lot of card tricks and cheating to fill up the evening. This must be so, because if ever a soothsayer or magician one day turned up on the stage and said, "I am very sorry, ladies and gentlemen, but I am badly disposed this evening; please ask for your money back," he would be finished. A man who wants to make a living in this way has to have, on the side, some means of cheating. But then investigators can catch him out, and the man is finished. The same argument applies here. If, however, we try to put it into the context of the story, then we see that a man who assumes that he knows the future and how things are going to be just falls into it, and that is Lucius again. He assumes he is not going to be involved in studying witchcraft, but has already one foot in it. Just where he would need his scientific accuracy and interest in watching out, it fails him, and that is the terrible thing. One cannot observe parapsychological phenomena with a cool, detached, and concentrated attitude, because then nothing happens. Jung, for instance, when he went to Africa, made an oath that whatever curious things might happen he would write down in his little diary and give an absolutely accurate report. Sometimes some typically African things did occur, and each time when he looked in his diary, he had not written about them! Why? He had gotten emotionally involved, stared and watched and gone through the events, and in the end he had naturally forgotten to write anything down. Synchronistic phenomena and parapsychological phenomena are borderline phenomena. In order that they may appear, the intensity of our ego consciousness must be turned down, for they use that energy to appear. One cannot have the penny and the cake; one cannot with one's normal, rational, observing scientist's ego go through such experiences. Parapsychology is still up against such a crux, but here it is different. Lucius is sliding off into the *abaissement du niveau mental* without noticing it. The Diophanes story shows that the man who is supposed to know is the one who walks into the trap.

At Byrrhena's dinner party people again tell stories. A guest called Thelyphron tells the next inserted story (*thelys* = "feminine," *phronein* = "to think, meditate"). The name would imply that this person has a feminine mental attitude or is someone who always thinks about women and the female, and the man bearing this revealing name tells the following story. He says that when he was a young man, after he had traveled all over Thessaly, he came in an evil hour to the city of Larissa and was in great need of money. There was so much witchcraft at that time that when anyone died, a guardian had to watch the corpse to protect it from the witches, who would sneak in and steal parts of the body for use in their charms. These would begin: Take the nails of a newly killed man—or the ears, or the nose, or whatever—and mix them with the blood, to make such-and-such a spell. Witches had, of course, to provide themselves with these ingredients, and corpses were taken from freshly dug graves in cemeteries. So Thelyphron takes on the job of staying up at night with a corpse to protect it from the witches. He is told that he must be careful because witches can transform themselves into animals or birds, and sometimes even into flies. He is taken to a house to guard the corpse of a dead man, and the widow shows him the corpse, which is complete in all its parts, and says that if it is the same the next morning he will get his money, but if not he will be punished by being mutilated in the same way as the corpse. The young man rubs his eyes and sings to keep himself from falling asleep, but about midnight a weasel creeps into the chamber and frightens him so much that he "marveled greatly at the audacity of so little a beast." But he tells it to go and it runs off, but when it had gone he "fell on the ground so fast in the deepest depth of sleep that Apollo himself could not well discern whether of us two was the dead corpse." In the morning he wakes up and, "being greatly afraid, ran unto the dead body with the lamp in my hand, and I uncovered his face and viewed him closely round about." The matron and the witnesses come in and find the body "in no part diminished."[3]

So he gets his money, but he makes some tactless remark and gets chased out of the house. At the funeral an old man suddenly comes out of the crowd, weeping and lamenting, and says that the man who is to be buried has been poisoned by his wife. There is a great uproar and the crowd says that the woman should be burnt, but she insists that she is innocent. In order to find out the truth, the old man produces Zatchlas, an Egyptian, a great magician and necromancer who has the power to revive dead bodies.

In antiquity this was supposed to be possible—the witch of Endor[4] was also capable of bringing the spirits of the dead up from the underworld and calling up the ghosts from the underworld and making them reveal the truth. Tibetan lamas, as Alexandra David-Néel describes, are also said to be able to do this. A lama who came too late to see his friend alive lies upon the corpse and warms it with his own breath. The corpse comes to life and the two dance together for a time and so have their last contact. Such things are still practiced in Africa. And here this Egyptian turns up and succeeds in bringing the corpse back to life, and the man says, yes, that his wife did poison him, and as proof of the truth of what he says, he affirms that while acting as guardian over the corpse, Thelyphron's nose and ears had been cut off by the witch, who had mistaken him for the corpse, and she had replaced these parts with wax. Thelyphron puts his hands to his nose and ears and they drop off. He realizes that he had been mutilated and had never noticed it.

Here we have to go into antique magic. Most African, Cuban, or South American voodoo magic is still valid all over the world. To bewitch somebody you need a part of his or her person, the fingernails or the hair, for instance. Thus one gets the most powerful "medicine" in the African sense of the word. For the primitive mentality, a part of a corpse is a kind of gruesome, numinous object which has a tremendously impure and, at the same time, divine power. Anything which you mix with fluid coming from a corpse or parts of a corpse is therefore a potent medicine.[5] There is a very good publication, the *Papyri Graecae Magicae,* edited by K. Preisendanz, in which there are a number of such recipes. For instance, a recipe for making any woman fall passionately in love with a man says: take two leaves of laurel, and a rose cut in moonlight, and the little finger of a newly buried boy, and mix it in such and such a manner, and say this and that, and you will see that that night the woman will stand burning with desire at the door of your house. Or, make the potion and when she is walking in the street, smear it on her back, and the next evening she will wail like a cat in love at the door or window of your house. There is an infinite number of such recipes, concerning such things as how to be lucky in gambling or how to get rid of an enemy.[6]

I think the story is relatively transparent: Thelyphron is an aspect of Lucius himself who wants to investigate sorcery, and directly, but unconsciously, steps right into the problem. Thelyphron has women on the brain and is, so to speak, the shadow of Lucius. He is really involved, in contrast to Lucius who only wants to look on with intellectual curiosity, but they both fall victim to the witch's trick.

While Lucius still continues with intellectual investigations, his shadow, the more unconscious part of his personality, is already overpowered by the magic aspect of the feminine principle. Thus, the adventure of Thelyphron plays the role of a dream, which warns the hero what can also happen to him if he is not cautious enough.

One of the most horrible effects of a negative mother complex is that it mutilates the man's instinct to find the right woman. A man whose mother was cold or neurotic or unsatisfactory has a great longing for warmth and love, and as the devil has arranged it, he has the wrong "nose" and will always choose the girl who is like the mother and either cold or witchlike. The nose is the organ for "flair," for orientation. It is the animal's most important organ. In the development of the brain, man's ability for orientation by the nose has diminished. It has also been said that shortsightedness is on the increase, that sight as well as the sense of smell is decreasing. Man is the animal with the smallest capacity for smell. In the whole animal world the nose is the organ for orientation and gives much needed information. The dog has the unattractive habit of smelling excrement, but by it he gains a lot of useful information, for if he follows the traces of a dog who has eaten well, he will find food, which is vitally important. This old instinct survives in spite of the fact that it is no longer necessary. The dog who urinates on the lamppost continues the old pattern by which he indicated his own territory. Formerly such habits were very meaningful, but their reasons have become blurred by civilization.

Animals in the zoo have also suffered disorientation of their instinctive habits, but the wild animal has its natural instincts. Jung has remarked that if a man gets syphilis there is something wrong with his instinct, for if he were in harmony with his animal nature he would "smell a rat"—his "dog nose" would tell him to keep away, but unfortunately most men have lost their "dog nose." Where there is a negative mother complex there is something wrong with the mother. She is an animus-possessed woman or neurotic or frigid, and then her instinct is blurred, so the son too has no nose. He falls for the wrong woman; he does not get the irrational warnings from his animal side. The ears are similar. Of someone who is very sensitive, we say that he "can hear the grass grow," his hearing is very acute. The man with a positive instinct may be fascinated by a beautiful woman, but a harmless remark may show him that she has no heart, and he can drop her in time. Another man would not notice and would continue to fall for her and one day discover that she was an icicle. But the man with good instinct can hear things. He has the awareness of the other person's being. One could say that the witchcraft of the negative mother complex robs the son of nose and ears whenever he touches the feminine world.

The group is delighted with the story, and Byrrhena talks to Lucius about the coming festival of the god Risus (god of laughter), which is to be celebrated on the next day, and says that she wishes he could "find or devise" something himself that might be in honor of so great a god. Lucius says that he would be glad if he could and then takes his leave. In the street his torch goes out, and in the darkness he has difficulty finding his way home. He sees "three men" of great stature "heaving and lifting at Milo's gates," trying to get in. Thinking that they are thieves, he draws his sword and slays them. He then knocks at the door, Photis lets him in, and he goes to bed dead drunk.

This is the end of a passage, and we have to look at this inserted story even more closely. In what preceded we took

Socrates as a part of Apuleius-Lucius, the Platonic philosopher who evades the anima problem and is overwhelmed in the unconscious by the dark mother goddess. Now the danger gets nearer. Thelyphron is a man who is exposed to the problem of women. Lucius, on the other hand, has only an intellectual curiosity about witchcraft and a sensual interest in Photis, while the problem of the anima is not yet a concern except in the intellectual realm. Thelyphron would therefore be a shadow figure who has been deeply damaged by the mother complex.

The weasel, like mice, owls, the hare, and many other little animals, is a witch animal. It is cruel and catlike in behavior and represents the cold cunning of the witch.[7] Obviously, one of the witches has turned into a weasel. She looks at him in a peculiar way so that he falls asleep, then she bites off his nose and ears. The weasel, because of its great cruelty on one side and amazing shrewd intelligence on the other, is in a way similar to the fox. It is an animal that represents this superhuman native shrewdness which is the shadow of the feminine principle of women as well as of the anima principle in men. The feminine has not a logos, a scientific mind, but in general the feminine in men, and in a woman by nature, has the kind of cunning which can sneak around and look round corners and get things indirectly. It is an aspect of what Jung called in women the so-called "natural mind," a kind of absolutely instinctive wisdom which can also be merciless and inhuman. It could perhaps best be illustrated by the woman who took a cure in Carlsbad with her husband and, looking at the beautiful country and setting sun, exclaimed, "Oh, John, if one of us dies, I shall move to Carlsbad!" She didn't think of what she was saying. That is the wisdom of the weasel! Generally women cover this up with sentimentality, but the anima has the same kind of natural shrewdness, which is a kind of thinking along nature lines and always concerned with death and inheritance. Some women know exactly when the man they are interested in is likely to be alone one evening, and then they remember that they ought to return the book that evening! Some are honest enough to know what is happening in the background, but some really are absolutely naive about it in consciousness. But their weasel shadow knows exactly that this would be the right evening to come and be very surprised, saying, "Isn't your wife in?" That's the weasel! The anima of man can do the same thing very well, only men are even more unaware of it.

If we apply Thelyphron's experience to Lucius, we can say that here he receives another definite warning. Inwardly he is preoccupied only with Photis, and, being completely bored with the conventional dinner party, he is only waiting for the right moment to disappear and get back to her. Therefore he is like Thelyphron—he has Photis on the brain. The story shows that, without realizing it, he is falling into black magic.

The Thelyphron story is also interesting because the truth is uncovered by an Egyptian priest, with the name Zatchlas. This seems to be a secondary motif, which the reader could easily overlook, but it points already to the events at the end of the book, when this whole underworld—which now only appears in this dark, uncanny, and gruesome story—comes to Lucius as his initiation in the Egyptian religion. One can see that already some threads of fate are being spun. Thelyphron would have been in a bad position if Zatchlas, the Egyptian priest, had not at the last minute, as a *deus ex machina,* clarified the situation for him. Commentators have connected the name *Zatchlas* with *Sôlalas,* which in ancient Egypt was a common name, meaning "he who knows." According to others, the name points to *Saclas,* a demon who was connected with the Egyptian word for "savior."[8] Necromancy was widely spread in the Egypt of antiquity. In the time of the Roman Empire, Egypt was famous for being the country of magic par excellence and at the same time the country of the greatest religiosity. One could say that the Greek and the Roman religion had already evolved partly into a philosophical system but had also degenerated into a kind of soulless institution that no longer included any primitive emotion. The cult became formal and sober as it is in our modern Christian Church. The essense of religion on the original level consists in being emotionally gripped, totally involved with the primitive, emotional part of

the personality. One could not imagine ecstatic dancing dervishes in a Christian Church. Religion is a total experience
which encompasses the primitive, affective, and instinctive
aspects of man; it should not concern us only from the waist
up. As at that time in these European religions, the emotional
element which was lost became projected mostly onto Egypt,
and further onto the Ethiopians. In the antique literature (since
Herodotus) one reads about the Ethiopians who worshipped
the sun, that they were the most pious and that they had the
most powerful religion. Later this was projected onto the
Brahmans of India, since the Greeks, through the conquests of
Alexander the Great, had come in touch with the Indians and
were impressed by the authenticity and completeness of their
religion. This projection survived into the Renaissance. For
instance, Giordano Bruno writes that the ancient Egyptians
were the only really pious and religious people. The same
projection is also at work here in our story, for it is the
Egyptian priest who knows the truth and reveals it. He makes
just a sporadic appearance and disappears again from the story.
The story of Thelyphron would be therefore like a second
dream. To make a comparison with Socrates, the unemotional
superior philosopher who falls completely into the witch, here
we have a young man who becomes a victim of witchcraft,
but only partly: Socrates is killed, whereas Thelyphron is only
mutilated. So one can notice a tiny improvement in the
"dreams" of Lucius.

When Lucius wakes up from his drunkenness, the police
come to fetch him and he remembers that he has killed three
people the evening before. Therefore he fears that his end has
come, and he remembers that he had been told that the people
who strolled about in the night in the streets were rich and
influential. So he thinks that he will have no chance. The case
is tried in court, and Lucius is accused and makes his defense,
but when it comes to the crucial moment and he is in tears and
thinks he is lost, everybody bursts into Homeric laughter.

Then the widows of the murdered men come weeping and
ask for vengeance and ask that the murderer uncover the
corpses of the murdered men. When Lucius is forced to do

this, he discovers that they are not men's bodies but blown bladders, mangled in diverse places. They are the goatskin bladders made for carrying water which he stabbed. For the crowd this was a great joke, the whole thing having been staged in honor of the great god Risus, but Lucius has lost his sense of humor and cannot join in the laughter.

Later Photis comes to his room and explains exactly what has happened and how she had been the cause of all his troubles, but had been forced into it by her mistress, Pamphile. Pamphile, she says, was in love with a young man whom she wanted to seduce, and in order to charm him to her side she instructed Photis to go to the barber and obtain some of his hair. Before Photis could get out of the barber's shop the barber saw her, and since she and Pamphile were accused of witchcraft, he ran after her and took away the hair she had managed to get hold of. Photis was frightened, knowing that she would be beaten. On the way home she saw a man shearing blown goatskins for water bags, and, as the hair was yellow and something of the same color, she took it to her mistress. With this hair and her other ingredients and confections, Pamphile concocted such a spell that "those bodies whose hair was burning in the fire received human shape, and felt and heard and walked, and smelling the scent of their own hair,"[9] came and rapped at the doors in place of the Boeotian, burning with passion as the young man was meant to be. These were the skins which Lucius had slaughtered. Photis begs Lucius to pardon her.

An analogy which occurs to one is that of Don Quixote, who fought against the windmills with true heroism. Here, too, a man fought with exaggerated effort and emotion against a hallucination, without recognizing the real danger that was sneaking up behind his back. That has again to do with the perversion of the instinctive functioning due to the mother complex. Such a man will say that all old women are witches and will watch out not to fall into the trap of the devouring mother, but eventually he turns up having married a super-witch and has not noticed it. That was what was slowly creeping up behind him. That is the tragedy of the perverted instinct, for the destroyed feeling function makes him fall for the wrong object. If you ask such a man wherein lies the great attraction toward his beloved, he will generally say that she has such "tremendous warmth," which usually means that she is good in bed. He has no capacity for differentiation and confuses physical passion with feeling. That is why the tragedy must take its course. It is of no purpose to preach against it, for the reason lies too deep. Men with such a negative mother complex are often engaged in fighting some intellectually represented danger, philosophical or ideological opponents, be it Communists or Jesuits. Such fights are shadow projections, for they do not see their own shadow, which is in the grip of the mother problem. The mock lawsuit against Lucius was displayed as an instance of this. Here it was in honor of the god of laughter. I have not been able to discover whether similar festivals were held in other towns. It is probably a spring festival, having to do with the fertility of the fields. In Athens, society ladies would meet and tell each other the most improper stories, which was supposed to further the fertility of human beings and the fields.

Among Jungians we consider that where there is no sense of humor such cases are serious. Especially in the case of a bad psychosis, it is helpful if one can get the patient to laugh about himself and not to take himself too seriously. If you can help a person who is possessed by an affect with a joke that allows him to see how ridiculous he is, this gives him a spark of objectivity, since for one second he can look at himself objectively, from the outside, so to speak. I would even say that it is the Self[10] manifesting in such a moment. The ego tries always to do the "right" thing but sometimes it behaves like a clown who rolls himself up in the carpet he is trying to lay. If you can see your own ego-clown and how incredibly funny you are for somebody else, at that moment you are in the objective center of yourself, there is a feeling connection with the archetype of the Self. But generally we lose our sense of humor the moment a complex is touched, and we become dramatic and serious, unable to look at our problem realistically.

However, as with all psychological factors, it can also be the other way around. Then we are dealing with the *negative* god of laughter, when laughter—as is the case here with Lucius—has a destructive effect. When someone has a damaged feeling function, he does not take himself quite seriously. He plays intellectually with his own life and does not see himself as really important. Some modern intellectuals are so poisoned by statistical thinking that they are convinced they do not matter, they are just casual existences, there are millions of people like themselves. Such people come into analysis and tell their tragic life history in the most casual manner. One man even said to me, "But you must hear such stories every day." He believed his tragedy would not affect me and assumed that I would deal with it only intellectually. He did not want me to be shaken by his tragedy and did not appreciate it when I took his life seriously, because then he also would have to take it seriously. So people make a joke in such cases and laugh about themselves. That is what happens to Lucius here, if we take the laughing people as being parts of himself. He suffers from intellectual irony, with which he can keep away all feeling reactions. Thus the shadow can get at him from behind.

4
The Ass

We now must go further into the cult of the god of laughter, which is obviously a parallel form of what we still have today in the form of carnival. It is mainly a festival at which people are licensed to make fun of each other and to take all sorts of liberties. In the very bourgeois level of society in Basel, for instance, where everybody knows everything about everybody else, including how much tax everyone pays, the people are stiff and narrow, stuffed-shirt people, but there is a kind of gentleman's agreement that whatever happens in the Basel Fastnacht never really happened. Even if you meet your neighbor naked in the street, dead drunk, you may never mention it later on. It is a day apart, when the other side may live and the most marvelous things may happen. Jung told a wonderful story of one of his uncles, one of those very honorable men, who got so drunk that he undressed and wanted to take a bath in one of the big fountains. His friends took away all his clothes and even his door key, so that the poor chap had to walk home through Basel completely naked, and when he arrived at his own door, he did not even have a key but had to ring. A very fashionable, elderly maid came to open the door, and he thought: Oh, my God, I can't face Marie in this costume! So he made her open the door and then caught the handle, saying, "It's all right, Marie, go to bed now." But she asked what was the matter with him and wanted to open the door more, so he repeated, "It's all right, Marie, go to bed now." They discussed this for half an hour, both pulling the door until finally it opened and he fell into her arms! So, if you want to know what the *Deus Risus* is, and the festival of laughter, go to Basel, for things still happen there nowadays.

Originally such things (which have now taken on a lighter touch) had a much deeper and more religious meaning. In Christian civilization it was still understood that a carnival belonged to the cult of the dead in antiquity. Those masked people, clowns and columbines and whomever one meets in the streets, are really ghosts. The dead come along in that form and you meet them halfway, you wear their masks. It is really a festival in which the underworld, the ancestral spirits, come back and you unite with them. In the inner parts of Switzerland at certain of these carnival festivals, which are also held before Christmas, these masked people whip the fields and the fruit trees in the fields, which is supposed to make them fertile. The dead ancestral spirits guarantee the fertility of cattle, of the fields, and of women. There takes place therefore a mystical union of the Beyond and the here and now. *Mundus infernus patet*, the underworld is wide and open and the masked ghosts go around, and the laughter has therefore a strange double aspect of being close to the gruesomeness of the ghost world and death. Here one could quote the famous saying of Heraclitus about these feasts in honor of Dionysos: "If it were not Hades, the god of the dead and the underworld, for whom these obscene songs are sung and festivals are made, it would be a shocking thing, but Hades and Dionysos are one."[1]

So we touch here the mystery of the shadow and of the *abaissement du niveau mental:* sex, in its purely impersonal, unrelated nature—fertility, shadow, dissolution, and the fertilization of everything. If we understand in this way the festival of the god Risus, we realize that here we touch on the whole process presented in this book, namely, the descent into the underworld, and that the god Risus, laughter, has a very dangerous, double-edged aspect. For instance, in the *I Ching,* hexagram 58, *Tui* ("the Gay," or "the Joyous"), says that "the joyous is close to murder and death." The joyous has to do with metal, death, and autumn.

One sees with Apuleius how much laughter, his sense of humor, which he obviously has, is an ambiguous thing. He sometimes uses it, like many people, in order to keep away from life. It is typical of neurotic personalities that when they get involved, when fate approaches them in the form of emotional involvement, they quickly make an elegant joke, turn it into something light and amusing, and hop out of it. I have had analysands who could not be serious. Whenever one touched something which could get pathetic or emotional, they made a joke to be out of it. That is a form of laughter which is used as a murder weapon, to kill life. It is an intellectual trick, a way of pretending to be old: it is the autumn of life and not youthful. Youth must be inwardly involved. This ironic attitude reveals that one is distancing oneself at the wrong moment, and it is utterly neurotic. The opposite is the freeing laughter. Schopenhauer even said that the sense of humor was the only divine quality in man. Jung always said that if a borderline case had a sense of humor, the chance of cure was ninety percent better.

Another problem for the normal personality is that when the deeper layers of the unconscious are touched, or if one tries to bring them up in active imagination, the unconscious tends to display an emotional and pathetic style which is difficult for modern man to stand. It is theatrical, childish, and pompous. For a long time I could not do active imagination, because a figure which turned up from the unconscious would say, "Harken!" or something like that, and I just switched off. Jung said that he had the same trouble, for it is very difficult to write down what seems to be a lot of theatrical, emotional stuff. But that is the style of the unconscious, although it shocks one's aesthetic and literary feeling. To jump into it and take it seriously, saying, "Well, after all, I am not going to publish this stuff, and if my soul speaks that language I shall write it down and look at it objectively," is a test of courage.

What is activated here is the psychic attitude of the primitive carnival festival, and the situation is bad, for it has a definitely negative effect on Lucius's consciousness. The big hoax and the collective joke they play on him destroy him completely, and strand him in a state of feeling inferiority, tears, and utter despair, so that the *abaissement du niveau mental* and the disintegration of the former conscious attitude are even speeded up. He loses the last bit of snobbism, or self-esteem, and is reduced to an absolutely helpless condition. But, if looked at from the outside, we can see that he is beginning to touch a more human level of his personality.

When he returns to Photis, in despair she confesses how great a share she had in this hoax by exchanging the hair, thus affording people an opportunity to laugh at Lucius. To make up for this, she offers to let him witness the secret magic actions of her mistress, Pamphile. As the continuation of the story will show, she makes another mistake by which Lucius gets even deeper into the mire. As I have pointed out, she must have had unconscious resistances because of his inhuman attitude toward her, which she pays back in the same coin. She allows him to go to the attic in the night and to see how Pamphile rubs herself with a certain ointment and, with the help of incantations, turns into a bird to fly and visit her lover. Lucius promptly is gripped by the desire to try this out on himself and wants Photis to steal the ointment for him, so that he might also transform himself into a bird. But she fears that, if he succeeds, he will never return. He swears that he will not try to escape; rather, he wants to be "a winged Cupid standing opposite her, Venus." This little sentence, which one hardly notices, refers to something that later is of importance: the fairy tale of Amor and Psyche. It is the first allusion to this motif. Lucius also says here that he wants to use magic powers so that he can identify with a god.

He gets what he wants, for he becomes a god, but in the form of an animal, for Photis makes a mistake in choosing the ointment, so that when he expects to grow feathers he instead grows a long tail and finds that he has grown into an ass, and though inwardly he feels like a human being, outwardly he can only say, "Hee-haw!" He looks with watery eyes at Photis, who says that the countermagic is very simple, thank God, that he just has to eat a few roses, and that then he will be back in human shape, and that tomorrow morning she will get them for him.

One has here to remember that all the Egyptian gods—the greatest gods worshipped at that time, and whom in the end Apuleius himself worshipped—wore animal heads. The gods in all original primitive religions were doctor-animals, spiritual, divine animals. Thus Lucius's grotesque transformation is an involuntary deification which he came to in the wrong way.

The motif of transformation into an animal is ambiguous because the animal can mean something positive or negative. On the one side, there is the motif of the helpful animal, the horse, fox, and so on; usually interpreted as the animal instinct showing us the way. As warm-blooded animals, we certainly have many instinctive patterns—hunger, fear of death, and many others—which are parallel to ours, and therefore if the animal appears in mythology or dreams, it would mean acting as it does. On the other hand, in myths there is very often the motif of a helpful animal which in the end asks to be beheaded. In the Grimm's fairy tale "The Golden Bird," and in many other fairy tales, the animal asks to be beheaded, and when this is done it becomes a human being and says, "I was transformed into animal shape and am now redeemed, having been cursed as an animal." What does that mean? Seen from the outside, I would say that probably shows the difference between animal instinctive behavior and human instinctive behavior. Emotionality is not reserved for the human being. Higher animals have perhaps the same feeling. But what animals probably do *not* have is an understanding of what is happening to them.

I do not think that animals, after having gone through a life experience, guided by their pattern of behavior, reflect about it afterward. Objective reflection on one's own behavior and experience seems to be confined to man, for it seems to be a

specific aspect of our species. Where does that impulse origi-
nate? The ego did not invent it. It comes also from the depths
of the instinct. You can say that our instinct has this deep,
human superstructure of reflection, which induces us not only
to live the instinct but to reflect upon it. Every species of
animal has a pattern of behavior in different situations—building nests, and so on. Every species has the same pattern with a
slight variation, a different nuance, yet it is similar. Man's
specific nuance would be the impulse to reflect and to build up
a certain continuity of consciousness. Therefore, if a man lives
as an animal, without reflection and without linking it up with
his conscious views, he is not living the totality of his anthropos pattern, and for this reason animals in fairy tales beg to be
transformed into human beings. For the animal instinct of a
man does not want to be lived autonomously. That is not a
disease of our civilization but belongs to the specific anthropos
instinct, which is different from that of other animals.

Then there is the question of the personal level. Let us take
the Naskapi Labrador hunter who lives to a great extent in
animal patterns. He has a philosophy about the interpretation
of dreams, a theory of where dreams come from, and that is a
thread of continuous interpretation and reflection. You have to
think about dreams. But there is no urge within these people
to develop to a more human level than that, except when they
are hit and wounded by an outer difficulty. You can say that
people always live on the lowest level of consciousness because
consciousness is such a terrible effort. Unless we are caught by
some trouble, why should we do more? But we get wounded
by disturbing influences which force us to think, and sometimes the wound comes from within. There are always among
a group of people some who are quarrelsome and restless,
inwardly hit by something, and not satisfied. They have the
Luciferian urge within them, which generally manifests as
dissatisfaction, irritability, nervousness, and so on. And where
this is followed up by attacks of depression, you find that there
is a specific urge to disturb the pattern in order to bring up a
higher level, and that I would call the urge to individuation.
This seems to be a tendency in man to reach a further level of

reflection and consciousness, and this comes from within and not always from outer disturbing factors only.

You could speculate a lot and ask, why is there such a thing as evolution in nature? And why does life on our planet always invent further situations? But that leads to philosophical speculations about an urge in nature to reach higher levels. What is the problem of mutation, and why does nature make groups in which some survive and some do not? To some people there seems to be a directive urge; we tend to believe in the teleological aspect, and see such a tendency within the human being, which would be only one example of the more general fact, namely that biological processes have to be looked at also from a final standpoint. It seems that in the human species there is an urge toward ever-increasing consciousness, which would give us a completely different theory of neuroses. It would suggest that in the neurotic person there is an indication of an urge to reach a higher level. If this is followed up, the neurosis disappears. One often cures the conflict by reaching a higher level.

I met two brothers, one a highly successful businessman who had been too much caught in the stuffed-shirt attitude and who had lost the meaning of life, his feeling and instinctive reactions. He had thus been forced to come to me, on all fours, because of awful compulsive symptoms which were so bad that he had no choice. Later, I met his brother, who presented exactly the same case, though not quite as bad. But, again, the stuffed shirt. He was eaten up by the persona and elegant and successful. He sniffed around for some time, but had not had a bad symptom. He was just generally dissatisfied, and he was not so caught in his profession. After a few hours, he got enough from analysis to realize that it would be painful if he went on. So he said he would come again if he felt bad, and later sent a message to say he was getting along all right. His brother had been forced by his symptoms to come, and he got somewhere, and got rid of his symptoms. He once asked me whether one absolutely had to take up all these shadow problems in order to get somewhere. Was it really necessary? And he mentioned his brother. I told him that he could thank God on his knees that he had had the symptoms, as otherwise he and his brother would have been just the same.

That means that the urge for individuation *is as strong as the symptom*. In one brother the urge was stronger, while the other got away with remaining relatively unconscious and wriggling through the situation. He was healthier, in a way, and in another way, looked at from the deeper level, less so. The younger brother had been forced into a realization, as his urge was stronger. It is shocking for a medical man to look at it from that angle. Jung sometimes spoke of a neurosis as a blessing, for behind the illness is the urge to reach the new level, and perhaps that is simply because the species, man, is still very much in a state of mutation. We know that the brain does enlarge and that we are still evolving, relatively quickly, so that the change can be seen statistically in a few generations. If a man acts like an animal, without adding the specifically human ingredient, he is behaving not instinctively right, for he is not living his real human pattern of behavior, which is a strange mixture: an animal that has to reflect!

In antiquity, transformation into an ass had a very specific meaning. The ass was interpreted not as a symbol but as a kind of allegory of lasciviousness. The transformation of Lucius is therefore characteristic, for the way he had behaved with Photis was the behavior of an ass. The ass is also an animal which belongs to the followers of Dionysos, and was therefore associated with the Dionysian ecstasy, sexuality, and drunkenness. More obviously (and, with Apuleius, certainly consciously) indicated is another connection, or symbolism, for the ass in the Egyptian religion is a symbol of the god Seth, who killed Osiris.[2] In the myth of Osiris, Seth invited Osiris, when they were at a festival, to get into a coffin, and when he did so, as a kind of joke, or to find out the measurements, Seth quickly put the lid on and poured lead on it and threw it into the sea. Seth is represented in the hieroglyphic text as an animal with a strange kind of long-eared head. It is not known whether what is meant is really an ass, but certainly in Hellenistic times it was interpreted as being the picture of an ass. Seth personifies in Egypt the principle of murder, lying, brutality, evil par excellence, the counterpart of the god-man Osiris. That Apuleius thought of this connection consciously is shown at the end, in the scene of his redemption, when Isis says to the ass, Lucius, "Get out of this shape of an ass, of the animal I always loathed." By this she alludes to the ass as the animal of Seth whom Isis naturally loathed.

In the Bible the ass has a still different meaning, if one thinks of the ass through whom God spoke to Balaam, giving him guidance, or the ass which carried Christ. In Christian symbolism, therefore, the ass acquired a slightly different meaning. At the time of Apuleius it was essentially associated with the God of the Old Testament, Yahweh. We have from that time a drawing by a student in a college who, to mock his comrades, drew the figure of the crucified Jesus as a man with a donkey's head. Obviously the student, for anti-Semitic reasons, wanted to mock his Jewish colleagues with this implication. To worship an ass was an insult to Jews and early Christians, who were at that time in the same common society, the Christians being regarded as a Jewish sect. In this way the ass acquired a different meaning, which then was picked up in the Middle Ages, when it had quite a positive meaning and very often represented a form of the old God, of a patient animal, the carrier animal of Christianity, a symbol of all those spiritual processes described in the Old Testament, which, in a hidden way, led to Christianity. Even that the birth of Christ in Bethlehem was witnessed by an ox and an ass was interpreted to mean that the ass represented the God of the Old Testament and the ox the God of the New Testament. These are later developments, but even at that time the ass was essentially associated with the Jews and Christians, who were thought to be worshippers of the donkey. If we know, for instance, that Christ was identified with Dionysos by many people, we can see the mental connection. The ass is the animal of Dionysos, and so of Christ. The image of Christ was not very precise; many people included him with all the youthful saviors, such as Attis, Tammuz, and Adonis, who dominated the mystery cults at that time. In astrology, the ass was attributed to Saturn and was seen as having the qualities of that planet, in the astrological sense of the word, which meant drivenness, creative depression, despair, heaviness, suffering, imprisonment, helplessness, and dehumanization.

These amplifications illustrate the psychological projections on the ass at these times, namely the strange, complex mixture with which we are now so familiar in the treatment of neurosis, of creative depression and drivenness. In some times of depression one finds that behind the constipation, the lameness, the headaches, and the continual low mood, there lies hidden a tremendous desire or drive which the person is intelligent enough to know cannot be lived. The person is convinced that a desire, or a power drive, or sexual drive, or any other strong instinctual drive, cannot be carried out, so that it is repressed through resignation and so constitutes the nucleus of a deep depression in the unconscious. That is why when you get people out of such a state they first turn into a hungry lion which wants to eat up everything, the depression having been only a compensation, or repression mechanism, because they could not cope with the tremendous drive. The same is true of real creativeness, which also has the aspect of violating the wishes of the ego. It attracts all the energies of the soul for its own purposes, so that in consciousness there remains only a deep melancholy, which then usually cures itself by an enormous creative élan. This mechanism was already known in the Middle Ages and in the Renaissance. In Marsilio Ficino's theory about melancholia one finds exactly the same problems described. Ficino suffered from very heavy depressions himself, and therefore he called himself a child of Saturn, and described exactly those states of depression, emptiness, *abaissement du niveau mental,* and listlessness, which in him always preceded great creative phases. This is also true of the painter Albrecht Dürer. The precreative depressions, if understood rightly, are actually helpful because they drive people into isolation, into their own depths, and into introversion, and therefore bring about favorable conditions from which creative ideas can arise from the unconscious.

We can therefore interpret the turning of Lucius into an ass either superficially, as has been done, in that he, so to speak,

has an *abaissement du niveau mental,* becoming completely identified with the sex drive, and by that completely unconscious,
and through this being turned into an ass; or we can take it in
a deeper way and ask what Lucius repressed. He certainly does
not repress his sex drives, but he does repress, to a certain
extent, his power drive. There is a lot of power drive and self-
preservation in him, looked at from a behavioral aspect, and
we shall see later what that and his aggression mean. But I do
not think that he is turned into an ass because of this. What he
actually represses most, and does not even have the foggiest
notion about, is his religious emotionality. Of what one could
call being moved by religious contents, he has no idea, and
that naturally overshadows his life, and depresses him literally
into an ass.

Here we must remember that first Lucius rode on a white
horse and then he came to Photis and Milo and had all the
experiences we have described. Next came Thelyphron's story,
the story of the man devoted to women, who was mutilated
by the witch. This, to follow the line of our sketch, gave a
slight improvement below the line, and a slight deterioration
on the upper level. The depression continues, for he gets into
a lower and lower state of mind. Then he gets turned into an
ass, and things go rapidly downward, but on the lower level
there is a slight improvement.

We have here what one always sees in treating a neurotic
split in human personality: consciousness becomes weaker and

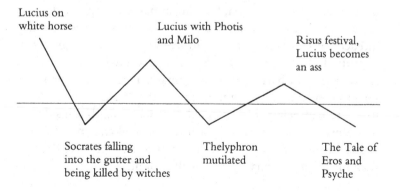

Lucius on
white horse

Lucius with Photis
and Milo

Risus festival,
Lucius becomes
an ass

Socrates falling
into the gutter and
being killed by witches

Thelyphron
mutilated

The Tale of
Eros and
Psyche

weaker and the unconscious comes up. Slowly, but only at the very end of the book, there is the sudden breakthrough of the two parts of the personality and the unification into one. But in the meantime there are all sorts of smaller ups and downs, with the main line showing a worsening of the conscious state, and a slow improvement on the unconscious. The ass makes visible the terrible and helpless imprisonment of the ego in depression, which now begins to take possession of Lucius, with all the drivenness, helplessness and lack of orientation. As an ass Lucius is not articulate, is incapable of expressing himself to Photis in any way, incapable of sleeping in his own bed or of having fun with Photis.

The ass Lucius goes down to the stable, parks himself where he thinks he belongs now, with his own horse and the other ass, and, to his absolute horror, where he expects to get a friendly greeting, he is confronted by the two animals turning against him in fury. This is his first great shock. This is actually a very subtle basic idea in the book. One feels that Apuleius cannot have thought that out consciously. Looked at from the modern psychological standpoint, if a human being behaves like an animal, he is not in harmony with his instincts. An animal which behaves like an animal is in harmony with itself. If a tiger behaves like a tiger, it is, so to speak, individuated. It is what it is, in the truest sense of the word. This is why Jung often said that the animal is the only really pious being on this planet, because it lives its own pattern and self-fulfillment. Only man is a split animal who fights against his own inner pattern. If we sink to an animal's pattern, we deviate from our own just as much as if we go off too much on the intellectual or conscious end. To live like a swine or an ass is neurotic for a human being. So the real animals reject Lucius, for he is not in harmony with animal nature. The tragedy of Lucius-Apuleius is that within his donkey's skin he still feels like a human being. He is treated like an animal, but inside, in his subjective inner world, he is not one. If taken symbolically, it shows that he lives below his own level, outwardly lower than his inner personality would allow him.

Then begins the whole series of "near-redemptions," which he always misses. In the stable he sees the statue of the goddess Epona. This Celtic goddess, protector of horses, had been imported by the slaves into the whole Roman Empire, and as the horses were generally looked after by slaves, this little statue was found in most stables. There is a wreath of roses around Epona's statue, and Lucius stretches to get it, but the slave sees him and beats him back from getting his quick redemption here. This is a little incident which carries a much deeper meaning, for in the late antique syncretistic religion, Epona was identified with Isis. So Lucius nearly reaches the goddess who could redeem him. The Romans and Greeks had quite a different attitude toward religions other than the Judeo-Christian one. It was based on the instinctual realization that there were the same archetypal patterns in most religions. As described before, they simply, for instance, established a temple in the conquered country in which a mother goddess was prayed to, saying: "O Hera, Juno, Epona, Isis, or whoever else you are." Historically we call this a syncretistic religion. By this means, naturally, the Romans got out of a lot of political trouble, for at least the conquered countries never revolted against the Roman Empire for religious reasons. Naturally, as the early apologists pointed out, it was a sloppy way of thinking, taking things not too seriously by skipping all the different nuances which a specific divine figure had. The historian Arnold Toynbee, who was rather attracted to Jungian psychology and read a lot of Jung, thought that some of our political and racial problems could be solved if we would establish a kind of syncretistic religion between East and West. He even published a kind of prayer beginning, "O Christ who is also Buddha; O Buddha, thou art . . ." and so on. His idea was to establish again the belief that there is a great spiritual savior god, whatever his name may be. Naturally, this is too intellectual. For Buddha, having grown out of Eastern civilization, implies certain emotional attitudes and other associations which one cannot simply skip over by saying, "Oh, that's more or less the same thing as our Christ. Let's just make a nice potpourri of it." But for a while the Romans did that quite successfully, as you can see here with the goddess Epona.

Here already the cure would come if Lucius could reach the roses of the mother goddess, but he is beaten back by a slave, by the completely undifferentiated primitive man.

At this very crucial moment robbers break into the stable. They have attacked Milo's house, whose inhabitants ran away or were killed, and have stolen everything. Probably the rumor has spread that Milo is rich. So the robbers come, take everything they can find, and load the animals with the things they have stolen. Because of this incident Lucius does not succeed in eating the roses. He tries to call out the name of the Roman emperor but can only produce animal sounds and gets beaten. Later he is forced to pass by a rosebush, which he dare not eat, because if he were to be transformed into a man at that time he would be killed at once by the robbers. So he has to continue with his load. After this second frustration of his redemption there follows the long account of how Lucius, as an ass, suffers under the hands of the robbers and must wait to be transformed back into a human being.

The thieves rob Lucius of human contact, and if you take that as an inner psychological dream, it would mean that they make it impossible for him to become human again. The robbers are the typical shadow of a mother-bound man. As Jung points out in *Mysterium Coniunctionis,* we have always to keep aware of the fact that the sexes are a contrast, which accounts for the "alchemical" attraction to each other. This is why the *coniunctio,* the union of these two opposites, is a symbol of the union of the greatest possible opposites. Therefore, if a woman can dominate her son, she generally opposes any symptoms of primitive masculinity, his robber qualities, so to speak, since she realizes that they will lead him away from her and be the basis of his independent masculine personality. She gives him a "decent education" so that he may not walk with dirty shoes in the drawing room and not spit or use coarse language, or eat like a pig at table, and so on. Every mother feels very justified in teaching her son such things, because otherwise he will not be adapted to society. She is naturally completely right, but there are two ways of getting about it. One way is to sympathize, as a real mother does, while thinking inwardly that, thank God, he is a real boy, and then trying reasonably to cut down the wildest shoots. Other mothers, however, instinctively hate that aspect of the son, scenting the germ of his independent personality, and they fight it. Theoretically it is because a good education requires that one should clean one's fingernails before eating, but underneath, the so-called good education has the purpose of castrating her son by laming any kind of enterprising masculinity.

The primitive masculinity of a man with a mother complex is generally damaged because the mother's animus has cut into it, so that it becomes an autonomous shadow and creates what one could describe as the incredibly inhuman brutality and cruelty of the weakling. A young man with such a mother complex becomes a weakling, and because he is not really masculine, he is inhumanly brutal, coldly brutal in the unconscious. He never dares to stand up like a man for what he wants and is a bit of a conformist, or wishy-washy, a mama's boy. And then from time to time, out pops this shadow quality.

The robber motif occurs just as much in women's as in men's dreams, and, with a grain of salt, I would say that it is the same thing. A completely related feminine personality may also have such fits of sudden brutality, directed either against her male partners or against herself. This means that the woman falls into an animus mood where she blots herself out: I am nobody and nothing, everything is wrong, and so on—a self-annihilation through negative opinions and negative judgments. That is very invisible. You do not see it outside, except that such a woman may look a bit pale and stiff, and be a bit not there, but the robbers have broken into the inner house and blotted out anything human and alive within by brutal judgments of the commonest collective value. Think, for instance, of the *tricoteuses* in Paris, who sat knitting and watching with delight while the aristocracy were guillotined. Sitting knitting, and enjoying the beheading! That's the robber!

Women who go wild and begin to display this robber or murderer animus are the women like Anna Paulker, or Mrs. Benjamin, the *rote Hilde*. Thus the robber represents in all cases primitive masculine brutality, which can also be positive. He is a nonconformist, which can be a very good thing. It implies not being bound to convention and tradition which tells you that you should not do this or that. He knows what he wants and goes for it, which is positive masculinity. He has initiative and is enterprising. He does not just sit and hope that the food will fall into his mouth, as the mama's boy always does. If the mama's boy does not have what he wants, he begins to cry, and mankind, or the state, or somebody else, has to run and help. The robber is the opposite. He says, "I want that, and I am going to have it." All that, if integrated, and controlled, and connected with the conscious personality, is masculinity at its best. It means to have a goal, to know what one wants and to go for it, instead of just sitting and hoping a parent will bring it on a silver platter. All that can be extremely positive. It all depends on the measure, and on how much it is integrated. It is not the robber, but his autonomy, that which pops in and out in sudden unrelated actions, which is wrong.

These robbers, as the stories show, endure many difficulties without too much fuss, and it takes positive masculinity not to collapse at once when things get disagreeable. But again, it is all wrong because it is autonomous, and that is typical for this setup. Here, falling into the hands of the robbers means falling into an *abaissement du niveau mental,* being overwhelmed by autonomous shadow impulses. Looked at from the deeper mystical aspect, it is approaching the layer where the god Seth kills Osiris, for it means approaching the instinctual, split-off layers of the personality from which positive masculinity will at last be born. So one has always to look at such things as a paradox, which is why it is so important to be conscious of what is happening. That makes all the difference.

We must think of robbers of that time slightly differently from what we would now associate with the word. The state police at that time were to a great extent inadequate to meet the people's needs and wishes, and also most of the state consisted of conquered countries not voluntarily adherent to the Roman Empire. Thousands and thousands of people were made slaves who, in their former country, had held quite important social positions. In a state in which the whole network of police and secret police did not function as efficiently as nowadays, numbers of people escaped into the woods and joined the robbers. They would have perhaps included a Celtic chief who had been made a slave and had run away because he would not be beaten to death by some low, foul Roman, yet he was not able to return to his country. The robbers at that time, therefore, were not all just plain criminals, but groups joined by runaway slaves of all classes, or by people who did not agree with the policy of the Romans, or who had got into some difficulty with the law in some other way. These robbers would fall into the category of the romantic children's book about the noble robber, the man who does not want to submit to Father State but wishes to live a free life in the mountains. There is still some of that spirit alive, for instance, in the Mediterranean smuggling trade in which there are quite decent robber-adventurers who consider it a kind of sport to outwit the police and the customs officials.

Observed from the psychological point of view, this motif means that so-called shadow figures overwhelm Lucius.[3] Later we will see even more clearly that their names represent all the different aspects of crude primitive virility or masculinity, something which Lucius, the mother's boy, lacks to such an extent. His whole life and good family background have made him what he is, and his mother complex has cut him off from this aspect of masculinity. We know of Apuleius that at least during his youth he was homosexual. This would indicate that he was cut off from certain aspects of his own masculinity, which he was searching for in projection with his male friends. Lucius is now overrun by the autonomous aspect of this primitive virility, which takes possession of him against his will. The cold, brutal, primitive man is in general a compensating, typical, even an archetypal shadow of the mother's boy.

The adventure has even a deeper meaning: these robbers are living with an old woman who drinks. They call her "Mother" from time to time, so it is obviously a man's society with one drunken old housekeeper. This strange group of men around the one female figure reminds one of the Greek and pagan mother cults, and the mother cults of Asia Minor. With the Greeks the young men were called Kuretes or Kabiri. They guarded the divine child, Zeus, and protected him. They were not considered human beings but demons. As with the case of the satyri later, they formed a group which gathered round the Great Mother. They represented at the same time the ancestral ghosts, and people believed that they could evoke madness, but also heal. The Kabiri were also identified with the demons who protected the smiths and ironworkers. In her book *Themis,* Jane Harrison deals with this situation from the sociological standpoint and makes comparisons with ancient primitive rites.[4] One can observe similar circumstances in the groups of unmarried young men all over the world. In ancient primitive cultures young boys were taken from their homes and were not allowed to recognize their mother, neither might they eat food cooked by her. They had to live in the men's houses until they married, and had to go through all kinds of torture. There was recognized permission for these men to be aggressive, primitive, and masculine, and in old Sparta they were *ordered* to steal and rob, to prove their independence and masculinity. That was the initiation into manhood.[5] Such an initiation not only involves instinctual behavior but also plays a role in the spiritual realm: it concerns, on the one hand, the animalistic, but on the other hand, it means an initiation in the spiritual life of the tribe. In other words, it has to do with a widening of the personality between the two extreme poles of instinct and spirit.

Therefore we can say that when Lucius falls into the hands of the robbers, he falls into the hands of these forces which would initiate him into a new masculinity. It is his initiation into manhood, even though in a negative aspect.

When the robbers have eaten, they recount their adventures. One band has lost its captain, called Lamachus ("the fighter"). He had tried to rob a rich man who lived as a beggar, but he was caught and his hand nailed to the door. The robbers, to save him, cut off his arm, but when making their escape Lamachus was too weak to keep up with the others and thrust his sword through his own body. Another leader, Alcimus ("the strong one"), tried to rob an old woman who tricked him and threw him out of the window so that he died. A third man, Thrasileon ("the courageous lion"), disguised in a bear-skin, helped his companions to steal gold and silver from the house of Demochares, but the dogs set upon him and reduced him to such a state that at last a man ran him through with a spear and killed him, while the robbers escaped with their treasure. Thus, one can see that in spite of their positive aspect, they fail and many of them are destroyed.

Mother's boys often have such sudden fits of doing something and then they go home to Mama to be spoiled, but they have no policy, no plans, which is why they fail in the end. Unconscious virility is of no use in this way, if it appears only sporadically. One can see from this that the robber world is a very ambiguous motif. It is a chance for Lucius to integrate his masculinity, or to lose it even more and in a worse way. It's just on the razor's edge, and depends on whether he realizes what it is and what is behind it. It is as though fate offered him an ambiguous possibility, either of initiation into manhood or of losing his identity still further and falling even worse into the claws of the Great Mother. What is still lacking here is the single most essential element of real masculinity—endurance. A man who can only be courageous in fits and starts, who can only do something sporadically, is not a man. Such spasms of virility without duration or planned consciousness are doomed from the beginning. They belong typically to a certain phase of a young man's fight with the mother complex. They resemble the sudden outbreaks which we now see in these horrible deeds which certain teenagers commit. They dare each other to pour kerosene on a man and burn him, and they think that that is a display of masculinity, but it simply lands them in complete failure and a breakdown worse than before. This kind of robber-shadow figure which unfolds its activity autonomously is doomed to run up against conventional society, which is quite justified in resisting such behavior. It is a typical state of delayed puberty transition. For example, in Switzerland most of the boys from better families belong to the Boy Scout movement. And on the one side they have a very decent Boy Scout life. They learn to bicycle and make knots, play football, and perform a good deed once a day. But many Boy Scout groups lead a nocturnal life which is most amusing: the older boys, disguised as ghosts or wild animals, frighten the younger boys, and a lot happens which comes sometimes within a hairsbreadth of an accident. But generally they are lucky, thank God! The really wonderful Boy Scout nights are when they go at midnight and jump naked into an ice-cold lake and such things, daring each other as to who can do even worse. When the boys are grown up, their shivering parents, who are thankful that they did not know at the time, are told all about it. So one can say that a certain amount of that is normal at a special age and belongs to the initiation of a young man and the assimilation of his virility. But at forty it is deplorable or difficult to catch up on these adventures. Such youngsters also have the daring without much perseverance, but later they begin to challenge each other in a much more refined way, namely as to who can endure for a long time. To endure a disagreeable situation represents a higher phase of development, the next step after the dashing, daring stage is past. At this stage, however, our robbers fail. But behind them is the drunken old woman who knows such beautiful fairy tales and who reveals to Lucius, for the first time, the archetypal background and the meaningful secret at play behind his tragic fate.

We must now examine why the old witch drinks. Again we come across, in this perverted form, an ambivalent element which could develop positively. The secret motivation behind drinking, as well as behind drug addiction, is, in most cases, the longing for an emotional experience of ecstasy, which originally and historically was a basic element in religious experience. Whenever people are cut off from this for some reason, being too intellectual or something else, then the longing for the spirit sometimes takes this rather concrete aspect, and is sought for in the bottle. We might, therefore, say that behind the mother complex, as represented by the robbers' mother, is a secret longing in Lucius for something spiritual which has not been fulfilled. The problem lies in the split-off part of his personality, split off because it is not connected with consciousness and lacks spiritual understanding. Expressed in biblical terms: the powers of darkness long for the light. The robbers' mother longs for something spiritual, but she takes it in this well-known surrogate form of liquor. Taken in the context of the whole book, it becomes more and more evident that behind the mother complex, even in the destructive form which is now slowly overwhelming Lucius, in the last analysis there is a secret longing for religious experience.

Furthermore, this old woman is not altogether negative, since, in order to comfort Charite, a prisoner of the robbers, she tells her the beautiful story of Eros and Psyche. Before we go into that, we first have to see what led up to the telling of the story. The robbers irrupted into a wedding party where the well-educated girl of a very good family, Charite, was to have been married to a young man called Tlepolemos. *Tle* means "to endure," "to stand," and *polemos* means "war." So he would be the warrior, the one who endures through a war, which is why he has the name of a famous Greek hero. The wedding ceremony of Charite and Tlepolemus is prevented, the robbers put the guests to flight, seemingly kill the bridegroom, steal all the wedding gifts, and abduct the bride. They do not harm her, for they are only interested in getting ransom money from her rich parents. The girl is in utter despair, and in order to keep her quiet the old hag tells her the story of Eros and Psyche.

It has already been pointed out by Reinhold Merkelbach[6] that the two couples, Charite and Tlepolemus as well as Eros and Psyche, undergo much the same fate at the beginning, for, as we will see later, Psyche is also separated from her bridegroom, goes through a tremendous amount of suffering, and in the end is reunited with her lover. Charite, the listener of the story, goes through the same process, except that for her everything goes wrong. So here there is a double couple:

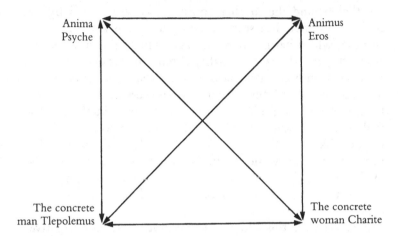

Charite and Tlepolemus, two human beings, and Psyche and
Eros, two divine beings. The constellation that appears thus in
their paralleled stories is the famous "marriage quaternio."[7]
Jung has pointed out that in every deep relationship between a
man and a woman there come indeed four elements into play:
the conscious ego of the man, the conscious ego of the woman,
his anima, and her animus. The figures of the animus and the
anima, owing to their numinous nature, were projected until
now (for instance in alchemy) upon royal figures or upon a
divine couple. Today, for the first time in history, we are
confronted with the problem of integrating these "superhuman" elements representing powerful aspects of the unconscious. If their integration does not succeed, then the hetero-
sexual elements of the unconscious overflood the ego: this is
one of the reasons for the increase of divorces today. In
Apuleius's novel the functions of the animus and the anima are
still represented by semidivine figures. However, one could
conclude from the "human" behavior of these figures that in
reality they are aspects of the human soul.

While various commentators have not realized the profound
relation of this tale in the whole context of the story of Lucius,
others recognized, especially Merkelbach, the mystical connection with the initiation in the Isis mystery cult, which is
described at the end of the novel.

Immediately when Lucius sees Charite, a beautiful, innocent young girl, the ass in him is awakened with interest in her. Even the drunken old woman has pity for her. In Greek mythology, Charis is one of the three Graces, those semigoddesses who are usually shown in a group of three, and represent grace and beauty. They were the companions of Dionysos. In Greek, the word *charis* means charm, intangible beauty, like that of the trees whose leaves are still completely fresh, or like that of a flower which opens up. The name Charite, and that of Tlepolemus, will become very meaningful later.

In this present condition the girl cries, not only because of the robbers, but because she had had a horrible dream in which she saw robbers kill her husband with a stone; she is therefore convinced that he is dead. We know that this is not true, because later he turns up, but is killed at the end by the robber Thrasyllus ("the reckless one") in a boar hunt. Although the dream does not correspond to the truth in this respect, it will become true later. Let us also bring to mind the fact that Charite commits suicide later, so the two are really already doomed to a tragic end.

The motif of the happy couple and of a masculine figure who disturbs the two is also to be found in alchemical symbolism. In *The Chymical Wedding* by Rosencreutz,[8] for instance, a Negro steals the bride, and she must be brought back by the bridegroom. The motif is also found in an alchemical parable, which Jung interpreted in *The Psychology of the Transference*,[9] where the thief who destroys the happiness of the couple is called Sulphur. It is the classical motif of the destructive masculine figure, the shadow figure of the man, or the animus of the woman, which disturbs the relationship. Jung interprets the thief as greed, the possessiveness of the ego, which makes the inner *coniunctio* impossible. Whenever one gets near the union of the opposites, the greedy ego wants to take the thing for itself and destroys the inner experience. This is true of the individual as well as on the level of the couple. This element destroys the love experience between two people just when it is going well, for then it awakes and destroys the whole relationship. If one remembers the attitude of Apuleius, then one can say that this male figure which disturbs the relationship with the female is the image of his own brutal shadow egoism, which disturbs his relations to women. It is his nonintegrated masculinity. The bride stolen by the robbers can be taken as a symbol of the anima who has been wounded by the chthonic masculine element. She represents the suffering feeling in the soul of Lucius. When a man falls for one-sided cold sexuality, he wounds the woman within as well as the woman without.

There is also a very revealing sentence, for the girl says that the robbers pulled her away "from the lap of her mother" and that is how her marriage was prevented. One would expect it to be "from the arms of her bridegroom." If we take it as a dream, it means that all feeling of Lucius-Apuleius under the aspect of Charite is still with the mother. With Photis, he experienced only sensuality, but his feeling is still sitting on the mother's lap. Men with a mother complex often prefer prostitutes to other women, and mothers who complain about such sons are really those who are most pleased about it, for they know that this is how they can keep their sons. But a suitable woman, whom he loves, would be a rival! In such a case the mother will say that she always wanted her son to marry, but not *this* woman. For she really feels that it is no longer only a matter of sexuality, but that this time his heart is pulling away from her. Here it becomes clear that Lucius is still dependent on the mother and that the robbers, despite their terrible deed, have done something positive for Lucius: through their intervention his feeling has at last been torn away by force from the mother, a necessary stage in order to be able to face the problems of life.

5
AMOR
AND PSYCHE I

Introduction to the Tale

I n order to distract Charite from her deep despair, the
drunken old woman who lives with the robbers recounts
to her the fairy tale of Amor and Psyche. Like all inserted
stories we will look at it as a dream.

The first two inserted stories of the novel one could call
"little dreams," but here we are dealing with a big archetypal
dream. The first story dealt with the murder of Socrates, and
the second with the adventure and mutilation of Thelyphron,
but this third mythological story occupies a large part of the
whole book. Erich Neumann has interpreted it independently
of the whole novel, using it as a model for the problems of
feminine psychology.[1] Taking Charite as a woman and Eros as
her animus, Neumann analyzed it in terms of the problem of
the woman getting away from the mother. He did not believe
that the fairy tale belonged in the context of the novel, but
thought it was a literary insertion. I do not agree with him
here, because psychologically it fits completely into the context of the novel, and also we cannot ignore the fact that the
book is written by a man who chose this fairy tale and inserted
it at a certain point. Therefore I am going to take it from the

standpoint of masculine psychology, representing the problem of Lucius-Apuleius.[2]

This type of fairy tale—the Amor and Psyche motif—is very widespread. "Beauty and the Beast" would be another example. The story is to be found in Russia, Spain, Germany, Italy, Greece, and even in India and Africa.[3] Typologically, it is the story of a young girl married to an unknown husband who appears either in an animal shape or in demonic form or who forbids her to call him by name or look at him in the light or in a mirror. Then she loses him by disobedience, and after a long, painful quest succeeds in finding him again and redeeming him. Usually he has been bewitched by a witch or wizard. Most philologists believe the story to be over two thousand years old. Apuleius, changing it here and there, inserted it in his novel, thus representing his own anima problem and preparing his initiation.

Before we go on with this essential jewel of the novel, I would like to remind the reader of the whole line of the book. The downward line shows, as mentioned already, the worsen-

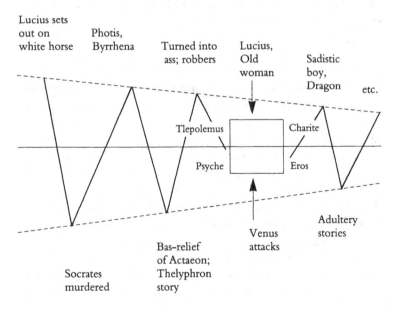

ing of Lucius's state of consciousness, whereas the upward lower line points to a slow progress in the unconscious. Lucius sets out on his white horse, he meets Photis, is turned into an ass, and comes to the robbers' cave, where a drunken old woman tells the story. He is then only an ass and the robbers' prisoner. At the same time a slight improvement in the unconscious takes place: at the beginning there was the gruesome story of the murdered Socrates, then followed Thelyphron's mutilation, and now comes the story of Amor and Psyche. The square drawn in the middle line of the scheme sets Eros and Psyche in connection with Tlepolemus and Charite.

As mentioned already, there is a certain parallel between the fates of the two couples. There are even late antique gems in which Charite is called Psyche,[4] so that even for a man of Apuleius's time, it was clear that these are two parallel stories with the difference that one couple consists of real people while the other consists of daimones, in the specific Neoplatonic sense. The mythological couple are mainly persecuted by the goddess Venus, while on the side of the human situation there stands the old woman, who recounts the story and who protects Lucius and Charite from the robbers. So the old woman and Venus are the forces which enframe this first encounter of the human and divine.

As I mentioned before, we are dealing here with the typical motif of the marriage quaternio, a scheme which, according to Jung, lies at the heart of every transformation process based on love, namely: a real couple, a man and a woman, and the corresponding archetypal aspects of their anima and animus, which are involved in every essential situation of mutual individuation between the sexes. The marriage quaternity is a symbol of totality. However, the first attempt at the realization of wholeness breaks apart within this story. Tlepolemus is killed and Charite commits suicide. Psyche and Eros are not killed, but they retire into Olympus, that is, into the distant collective unconscious. They do not realize themselves in the human reality. So this encounter means only a first abortive attempt to form a union of the two worlds. One reason why it is abortive is that Lucius, instead of taking part, is only an onlooker. He listens to the words of the old woman's story completely passively and in his donkey form. If he had entered this formation of the quaternio, if he had taken the place of Tlepolemus, then perhaps the whole coming together of the upper and the lower layer, the conscious and the unconscious worlds, could have taken place. But because he only listens, without entering the process except a little bit at the end, the whole thing falls apart again.

One might say that the fairy tale had relatively no effect upon our hero, that it was just a nice story, after which the main story about the suffering of Lucius-ass goes on. But as we shall see this is not true. Just as a dream that is not understood still has a certain effect upon consciousness, this story leaves behind a deep emotional impact. For after he has heard the fairy tale of Eros and Psyche, Lucius decides to run away with Charite, so he gets at least an impulse to try to free himself and return to a more human life. There is one more important detail: Charite sits on his back when they run away together, and Lucius, with the excuse of wanting to scratch his neck, tries to kiss Charite's feet. There one can see a tiny attempt on Lucius's side to become Charite's savior and lover, that is, to replace Tlepolemus. Although this small attempt does not have any effect, one sees that the fairy tale has had a certain impact upon him. It has aroused the impulse of the conscious personality to enter the game and become involved, but typically enough Lucius only tries this flirtatious donkey kiss. He does not have yet a serious feeling in what he is doing. It is as if, for the first time, the inner totality, or the structure of the Self, turned up from the unconscious, touched consciousness slightly, and then fell apart to sink again into the unconscious. Afterward, and probably because this attempt toward an integration has failed, things get rapidly worse. Lucius falls into the hands of a sadistic boy who nearly kills him and whose witch mother tries to castrate and burn him. If an attempt toward integration has been built up by the unconscious and then fails, then there follows generally a new and especially bad depression before the possibility of a further integration offers itself.

We must now go more into the two main figures of the fairy tale, Eros and Psyche, so that we may understand what the whole tale is about. Eros is a god, and, as Richard Reitzenstein[5] has proved, both he and Psyche are divine figures worshiped in local Greek cults. The goddess Psyche is of later origin than Eros, but she too had temples of her own in which she was worshiped. Both are relatively human figures, but are of that type of minor gods which the Greeks called daimones. The Romans called them genii. This Neoplatonic idea has its origin in the classical text of Plato, the *Symposium,* where Diotima explains:

> You have thus admitted that Love (because of what is lacking in the good and the beautiful) desires what is lacking.—I admit it.—How, then could he be a God, he for whom the good and the beautiful are faults?—In no way, apparently.—You see then, she told me, that you cannot consider Love a God.—What then, I said, is Love? A mortal?—Certainly not.—What then?—A superior being, an intermediary between the human and the divine.—What is he then, O Diotima?—O Socrates, he is a great daimon. Because the nature of daimones is intermediary between men and Gods.[6]

When Apuleius writes a fairy tale in which the central figure, Eros, is a daimon, he means not a personal, but a superpersonal daimon. And the goddess, Psyche, would also be such a figure.

The idea of the god Eros went through a long development up to the late Greek-Roman culture, for originally he was a Boeotian god, and the Boeotians were looked upon as primitive, rustic, and uncouth. He was worshiped by them in the form of a big wooden or stone phallus or just as a stone; he was thought of as the creative chthonic god who effected the fertility of the cattle and the fields and protected the wells. He was attributed with the special ability of protecting the tribe and its freedom in wartime, as well as its love life, especially homosexual love. In ancient Sparta the groups in men's societies were usually homoerotic and, thus united, became the protagonists for freedom and the protection of the country.

Homosexuality formed a kind of bond which led to a heroic attitude and also to a strengthening of the inner political life. Thus Eros is very close to the Greek god Hermes, who was also worshipped as a phallus in stone or wood or as a man with an erect phallus. In earliest times Hermes and Eros were practically identical. In Plato's writings, Eros is also considered the source of fertility and an inspiring force in all spiritual achievements. Later he became a literary figure and lost much of his original impressive power.

There are few large images of Eros left in antique art, but many little cut stones and gems on which he is represented as winged, sometimes as a winged being who shows his genitals, and frequently as a hermaphrodite. Or he is represented as a winged youth smelling flowers with a zither in his right hand, or as a winged phallus with a head on it or a small boy with a divine snake or a grown-up winged youth with a bow and arrow, as in Renaissance art. Or he is represented as a boy riding on Psyche as a butterfly, or sitting on the lap of his mother, the goddess of love, Aphrodite, or playing with her. Besides these representations the god Eros is also found in many Greek and Roman tombs as the protecting spirit of the dead or as the spirit of the deceased person. He is frequently shown holding a torch downward, the symbol of death. Again he is represented—and this comes closer to our fairy-tale motif—as holding a butterfly and sadistically burning it with his torch, which represents the idea that Eros, the god of love, is a great torturer of the human soul and at the same time its great purifier.

Love with its passion and pain becomes the urge toward individuation, which is why there is no real process of individuation without the experience of love, for love tortures and purifies the soul. Expressed differently, Eros presses the butterfly painfully against his chest, representing the soul being developed and tortured by the love god. On one beautiful gem the goddess Psyche, with her hands behind her back, is being tied by the god to a column which ends in a sphere. One could say that this image expresses in a beautiful way the process of individuation. Eros tying Psyche to the column surmounted by a sphere, the symbol of totality which is realized by suffering. Sometimes one would like to run away from the person to whom one is tied, in order to run away from the dependence, but Eros forces us to become conscious through this tie. Love makes us dare everything and leads us thus to ourselves. Therefore one of Eros's main epithets, which he had in antiquity, was "purifier of the soul."

One of the most beautiful prayers which I know is addressed to this great god. It has been preserved in a magic text:

> I call to thee, Origin of all Becoming, that spread your wings over the entire world, you the unapproachable, the infinite, that inspires the living thoughts of every soul, who has joined all things by your power. First-born creature of the universe, of the golden wings, dark being, you who veil reasonable thoughts and inspire with dark passion, you who live secretly in every soul, you create the invisible fire, touching every living being, the untiring torment of sorrowful pleasures and delights, since the universe has existed. You bring suffering in your presence, you who are sometimes reasonable and sometimes insane, you for whom men violate their duties with bold endeavors and that they call to help them, you the dark. You the last-born, the lawless, the merciless, the inexorable, the invisible generator without body of passions, archer, carrier of the torch, lord of all spiritual perception and of all things hidden, lord of the forgetting and father of silence, by whom shines all light, young child when you are born in the heart, old man when you are consummated. . . .[7]

Eros is very close to the alchemical Mercurius, who also has the arrow of passion and the torch, representing the torturing and painful aspect of love. At the entrance of the Aesculapian temple in Epidaurus, where the sick came to be healed of psychological or physical diseases, were the pictures of the two healing principles of Eros and Methē (drunkenness).[8] Love and drunkenness are the great healing forces for soul and body. The drunkenness referred to here is not that obtained through alcohol, though this vulgar aspect is in it, for in drunkenness you are out of your narrow ego confines and are lifted ecstatically to another world beyond the worries of everyday life. This experience of elevation and of eternity links us again with the archetypal basis of the psyche and has a healing and transforming effect.

Eros, one of the healing gods in ancient Greece, is also the "divine child" in some of its mystery cults. In the Eleusinian mysteries there took place the birth of a mystical divine child sometimes called Plutus, Iacchos, or Triptolemos and also sometimes called Eros. The central archetypal idea is that the divine earth mother gives birth to a divine boy, who is at the same time redeemer and god of fertility. He corresponds to the Mercurius in alchemy. All the later associations and ideas about love in medieval times absolutely coincide with what was said of Eros in earlier antiquity, and he is therefore a symbol of the Self. In the symbolism of alchemy there is always the divine couple: a god and a goddess, or a king and a queen, who represent the transcendental personalities, and a cock and a hen as the empirical personalities. Psyche would be the divine feminine partner of Eros, but in our fairy tale she is an ordinary human being, though in some other instances she is looked upon as half-divine, like Eros himself.

Psyche appears less as a divinity in late antiquity. She is nearly always represented together with Eros, sometimes without wings when she corresponds more to our figure in the story and is more in contrast to the immortal god, Eros. More frequently, however, she has wings, with the typical points or dots or circles which characterize butterfly wings. Then she is more a figure of the type of the divine young girl, Kore, the central figure of the Eleusinian mysteries.[9] In the Eleusinian mysteries, which, according to Jung, are mainly mysteries of the feminine psyche, the main theme is the story of Demeter, whose daughter, Kore (the divine maiden), was abducted by Hades-Pluto, the god of the dead and of the underworld. Finally, through the mediation of Zeus, she is allowed to have her daughter back from time to time. But this is only one aspect of the story. There must have been many more components of the mysteries which we do not know. But we do know that Kore gives birth to a mystical child, generally called Iacchus or Brimos ("the strong one") and in some late texts also Triptolemus or Eros. That was the great event of the night of initiation into the Eleusinian mysteries. Exactly what the mysteries were has never been betrayed, and we know them only through certain allusions by the Church Fathers who were initiated before their conversion to Christianity. But even after becoming Christian, they seem either not to have had the courage or to have had too much respect for the mystical content of the mysteries to give away what actually happened. They sometimes merely made some allusion to them, so we have to reconstruct what really happened. We know that, after long fasting and many rituals, those elected to be initiated were called at midnight to a central part of the temple and a priest carrying an ear of corn said, "I announce the good tidings: Brimo has given birth to the divine child Brimos" (or, according to another text, Iacchus). In the museum at Athens there is the famous relief of Triptolemus— Triptolemus is another name for the same god. It shows Demeter, with her hand on the head of a youth of about fifteen who is standing in front of her, while Kore stands on the other side. As mentioned already, we do not really know enough about these mysteries, but we do know that they had to do with the mother and daughter mystery and the birth of a son-divinity. Ovid gave to Iacchus, the divine child, the festive name *puer aeternus*.

On later gems Psyche is usually identical with Kore; she would be therefore the mother of Eros. But it is typical of mythological relationships that the woman is always the mother, sister, wife, daughter of her husband, father, and so on. It is also the typical relationship all gods had to each other, for instance, Isis and Osiris.

On his part, Eros was also a central figure in the Orphic mysteries, but this leads to difficult, controversial ground, for in antiquity there was an early Orphism and a later Orphism. The early Orphism was influenced by Egyptian religion. According to their cosmogony the world came into being from an egg whose upper half was gold and lower part silver. The egg burst apart and out of it came a god called Phanes-Eros.

Phanes was a divine youth and a creator god of the world. Similarly, in Egypt, Osiris was characterized as "the seed of the noble and magnificent egg."[10] There is a question as to whether and how far the old Boeotian god, who was worshipped in rural countries as a stone phallus, played a role in the early Orphic mysteries, or whether there was only a later connection between the two principles. Certainly in the time of Apuleius, Eros was worshipped as a world-creating principle par excellence; he also played a role in the Mithraic mysteries, where he appears as partner and redeemer of the goddess Psyche.

Commentary on the Story

The fairy tale of Eros-Amor and Psyche begins with the story of a king and a queen who have three daughters. The youngest is so beautiful that she attracts all the collective admiration, and a rumor spreads that she is an incarnation of the goddess Venus. The people begin to prefer this concrete incarnation to the rather abstract Olympian goddess and begin to worship her, which raises her to the status of a goddess, thus making her lonely and making it impossible for her to find a husband. She also attracts the jealousy and hatred of her less beautiful sisters and of Venus, who discovers that her temples and cult are deserted. The people's idea that this beautiful girl, Psyche, could be a human incarnation of Venus is not just a naive opinion. We will see that this corresponds to some extent to the reality, which is why Venus gets so angry with her.

Psychologically, Venus would represent the archetype of the mother-anima figure. From Jung's point of view[11] the anima figure in man is a derivative of the mother figure, which is the first feminine figure to impress the young male child. She means his first encounter with the feminine, which, so to speak, shapes his disposition for reactions toward women and gives his anima certain characteristics. Thus, in an undeveloped state, the mother and the anima figure are more or less one in the man's unconscious. Hence, one could say that Venus embodies the mother-anima archetype per se. Every man has by nature a predisposition to live such an experience, since its structure exists latent in the collective unconscious, somewhere "in Olympus," to use the language of Apuleius. There is no primary connection with that structure until it becomes visible by a human drama: the anima experience of a man begins, for instance, when he is interested for the first time in a woman. The feeling which he experiences thereby does not involve his personal conscious memories only; rather the whole mother-anima archetype comes into play and leads him to the love experience, with all the richness of the relationship to the other sex, as well as its difficulties and complications. Later still, it can lead to the realization of an inner psychic factor, independent of the outer woman: to one's own anima. For a human being, the experience of this realm of the psyche brings a fertile widening of the personality, which is why it has a healing effect. Here lies also the reason why Eros and Methē in Epidaurus were worshipped as healer gods. Psychological healing always entails a widening of the personality. It brings more life and more aspects of the personality into activity. One can say that the greater part of neurotic disturbances is due to the fact that the ego has its shutters too closed against those realities of life which want to enter. Therefore, healing coincides with a widening of consciousness. To the human being this means an access to religious experience, a discovery of the deeper meaning of life and of healing emotions. But in the mirror process it also means pulling down a brilliant omnipotent god into the miserable narrowness of human existence. A concept of the Christian theology illustrates this: the process of kenosis (from the Greek, "to empty oneself," "to dispose").[12] It means that Christ (when he was still with the Father, before his incarnation, as the Logos, the Johannine Logos) had the plenitude of the Father, the all-pervading oneness with the divine world, without definiteness. After that he emptied himself—*"ekénose heautón,"*—as Saint Paul writes—which means he emptied himself of his all-embracing plenitude and oneness in order to become a mortal. Man is heightened through the realization of the inner Christ (for instance, by getting Christian teaching), and Christ is lowered by his descent into the human world. This is also expressed by his birth in the stable.

What Christian theology says about Christ's kenosis is really a specific representation of a general archetypal event. Whenever a god incarnates, there takes place for him this process of kenosis, of narrowing, while at the same time human consciousness widens.

The problem of the incarnation of Venus is still pendent: a modern English writer, John Erskine, wrote a book about it entitled *The Lonely Venus*. Erskine is very amusing and must know a bit about feminine psychology, or must have become a bit conscious of his anima. He wrote another most amusing book called *The Private Life of Helen of Troy*. It is the story of Troy after conquest. Menelaus is furious and is forced by convention to kill his unfaithful wife, who by running away had started the whole war. Blazing with fury and conformist indignation, he storms after Helen, but the latter meets him with her natural charm and first makes a gesture of devotion, showing her beautiful breasts, and saying that she completely deserves it and he should please kill her. In a bitchy way, she slowly reconquers the whole situation. She comes home, where the old servants are indignant and treat her as a prostitute. But Helen, humble, friendly, and typically feminine, modestly and slowly takes the reins in her hands, and at the end of the book she rules Menelaus and the household, and people begin even to think that it must all have been Menelaus's fault.

Erskine had certainly got a whiff of certain problems, and is very well orientated in antiquity. *The Lonely Venus,* Erskine's other work, is the story of the love affair of Venus, who is unfaithful to her crippled husband, Hephaestus, and falls in love with the war god, Ares. In this way she gets mixed up with human affairs. In the Trojan war, in contrast to what Apuleius writes about the Olympic gods, the gods were very much involved. Zeus and the other gods tried to keep out of human dirt, but Ares went to fight on the side of the Trojans, and through that Venus got pulled into it. In the end there is a regressive restitution of the persona of the Olympic gods. After the burning of Troy on earth, the gods retire and become aloof again. The end scene has Zeus and the other Olympic gods looking down from a kind of balcony in the Beyond onto the burning city with all its dead and the destruction of war. Only Venus, by having fallen in love with Ares and having therefore been more deeply involved with human affairs, is unhappy and restless and cannot make peace with the aloof attitude of the Olympic gods. In the last sentence of the novel she suggests that the gods should really become man—an allusion to later Christian development.

Looked at broadly, what happened then was that at the end of antiquity the Olympic gods had worn themselves out in their aloofness and inhumanity and had become obsolete, and then came the great new myth of god becoming man. Historically, the masculine godhead has become a man, Christ. Incarnation has taken place on the masculine, not the feminine, side of development. But actually there was a germ or beginning of the development in late antiquity by which the feminine goddess should become a woman, and incarnation should not be only on the masculine side, but on the feminine side as well. Erskine, interestingly enough, has projected that into the love stories of Venus. In Virgil's story of Dido, Venus, more than the other Olympic gods, again gets involved in human affairs and, so to speak, elects a woman to act out her plans. Venus is the mother of Aeneas the Trojan, and in order to have him well received in Carthage she arranges that Dido, the queen of Carthage, should fall in love with him. Later, because politics advise otherwise, the love affair is ended, Dido is deserted, and she commits suicide. So one could say that Venus always has a tendency to get involved in human affairs, but generally the women she uses for her purposes get destroyed or are deeply unhappy. These tendencies toward an incarnation, or a linking of the feminine goddess with a human woman, therefore remained scattered attempts and did not lead to a great new religious, mythological event, as in the birth of Christ.

One can say that the incarnation of the feminine principle in a woman is still on the program for the coming centuries, and is beginning to become urgent today. Seen in this context, the fact that the people wanted to worship a human Venus in the form of this girl Psyche, a king's daughter, is most meaningful. For it expresses the wish of the people that Venus should also become human and change in that way. If we look at the process of the incarnation of a godhead in psychological terms, then it is the mirror effect of a realization by man, or the archetypal background of a psychological realization. We think generally of modern man having an ego, then a threshold of consciousness, with the unconscious below. In dreams we distinguish the personal unconscious from a structure underneath (that which we call the collective unconscious), the energetic nuclei of which would be the archetypes. Normal man has no idea of this reality and experiences it therefore in projection. Through modern Freudian and Jungian analysis one has begun to discover this substructure of the human psyche and to see that the motivations behind our fate stem from there, and, coming through the filter of the personal unconscious, modify and influence consciousness. In the analytical process we use the word *integration* for what happens, meaning that the ego relates to these contents, has an *Auseinandersetzung,* a confrontation, with them, recognizing them as the deeper part of its own psychic substructure. Now, what happens, actually, if you take a mirrored, symmetrical standpoint and look at the thing from the side of the archetypes? The archetypes are the gods of polytheistic paganism. The Greek gods are the archetypes in the collective Greek psyche. What happens to the gods if this process of integration takes place? A relationship is never only a one-way thing, so the gods get pulled into the human realm and, in the countermovement, the ego expands its conscious awareness. That is the process of the incarnation of a god. Actually, the beginning of this process is not here. We very often see in the impulse toward individuation and integration it is the god who wants to incarnate. Only secondarily is the ego touched and pulled into the process. This explains why initial dreams in analysis frequently are not that the ego meets divine figures, but that the god has decided to incarnate. The ego has no idea of this but is looking somewhere else, has had money or marital troubles, and does not know yet what is being played out on the other side. Very often the creative initiative of the process of individuation comes from the other side.

In our fairy tale, then, we can understand that Venus does not like to incarnate in a human being and resents being robbed of her all-encompassing divinity. She feels a typically feminine and rightful jealousy toward the girl Psyche.

Reinhold Merkelbach has taken great trouble to find out, step by step, the analogy between Isis and Psyche.[13] He is convincing to a certain extent, but he stumbles over the fact that Psyche as well as Venus can be looked at as identical with Isis. That Venus is a parallel to Isis is clear, but that would mean that Isis fights Isis! We are dealing here with a split within the symbolic figure. A fight arises between one part of the archetype which wants to remain in its original form, in its inertia, and the other part which wants to incarnate into human form. The conflict is represented in a projected form as jealousy, when Venus says indignantly, "And now a mortal girl, who will die, walks about in my shape," which very clearly expresses her feeling. She protests against the narrowing of her immortal omnipotence.

Venus then orders her son, Eros, to make the girl fall in love with the lowest of all human beings, but Eros, on seeing his victim, elects to be that lowest human being himself. Then it is arranged that the king, because his daughter has not married yet, is told by the Delphic oracle that she will never marry but is destined for a terrible dragon, or monstrous thing, and that, therefore, she should be exposed on the top of a mountain. This is a typical Greek version of the fairy tale.

In all the more modern folklore stories[14] it is the girl who brings this fate upon herself. Some versions run: A father or a king has three daughters. He goes for a journey and asks them what he should bring back. One wants clothes, the other money or jewels, but the youngest girl asks for something nonexistent, something fantastic. For instance, she wishes *"ein singendes, springendes Löweneckerchen"* ("a singing, springing lion's lark"), or a squirrel called Sorrow, or a white bear named Valemon, or a white dog from the mountains, or some such apparently whimsical thing. And when the father finds it—the lion's lark or white bear or wolf or a squirrel called Sorrow—it says, "All right, you can have me, but in return your daughter must marry me." So, by a kind of wishful fantasy, the girl brings this fate upon herself. Here it is replaced by the Delphic oracle, which is not much different if one realizes that the oracle was simply the place where people asked, with the help of a medium, for an explanation of the present constellation of the collective unconscious. Even before the greatest military and political enterprises, the Greeks never omitted first consulting the collective unconscious constellation to find out whether it was favorable for a war or not. That was very wise and corresponds to the fact that until the First World War the Japanese parliament still officially consulted the *I Ching* before great actions, and I think if they had consulted it before the Second World War they would perhaps have been better off. There they were already "enlightened" by our not doing so.

One could therefore say that something from the collective unconscious voices the wish for a union of Eros and Psyche and for an incarnation of Venus. It is the wish for a divine marriage between the masculine and the feminine principles. Because Venus is the mother of Eros, and Psyche is Venus, we are dealing here with the famous mythological *hieros gamos* ("sacred marriage") between the mother-daughter-sister and her own son, but this time in a partly incarnate form, since it is not only that an archetypal image of Venus is approaching the human realm, but also that the whole image of the sacred marriage is coming down onto earth.

The girl is exposed on the mountain and left there for a death marriage. The *hieros gamos* is often mythologically identical with the death experience, so this is not only a play on the words of Apuleius, for Psyche goes through a kind of anticipation of a death experience. This has also been pointed out by Merkelbach, who says that this first part of the love affair of Eros and Psyche is really something which happens in the Beyond, in the underworld of death, though in its blissful aspect. It is so, because Psyche is carried away by the wind into a kind of unreal, beyondish, magical situation, far away from all human experience and existence, where she is served by invisible servants and united with an invisible partner.

The underworld, which is identical with the unconscious, here shows its paradisiacal, fairylike, alluring, and soporific beauty, and Psyche is caught into its magic realm. Whenever a deeper love experience between a man and a woman takes place, there has opened up another dimension of reality; a divine dimension breaks into the psyche and washes away its egocentric pettiness. There is an element of romantic unreality about it which every passionate love experience also generally contains, at least in its beginning stages, a kind of Olympic spring blossoming where everything is divine and somehow uncannily real. That is why people in love are laughed at by those around them. If they are wise they disappear out of human society, they fall out of it, because they are now in the realm of the gods. In spite of its divine beauty, there is also an uncanny feeling of having lost something which essentially belongs to the human realm—the pettiness, the jealousy, the narrow-minded cynicism, and all the other not-so-nice qualities of the higher mammals. This condition brings up the jealousy of Psyche's sisters.

The classical philologist C. S. Lewis has written a famous novel, *Till We Have Faces,* in which he created very aptly a kind of modern paraphrase of this story of the jealous sisters. He interprets them as the shadow figure of Psyche. It is a little dangerous to use the word *shadow* in this respect, because if Psyche is a daimon, she is not a human being. Does a daimon also have a shadow? We can say yes, but then it is a slightly different use of the word. *Cum grano salis,* these sisters are the shadow of Psyche, the other aspect of the humanization of the goddess, namely, of being pulled into the human, the all-too-human, realm. Young people generally do not see this realistic and cynical side of love. Only in later life, when one has experienced the true and divine aspect, can one become immune to the cynical, inferior side of human relationships. If the ideal side of love prevails too much, the dark side is blotted out or repressed, and then it naturally develops into a dangerous outside factor. No grown-up person can be only romantic; one has had too much experience of life not to know that there is an all-too-human aspect of love. This aspect is embodied in the sisters. Here they instill distrust into Psyche's ear and heart, and make her disregard what Eros has demanded of her. The main figure in C. S. Lewis's novel is, characteristically, one of the jealous sisters, and he tries to show that it was she who destroyed the first relationship of Eros and Psyche. She personifies the woman who refuses the love of the god.

Psyche herself could best be compared to all the young mythological daughters of the great mother goddess. From Kerényi's paper on the Kore myth, and Jung's commentary on it, in *Essays on a Science of Mythology*,[15] we find out more about these two figures. One could take Psyche as a variant of the Greek goddess Kore. Besides the mature woman there is the young girl who simply represents the mother goddess in her rejuvenated form. Mother and daughter are one, in the same way as the Father and the Son in the Christian religion. We have to ask, however, what the difference is between the mother and the daughter goddess, and in general we can say, looked at *mutatis mutandis,* that the daughter goddess is closer to the human than the mother goddess, just as God the Father is more removed from man than Christ. The same difference is true in regard to Kore. The girl goddess is closer to humanity, being a more incarnated form of the mother goddess, and Psyche would correspond to a more humanized form of the Great Mother, a form which has almost completely reached the human level. Only her name still implies that she is divine. In the great Demeter-Kore myth, Kore sometimes has to live with her mother in the upper world, and sometimes with Pluto in the lower world. Psyche, too, is connected with the underworld through a daimon who seems to be a god of death. Only at the end is she redeemed and taken up to Olympus. So one sees that her fate is a new variation of the old Demeter-Kore myth, and that she herself is an incarnated form of the Great Mother. In a man's psychology this myth represents the problem of making himself conscious of and integrating his anima.

If a man is capable of integrating the anima, of establishing human contact with his anima, then he brings something archetypal into the realm of his humanity. From the man's side this would be making the anima conscious, but seen from the side of the unconscious itself it means that the archetype incarnates. As Apuleius believed, the gods are removed from man and cannot be contacted directly. When the archetype appears as a synchronistic phenomenon you cannot do anything with it. You can see a meaning in it but you cannot influence it. Gods are, so to speak, the archetypes among themselves, and among them is the mother archetype—the great queen of heaven. Closer to man comes Kore-Psyche, the archetypal image entering the personal field of a man's ego. I would like to illustrate this with an example.

A young man who had a positive mother complex dreamed of a mother goddess, a huge green woman with huge green hanging breasts, who was quite terrifying. He ran away from her in many dreams, so I got him to do an active imagination on the dream, that is, to take up contact with her in a waking fantasy.[16] He approached her in a little boat and tried to enter a conversation with her, but he could not get close to the figure, for she was too frightening. All the same he saw that the whole had to do with his mother complex and his romantic veneration for nature. Then in outer life he got into contact with a beautiful, hysterical woman who behaved as a nature demon would. I said that he should talk to this woman inside himself, and when he did this, she said, "I am the same as the green one with whom you could not talk." This irrational, catty woman said she was immortal! He said that he did not accept that, but she answered that she was the beginning and the end, meaning that she was God. Then a long conversation started in which the whole of his *Weltanschauung* had to be rediscussed. He had to review his whole attitude to life, which she pulled to pieces bit by bit. The green woman on the first level would be practically unapproachable, and the next step would be the Kore figure, which had a personal connection with him and with whom he could make contact.

Ovid speaks of Eros as the *puer aeternus*. That is giving him the highest inner value. It has become a habit to speak of the *puer aeternus*, meaning by that a mother's boy, as a bit homosexual, idealistic, and unadapted, someone likely to be artistic and to have megalomaniacal fantasies. But in labeling a man like this, we forget that we are using the name of a god. It is the name of the genius, Eros. Eros is the *puer aeternus*. He represents the phenomenon which we know mostly in its negative context. If a man is a mother's boy and lives as though he were eternal, as if he did not need to adapt to reality and a real woman, if he lives in savior fantasies as the man who will one day save the world or be the greatest philosopher or poet, he is wrongly identified with the *puer aeternus* figure. He is identical with a god, and he has not yet detached his ego complex from it. It has not yet grown out of the archetypal background, and the *puer* is sheer destructiveness. Such boys, who are stuck in the mother complex, are absolutely unformed, and the collective scheme fits all the cases. When I lectured on the *puer aeternus* case, many people came up afterward and said that they knew who he was, and a lot of young men were named. However, I was lecturing on the case of a man who had never been in Zurich. It was just that the characteristics fitted an innumerable number of cases.

The positive mother complex in particular constellates the divine son-lover of the Great Mother. Both together play the role of goddess and god, as Jung describes it in the first chapter of *Aion*. For a young man it is a great temptation to stay with the eternal mother, and he joins in by being the eternal lover. They help each other to stay outside life and do not face the fact that they are ordinary human beings. The son cannot separate from the mother and prefers to live the myth and the role of the young god instead.

That is the negative aspect. If he grows up, however, and realizes that he has to adapt to reality and to leave the paradise of the mother, then the *puer aeternus* becomes what he always has been, something positive: an aspect of the Self.[17] If he does not grow up, neither his ego nor the Self are pure, because everything is too contaminated. The ego is inflated, that is, it assumes the role of the archetype, and the archetype is not free either. Man assumes the role of a god, and the unfortunate thing for him is that he becomes unadapted, ill, and neurotic, and then the *puer aeternus,* in his aspect of the Self, is also infected and becomes poisoned from his contact with human nature.

If we ascertain that this or that figure represents the Self, then this is a somewhat indefinite statement, for the Self has many facets. Eros would represent therein the aspects of creativity and vitality, as well as the capacity for being gripped by and feeling the meaning of life, for devoting oneself to the other sex and the search to find the right relationship, for being able to lift oneself beyond the boredom of life, to be moved religiously, to look for one's own *Weltanschauung,* to support other people and to be able to help them. A person who meets someone in whom Eros is alive feels the mysterious inner nucleus behind his humble human ego, for he has creativity, life, and vitality. A man who has assimilated the *puer* will, when he deals with a problem, shape it anew. One knows from literature that people of genius have a way of discussing problems from entirely new angles. There is a source of creativity within them which is a specific manifestation of the Self.

The image of the Self does not appear only as the *puer* but often also as the "wise old man," but as *puer* it is eternally youthful and gives a creative impulse to man which enables him to see life from another angle. This can be felt especially in Goethe's poems. In the "West-Eastern Divan," for instance, the poet uses Islamic mysticism as the outer form: the tired old man calls a young slave to bring him wine, and he speaks to the youth with a slightly erotic tinge. That is an experience of the Self. The *puer aeternus* always conveys the feeling of eternal life, of life beyond death. On the other hand, where there is an identification with the *puer* one finds the neurosis of the provisional life; that means *someday* the boy hopes to become an important man. Such youths live in the wrong idea of immortality, missing the here and now, which has to be accepted because it is what makes the bridge to eternal life.

In the case of a positive mother complex the young man identifies with the *puer aeternus* and must give up this identification. In the case of the negative mother complex the man refuses completely the identification with the *puer aeternus* quality. He tends to be cynical and not to trust his own feeling, or women. He is in a state of constant restraint. He cannot give himself to life and smells danger everywhere. One could say that in our novel, Milo symbolizes this kind of stinginess, he who does not risk anything and who always sees "the snake in the grass." Therefore, in the man with the negative mother complex, the *puer aeternus* becomes a very positive *inner* figure which has to be assimilated so that he can progress out of his psychic narrowness and counterbalance his frozen attitude to life.

We know that Lucius wants to investigate the negative mother complex and therefore his big problem is the *puer aeternus* whom he must find. Contrary to Lucius, Eros himself has a positive mother complex. He has an incestuous dependency on Venus and therefore has some difficulty in marrying. His problem is exactly the opposite of Lucius's.

Remember that at first Eros and Psyche live happily united in the darkness of a faraway castle. She is happy but does not know what her husband looks like. Her jealous sisters find out about this hidden happiness and instruct Psyche to take a knife and kill him, because, they say, he is a snake or a dragon. We have to think what the jealous sisters stand for inwardly in a man. Erich Neumann takes them as shadow figures of Psyche. If we take it as a problem of a woman, this is true; her shadow is then projected onto her sisters, who want to destroy her happy marriage with the man she loves. If we take it as an anima problem, the sisters would represent the negative aspect of the anima. Her outstanding characteristic is jealousy, which would cause the poisoning of the anima through the negative mother aspect. The feelings coming from the negative mother poison the inner experience of life. The negative sisters who ruin Psyche are both unhappily married, having married for money and power, and they obviously represent a destructive side of the power complex, which destroys every true feeling relationship. They symbolize the greedy, envious force, the jealousy, possessiveness, and miserliness of the soul which does not want to give itself to an inner or outer love experience, together with the inability to get away from the banal aspect of life.

The man with the positive mother complex does not know this, for in his conscious behavior he tends to trust women too much. But if one knows him better, one discovers that he has this distrustful jealousy somewhere in the background of his feeling. Where there is a negative mother complex, the man will be jealous, distrustful, possessive, and anxious in his behavior toward women, but in the unconscious behind that, he remains very naive and shy, only because he is afraid to expose his feelings too much.

I once analyzed a man with a negative mother complex who had lived with his aunt. She was a hysterical, horrible old woman. It was really a fairy-tale-like story. She imprisoned him to such an extent that he could not even leave the flat during the day. He had to make the beds and clean the floors, was never allowed to go out, and was even forced to live with her sexually. This was in 1940 in Switzerland! The man escaped his aunt, entered analysis, and spoke of all women as damned witches. After some time he decided to give up his homosexual leanings and intended to take up connections to young women. But one cannot escape such a problem by conscious decision, so he had to work a lot more. For some strange reason he trusted me completely from the first day, but in such an unreal way that my heart sank. He asked for the meaning of his dreams and believed everything I said. I was apprehensive because nothing is more depressing than to be trusted more than one deserves. He did not see that I was an ordinary human being, but took everything I said for gospel. The result was a miraculous cure: his symptoms disappeared in two months. It was uncanny to me and reached the borders of magic; then he fell too much into the optimistic *puer aeternus* attitude, the reverse of the negative mother complex. Fortunately, after much more analytical work he really came out of his troubles.

Since then I have learned to expect such a reaction, knowing that where there is a negative mother complex, suddenly the *puer aeternus* will come out in the divine form, a divine naiveté which is not up to life as it really is, or women as they really are. After having switched from one to the other, he had to grow up to a middle attitude and learn to go into relationships without complete distrust or the limitless trust of a little boy. But I could have done nothing for him if I had misused my power. I had to wait and avoid every power attitude. I tried from time to time to put a little skepticism into his trustfulness, and when I gave him the interpretation of a dream, I asked him if he really believed it, trying to get him to be more critical and to listen to his own judgment instead of saying, always, "Yes." At the end it so happened that one day he needed me badly. At that time I had the flu and could not see him. That gave him a shock, and suddenly he saw that I was an ordinary human being who could even fall ill. For the first time he realized that I was not a divine daimon or goddess but could get the flu, and that gave him a hint that he should grow up, that to leave everything in my hands was not quite safe. So he pulled himself together and began to think about his relationship to me and what it meant.

In our tale one can say that in the figure of Psyche is personified a positive feeling relationship of man to women and to the unconscious, but one which is naive and still living in paradise, where everything is positive. At the same time, the jealous sisters are too skeptical, too cynical, and too much aware of the banal aspect of life. If one walks in the woods and sees the young couples who are in love with each other, then one realizes that they are living in a divine world. The people who pass by have a double reaction, for, on the one hand, they recognize that the lovers are in a divine world, and, on the other, everything looks so utterly common and banal. It is "the eternal Harry and the eternal Harriet," and, like the jealous sisters, the passers-by make mocking remarks because they are aware of the couples' banality and incompleteness, while the couples themselves see only their fairy-tale aspect. The two aspects are too far apart and one-sided. One who sees such a thing from a more mature attitude will know that there is always both, the divine and the banal aspect, and that is one of the greatest paradoxes our feeling must learn to accept.

A woman who was occupied with this problem, and who asked herself whether her love relationship was a divine experience or a banal love affair, dreamed once of a king and a queen wearing radiant crowns, walking ahead of her, accompanied by a cock and a hen. And a voice said, "These two pairs are one and the same thing." This image represents fittingly the paradox of love, but practically it is a great problem, and to stand it, great maturity is required. In alchemy the symbol of the *coniunctio,* a union of the divine couple, can be represented equally as king and queen, as god and goddess, or as two mating dogs.[18] The alchemists knew that these are all aspects of the same union, symbols of the psychic opposites in the unconscious wholeness of the personality.

6

AMOR
AND PSYCHE II

We have seen that Psyche and Venus are two aspects of the same archetype, Venus symbolizing more the anima which is mixed with the maternal image and Psyche the actual anima which is no longer contaminated with the maternal image. One could imagine the archetypes like atomic nuclei in the field of the unconscious. Most probably, there they are in a state in which every element is influenced by all the others. Thus an archetype in the unconscious is in some way also identical with the whole unconscious. It contains in itself the opposites: it is everything, masculine and feminine, dark and light, everything overlaps. Only when an archetype approaches the threshold of consciousness does it become more distinct. In our story, Venus resents that she, the omnipotent goddess in the Beyond, has now a rival on earth. This is a widespread problem in late antiquity. It appears with variations, for instance, in the so-called "Songs of the Fallen Sophia," which were written about the time of Apuleius. According to some Gnostic systems, especially in the book *Pistis Sophia*,[1] there was with God at the beginning of creation a feminine figure or companion: Sophia, Wisdom. In the Apocrypha of the Old Testament, too, she is represented as the Wisdom of God. (See the Song of Solomon,

Jesus Sirach, and Proverbs.) There she says: "Before God created the world I was there. I played with Him. . . ." But, since according to Christian teaching God is not married and has no feminine companion, the interpretation of these texts gave some trouble to the Church Fathers, who therefore said that this was the pre-incarnate form of the "anima Christi" before his incarnation.

In many Gnostic systems it is said that Sophia was with God at the beginning of, or before, creation, but later she sank down into matter and was cut off from God. She had lost her connection, and in seeking Him when looking down into matter she saw a lion-headed demon, Jaldabaôth, and she thought that that was God the Father and went down, and Jaldabaôth caught her. There are very beautiful songs and poems in which she calls back to the Heavenly Father asking for his help to free her from matter and from her contamination with the demons and with Jaldabaôth. The Gnostics in late antiquity were the philosophers and thinkers in the early Church, and it is not by chance that they have amplified the myth of the fallen Sophia, because as Jung says, if a man identifies with the Logos or the intellect, his emotional and feeling side falls into the unconscious and must be redeemed from there.[2] His soul then becomes contaminated with primitive chthonic passion. This myth, developed especially by the Gnostics, was forgotten after the Church decided to expel the Gnostic philosophers and declare their system as heresy.[3]

Were we to compare the incarnation of the Father God in Christ with the incarnation that occurs in the story of Amor and Psyche, we would have different images. God comes down from the heavenly sphere, carefully purified from any *macula peccati,* and takes on human form. In the parallel of our story, the incarnation of the goddess is not the same. Venus does not come down and incarnate in a feminine being, but instead an ordinary feminine being is elevated and regarded as a personification of Venus and rises slowly up to Olympus. In the development of the Catholic teaching, too, the Virgin Mary is first an ordinary feminine being who slowly, through the historical processes, is elevated to nearly divine rank. Thus, in

the incarnation of the male god there is a descent into humanity and into matter, and in the incarnation of the female
goddess, an ascent of an ordinary human being to a nearly
divine realm. We are dealing, on the one hand, with the
materialization of the abstract *logos,* and, on the other hand,
with the spiritualization of matter. The latter process is still
today in its beginnings. Psyche, who is looked on as an
incarnation of Venus, incurs her wrath and is condemned in
the Beyond to marry the lowest of men. But Eros, falling in
love with her, decides to be her mysterious bridegroom.
Psyche is placed on the summit of a rock for her funeral
marriage and left there. But a soft wind lands her in a paradisiacal country where she lives very happily with her husband,
who remains invisible, only visits her at night, and forbids her
ever to look at him. In contrast to what happens later, the first
descent of Psyche into the unconscious has a misleading aspect,
which takes her into an ideal place, a fool's paradise of happy
love. And, as with all fairy tales which run parallel, this cannot
last. In this form, her process of becoming conscious is delayed, since for Psyche the event indeed seems to be lucky and
a great blessing, but from the human realm it means a loss. In
the human realm a feminine being, who has already carried
the first characteristics of Venus in an incarnated form, has
disappeared into the unconscious, and in this the human world
has suffered a "loss of soul." At the beginning of the coming
up of a new content from the unconscious, energy is being
used, and hence there arises often on the other side a loss of
libido, a depression or emptiness, until one discovers what
comes up from below and what has happened there. Therefore
we cannot be too angry with the two sisters, who, with
jealousy, learn of the secret of Psyche's happiness and who
weave their poisonous intrigues by telling her that Eros is a
dragon.

The slander that Eros is a monster is in itself meaningful
because in antiquity Eros was very often represented as a
dragon or a snake. In alchemy the snake or the dragon is a
symbol of the *prima materia* of the "stone of the philosophers"
or a symbol of the "divine child."[4] So the two sisters are not

too much off the mark. In a way they are even right: if the whole love problem has again regressed into such deep layers of the unconscious, one could say that it was completely inhuman and cold. The dragon and the snake always refer to something in the unconscious which is inhuman, either in the positive sense of being divine or in the negative sense of being demonic. In either case they are not human and lack the possibility of human contact. Jung always pointed out that wardens in zoos say that from the snake on downward even the specialist in animal contact cannot make any feeling connection. One can tame and handle a snake for years, but one day it will bite, and even a very experienced warden cannot foresee such a reaction. With warm-blooded animals, on the other hand, someone with enough experience and knowledge can foresee or guess their reactions. If we live close to warm-blooded animals, we can have an empathy with them that we cannot have with snakes. As soon as a content in the unconscious appears in snake form it is therefore often difficult to make the meaning understandable to the dreamer. He does not feel any empathy toward this content of the unconscious, which sometimes shows itself only in physical symptoms, especially in those which involve the sympathetic nervous system. It is therefore almost impossible to come in contact with something which is stirred in this form in the deepest layers of the unconscious. We feel, quite innocently, that this has nothing to do with us, and generally it takes, in my experience, months before such a content becomes visible enough for one to be able to say, "Now, that is the snake." Therefore, if the sisters slander Eros, calling him a snake, they describe it in the way Eros appears when seen from outside. It is too far away from the human and therefore the unreal, divine paradise in which Psyche lives has to be destroyed.

Naturally, one can also connect the sisters with the power drive, which works in them, although this drive has a positive value, as power and self-preservation are very closely connected. If an animal expands its territory by fighting a neighboring animal, is that self-preservation fighting to have enough food, or is it power? In a certain measure it is simply self-preservation, but if it goes beyond that it begins to become what we would call power drive. There is only a thin borderline between the two. This instinct of self-preservation, contaminated with evil power, breaks into the paradise of Psyche. She is induced to take a lamp and a knife and to throw light on her bridegroom in the night. If she should find that he is a dragon, she intends to kill him. So, with no less intention than murdering Eros, Psyche lights the lamp. But then she discovers that her husband is a beautiful winged youth, and she is so shaken by this overwhelming sight that she drops the knife, and a drop of hot oil from the lamp falls onto Eros. He wakes up and gives her the greatest punishment this god can give: he leaves her. To be left by the god of love is really worse than anything else he could have done to her. Psyche now is completely in the dark, and now her real deeds begin with the long and agonizing search to find Eros again.

The symbolism of the lamp, whose oil burns Eros, is double. In a modern German parallel, recorded by the brothers Grimm,[5] it is the light (not the oil) that drives away the hidden lover. In mythological context light symbolizes consciousness. The light of a lamp represents in particular that which consciously is at the disposal of a human being and can be controlled by him, in contrast to the light of the sun, which is of a divine and cosmic nature. Jung has pointed out frequently that it is not possible to describe the unconscious life of the soul with the help of conscious and logical categories. Too much "light" damages the soul. Symbolic analogies are much more adequate, because all psychic reality is never "nothing but" this or that; rather, it is a living entity with innumerable facets. Moreover, the hot oil of the lamp makes Eros suffer greatly. In every devaluating interpretation of the personification and of psychic events of this kind there lies hidden a secret motivation: the wish to escape the "divine" aspect, which is manifested in all archetypal manifestations of the deeper layers of the collective unconscious. The true motivation of this rationalistic devaluation is fear. We see this depreciation at work in the common modern psychological theories, in which the great divine symbols of the unconscious are looked upon as "only" sexual or involving the power drive.

Beyond the fear there is contained in the oil of the lamp still one more element, namely, "burning" passion, but a passion which has more to do with demand for power and possession than with true love. Psyche personifies here some *personal* traits of the anima of Apuleius-Lucius: his passionate longing for knowledge *(curiositas)* and his inclination toward magic, whose purpose is to manipulate the divine forces instead of serving them. These intellectual qualities of his anima have prevented Lucius until now from getting to know the goddess Isis through personal experience and subordinating himself to the unexplorable mysteries of the soul. Love can endure neither an intellectual standpoint (these are "nothing-but" interpretations) nor the passion which strives for possession. That is why Eros runs away, deeply wounded, and Psyche must suffer long trials before she can find him again.

As Erich Neumann[6] has pointed out, in that moment when Psyche begins to love truly she is no longer lost in the unconscious of a distant paradise of joy and death; rather, she awakens and behaves toward Eros like a loving partner. The personal love has taken the place of a purely collective pleasure principle, but exactly in this moment love becomes tragic.

Generally in fairy tales the woman achieves individuation by suffering, while the male hero is more active. There are exceptions, but the hero slays dragons, fights with giants, or climbs mountains, while the heroine more frequently completes her quest by enduring suffering without giving up her love. Psyche is a typical example of the latter. There are innumerable fairy tales in which the girl goes to find the water of life, and so on. There are also the texts of late antiquity, as I have mentioned, which described endlessly the sufferings of the goddess Sophia and her descent into hell.

There is a certain amount of the same motif in the Jewish teaching that the divine aspect of the feminine in God, the Shekhinah, has to be redeemed from matter and return to God again. These Jewish Shekhinah tales were probably influenced by Gnostic traditions, or they may come from the same source. Jung mentions this in his book *Alchemical Studies*. He says that wherever motifs come up in which the feminine side of God has gotten separated from the male, this is the separation from the anima through the Logos, who wants absoluteness and the victory of the spirit over the sensual world. The more a man wants to establish order in consciousness, the more he will cut himself off from the anima, and she therefore falls into the lower level, into matter. This means that he is dissociated from his anima, who sinks down into suffering and endless emotions. Where the man does not consider his anima and keep in contact with her, she becomes more and more involved in sensual impulses and primitive affects. That's why the academic man often has a worse character than the man in other professions, for he is the type who tends to reject the anima and who therefore regresses onto a lower level. If you take away the academic persona from the professor, you may find just a baby. He is often the man who marries his cook, for he is too lazy to find a proper wife and has no time to develop his feeling and woo a decent woman to whom he might have to give in to a certain extent. The man who is absorbed in his books all day needs someone simple, so he marries his cook because she is there, and after a few years she rules him! He has devoted himself to the Logos, and the anima has regressed into primitive sensuality, affect, and emotion. Naturally, this is only a caricature of what happens when the man rejects Eros too much. And that is mirrored in the motif of the anima falling down from heaven and having to go on a long quest. As stated earlier, mythologically, the woman usually reaches the goal more by suffering than through action. It is a quest of endurance, and of more and more suffering, while the hero often has to be active, though this is not always the case. Like the suffering, fallen Sophia in Gnosis, she accepts her suffering and goes a long way to find Eros. In the tale of Eros and Psyche, one fact, however, is definitely altered by the interference of the wicked sisters, a little fact which Neumann skips in his book, but which is an important point for me: in leaving her, Eros says to Psyche that the child which she has in her womb will now become a girl instead of

a boy. "If you had not broken the secret," he says, "it would
have been a boy, but because of what you have done you will
not lose the child, but will give birth to a girl." We know that
at the end of the story, when she is on Olympus, she gives
birth to a girl called Voluptas, sensuous love. She would have
given birth to a boy, whose name we do not know, if she had
not broken the spell.

If we interpret this turn of events from the human aspect
and connect it back to Apuleius, then it becomes clear that
Charite and Psyche are a personal aspect of the same figure in
his unconscious, which is tied up with the positive aspect of
the mother complex and with a great *puer aeternus* naivité.
When a man has a positive mother complex he identifies
directly with the divine child. He behaves like a winged god,
refusing all the essential tasks of life, such as taking a firm
standpoint of reality of his own, earning his own money,
finding his appropriate line of work, and similar hardships.
Lucius has a negative mother complex, as we saw in the
beginning. One could say that he, the ass, is completely
imprisoned by the negative aspect of the mother archetype.
The Psyche-Eros mythos now shows an *enantiodromia*, a beginning turn into the opposite. But since this positive aspect is
still completely unadapted and unrealistic, the sisters can break
into it.

This leads us to the question of what the "masculine child"
who is not born could have been. The answer is: the child of
the anima, that is, the Self. The result of the *hieros gamos*, of
the sacred marriage of Eros and Psyche, would have been the
birth of a symbol of the Self. A divine child would have been
born, which we could have called the emergence of his Self in
relation to Lucius. In a man's psychology, the girl who will
now be born is a renewal of the anima. It comes up as Voluptas,
as sensuous lust, of which one would think Lucius had already
enjoyed enough. Although born on Olympus, this girl Voluptas is closer to the human, so there arises with her a humanization of the pleasure principle, which is, however, almost
immediately swallowed back into the collective unconscious.

A similar, and to a certain extent parallel, process is represented in the Apocalypse of Saint John, on which Jung commented in *Answer to Job*.[7] A woman appears with a crown of twelve stars on her head and is pursued by a red dragon. She should give birth to a new savior figure, but she is removed to heaven again, and thus the divine child is not incarnated on earth. Here we also have a description of the possible birth of a new symbol of the Self, which, however, again sinks back into the unconscious. This means that the time has not yet come when this aspect could have come into the collective consciousness. Also this is a parallel to the Leto-Apollo myth and the not-yet-dead paganism of late antiquity. Here, too, is a description of the possibility of birth of a new symbol of the Self, which is again removed into the unconscious. There are only germs of such realizations here and there, which then get lost again. We must see the abortive birth of a boy in our story as a parallel to the Apocalyptic story; "only" a girl is born instead, and she is taken away into the Beyond. The question why it is specifically Voluptas, sensuous lust, I would like to leave until the end of the story when we have to comment on the beauty box Psyche finds in the underworld, for it is connected with that.

The bringing together of the divine, elevating, transpersonal, and freeing aspect of the *hieros gamos,* the sacred marriage motif, with the incompleteness and disappointing narrowness and dirt of human life, is still one of the greatest of unsolved problems. People either let themselves be intoxicated by the "divine" and romantic aspect of love or cynically remain in its banal aspect. There is a beautiful representation of this problem in the novel *Aurélia* by the French author Gérard de Nerval. He was a deep-feeling and romantic poet, which is a very unfortunate predisposition for a Frenchman, and he liked therefore to live in Germany, where he felt much better. This he occasionally was able to do, visiting a German uncle in the Schwarzwald. As a young man and a gifted writer, he fell very much in love with a little *midinette*. Completely overwhelmed by his feelings and emotions, he wrote poems about her. He felt that Dante's relationship to Beatrice could not be greater than this experience. But then suddenly the

French rationalism and Gallic cynicism came up, and he decided that, after all, she was just *une femme ordinaire de notre siècle,* an ordinary woman of our time. So he threw her over. The girl really loved him, and she fell into despair. Later a woman friend tried to bring them together again, but somehow, probably because of the cynical way in which he had thrown her over, really destroying his and her own feelings, the break could not be mended. When this woman brought them together again, the girl looked at him rather reproachfully and with tears in her eyes. That hit him very badly; in the night he dreamt that he went into the garden and saw that the statue of a beautiful woman had fallen onto the grass and broken apart in the middle. This dream shows what really happened in Nerval. His anima had split, because now the woman was for him either the unobtainable goddess or *une femme ordinaire de notre siècle,* with whom you can just have a little pleasure. He could never bring those two aspects together again. He then slowly slithered into a psychotic crisis, which at the end overwhelmed him, and finally he hanged himself in a fit of mental confusion. He was a sick man, but he could have probably overcome his split if he had only understood that the *hieros gamos* and the ordinary aspect of every deep human relationship is a paradox. Love is a moving, divine, unique mystery, and at the same time just an ordinary human event. This split is constellated in the same way here: at first the pendulum goes too much toward the divine Beyond aspect, where Eros and Psyche live in a kind of paradise, and then follows the countermovement initiated by the interference of the sisters, who, through bringing in all the most wicked and cynical aspects of life, destroy the connection. I believe that a sense of humor is the only divine quality with which one can hold together these irreconcilable aspects of every deeper love experience. But people like Gérard de Nerval lack that; and so he became psychotic. He had no sense of humor at all, and thus he could not accept the paradox and say, "Yes, it is both, she is Beatrice, the experience of the divine woman, and also *une femme ordinaire de notre siècle.*" When a woman goes through such a process, generally the animus is the cynical commentator who tries to destroy every deeper movement of feeling.

C. S. Lewis, in his novel, retells the story from the standpoint of one of the wicked sisters, who in our fairy tale are described as weak, jealous, intriguing, and witchlike women. Lewis, however, projected onto this motif a rational woman who serves the idea of power and duty. She takes over the throne from her father and rules the country. She is in opposition to her romantic sister, who falls into Eros's clutches and seems to be lost in a romantic dream. But at the end of the novel, in a moment of truth, this jealous sister realizes that she has missed the point and has betrayed the principle of love. Lewis has therefore confronted the domination of Eros with opposing drives: sex and self-preservation. That conflict exists already in nature. The female sacrifices herself for the young, and the male often ignores his own self-preservation in the moment of sexual drive. These drives are the basis for many human conflicts, for here two genuine human urges do not coincide, and the still deeper drive to be oneself has to be constellated in order to overcome the difficulty.

One could ask now what would have happened if Psyche had not disobeyed her husband. The answer is that mythological laws are *always* transgressed, otherwise there would be no story! But there may be more to it than that. Such stages of unconscious harmony, like that in the story of Paradise, result in the stagnation of life, and naturally certain disharmonious or evil impulses are excluded. Some people by a great mental and psychological effort will sacrifice the *one* pole of an essential conflict in the hope of establishing peace in their souls with the remainder. For instance, in the monastic life money and sex are cut out, and with them the source of innumerable conflicts, and by retiring from these difficulties the establishment of peace in the soul is sought. The whole Christian idea of inner peace is in this direction; that is, one first cuts out a certain aspect of evil which seems impossible to integrate, and then one tries artificially to establish harmony with the remainder. All over the world mankind has a tendency to go in this direction. It is probably inevitable, for one needs from time to time to be able to set aside an insoluble problem. It is as though there were rest places where one has a moment of peace, though one has the dim feeling that the conflict is not solved and will reappear after a time. One can observe this in people who draw mandalas[8] and in doing so leave a part outside. They put the dark things outside the border of the mandala and imagine that they have now reached a state of relative wholeness and totality. But in this way they exclude certain aspects, and they can be sure that this state will not last. Some of these left-out elements will break in and a new process of integration must begin. At this point we have the essence of the whole novel, for all through it (though sometimes the author seems to be gripped by feeling) a mocking, skeptical tone creeps in, a devaluating judgment which works like the knife in Psyche's hand. When things go well, a devil whispers in our ears that it is "nothing but," a rational devaluation which destroys everything. In a woman it is generally the animus who is the artist in this field, and in a man it is a certain aspect of the anima. The more sensitive and delicate and untouchable a man's feeling is on one side, the more he tends to mock himself. The Swiss recognize this type of man in their poet Gottfried Keller, whose feeling, on the one side, was extremely delicate, while on the other he showed the typical mockery of an old bachelor. That was his defense against his own hypersensitivity. He drank too much and was incapable of dealing with the anima problem. Apuleius-Lucius has some of the same characteristics.

We come now to the different stages of Psyche's journey in her search for Eros. Back in heaven, Eros is imprisoned by his resentful mother. In her despair, Psyche wants to kill herself and throw herself into a river, but the god of the running waters brings her back to the shore, where she meets Pan, the goat-god; with his great wisdom he advises her not to end her life but, on the contrary, to honor Eros, "the most exalted" of all gods, with her prayers. The great god of cosmic nature therefore helps Psyche to go on living. In between, the enraged Venus searches for her everywhere. Finally, Psyche surrenders herself to her and as Psyche arrives at the heavenly palace,

Venus has her seized by her servants, Sorrow and Sadness, who torment her and then bring her back to face Venus. This part, I think, is understandable to anyone who has ever experienced an unhappy love affair. Venus then orders Psyche to sort out a quantity of different kinds of seeds during the night. The sorting out of grain is a motif found in numerous fairy tales, for instance in the Russian tale "The Beautiful Wassilissa," in which an unhappy girl comes to the great witch, Baba Yaga, the nature and death goddess, and there she must also sort out seeds or corn. According to Merkelbach's interpretation, this could have to do with the Eleusinian mysteries, for corn is the mystical substance which represents the mother goddess as the goddess of corn.

A chaotic host of seeds is, in a way, an image of the collective unconscious, which seems to be, at the same time, a single essence and a multiplicity of images and creative impulses. One could say that as long as the archetypes of the collective unconscious are not realized by a human being, they are not real. They only become psychologically a reality if they are experienced by the human psyche. It is for this reason that the archetypes of the collective unconscious resemble a host of chaotically dormant "seeds" inborn in every human being, which, if not activated through contact with human consciousness, could just as well be regarded as nonexistent. We can perhaps guess what such a heap of potential archetypal contents looks like if we observe a person in a psychotic episode. On the one hand patients in this condition pour out, at terrific speed, one archetypal fantasy after the other. But two minutes later they do not remember anything they have said. The most amazing, beautiful material pours through them, but they have no memory of it. Thus the collective unconscious is seen as a kind of chaos of contents, all of which have the latent possibility of becoming something meaningful within human consciousness. But instead there is confusion, and consciousness is too weak to stop the flood.[9] Jung spoke of a patient he had, a woman, who talked a lot of absolute nonsense all the time, but then she would suddenly stop and say, "Hello, yes, ah-ha, thank you." And after this "telephone call" she would be all right for a while, and Jung would succeed in worming out of her what she was really doing, and she would say that she had been telephoning to the Virgin Mary, who was very helpful to her and who would say, "Now don't talk so much nonsense!" And that would quiet her down for a while, but then it started again. One saw that there the normal personality somewhere still functioned but could not hold its own.

One could say that a good mind is needed to sort out the material, but that does not help either because one cannot bring any intellectual order into these things. What is needed is the *feeling* function, the function of choice, which says, "Now I will fish out this and discard the rest" and "I will relate to what has become conscious to me and stay with it." Without the evaluation through the feeling function one cannot know what is important and what is not. One cannot sort the chaff from the corn in the unconscious.

In the tale Psyche cannot cope alone with the corn. But there is still something that can rescue her, for ants turn up and sort out the grain. The chaos of the unconscious always contains a relation to order as well. In talking about the unconscious one must always talk in paradoxes, and when we emphasize its chaotic aspect we know at the same time that the unconscious is not only chaos but is also order. In the last analysis, only unconscious order can overcome unconscious disorder. Man cannot do anything but be attentive and make the utmost and, so to speak, hopeless effort, until order is established again by itself.

This is something which Christian theologians would call faith. Having faith and doing one's best, when one is faced with what seems hopeless, gives one the underlying feeling that, even when one is lost, one has at least done what was possible. This is essentially human and it is a behavior which a god or an animal could not do. Here in our story the same unconscious which is chaotic manifoldness cures its disorder by another chaotic manifoldness, the invasion of ants. We, in our Western countries, often speak of ants negatively, saying that "if we go on like this we shall soon be an ant heap." This is naturally a negative metaphor for the complete blotting out of the individual, but the ant in itself, in mythology, is generally a positive insect. For instance, according to an Indian myth (recorded by Herodotus), it helps to carry the sun in its night journey under the earth. In Egypt the scarab does that.[10] In some Greek sagas the ant extracts gold from the earth; it is the symbol of the secret orderliness of the collective unconscious, contrary to our bureaucratic state organizations. Karl Kerényi has connected the ants with the people of Myrmidones, who, according to a Greek myth, were the first inhabitants of their country:[11] the Greeks believed that these people were born directly from the earth mother. Thus, in the Attic comedies, whose texts are unfortunately lost, there were antpeople, "Myrmekanthropoi," who represented the first inhabitants. Contrary to the destructive mother Aphrodite-Venus, these "children of the earth mother" help Psyche. The ants, and especially their cousins, the termites, have also in reality very mysterious and unexplored qualities. One knows that hundreds and hundreds of termites will build a complete architectural structure. In an experiment to try to find out how they communicate when building, a lead plate was put through the center of a termite building at its beginning; the termites of the left half built their parts for the whole building in a way that met exactly with those on the right half. One could take the plate out and the two halves fit. So one knows that they have no telegraphic signal, but work synchronously in a complete organization, which is something still unexplained. We know of bees that they signal each other when they wag their tails, but we do not know anything yet in this respect about termites. One sees, therefore, that this beautiful image is more than just a simile really, for these things also happen in reality. An artist who had lived for a long time in Bali described to me the same process: a temple had fallen into ruins, and for some reason the villagers decided to build a new and bigger one. To his amazement there was no organizer, no plan, and no architect, and practically not even a stone mason to organize. One villager sat in one corner and made a column, another sat in another corner preparing stones. No communication went on, but everybody worked extremely zealously. In the end they put the temple parts together and every stone fit! The artist could not find out how the Balinese did this. They worked together inwardly via the unconscious. The temple lived simply in their inner vision. That is the whole explanation. So one can say that in the right way faith is a great achievement, or rather *pistis:* loyalty to the inner law. When this loyalty or feeling constellates, it calls forth the secret order which is in the chaos of the unconscious.

After having fulfilled the first task, Psyche must fetch the golden wool from dangerous wild solar sheep, or rams, which are very difficult to approach. Here she is helped by reeds which tell her that the rams are unapproachable at midday and that she should wait until evening when they get cooled down in their temperamental wildness. If Psyche approaches them too early they will tear her to bits. The reeds, as Merkelbach points out, had a great meaning in Egypt: the hieroglyph for "reed" represents the king of Egypt and Horus, the new sun, the reborn sun god, the new king of Egypt. The reed represents the king in his rebirth form.

In many fairy tales, the reeds betray secret knowledge. In antiquity there are many stories where somebody is murdered and buried in a swamp. A shepherd comes along, cuts a reed, and makes himself a flute, and the flute sings and reveals the secret of the murder, and the murderer is discovered and punished. The reed can also betray or convey divine wisdom to man by the wind which whistles through it. There is an instinct of truth in the human psyche which, in the long run, cannot be suppressed. We can pretend not to hear it, but it remains in the unconscious. And Psyche in our story has a kind of secret inspiration about how she can solve the task. The whistling reed, like the ants, corresponds to these tiny hints of truth which we get from the unconscious. Jung always said that truth does not speak with a loud voice. Its low but unsuppressible voice announces itself as a malaise, or a bad conscience, or whatever one may want to call it. Great quiet is needed in order to feel these small hints. When the unconscious begins to talk loudly and to manifest itself with car accidents and such happenings, then the situation is already very bad.

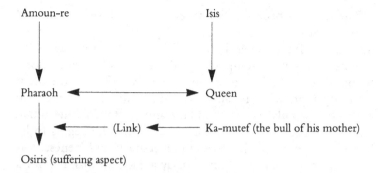

But in the normal state it has been whispering softly for years, before the thunderclap comes with accidents or other bad things. That is why we have analysis, where we try to hear what the reed says before the catastrophe comes.

The reed, as we have seen, is connected mythologically with the rebirth of the sun god in the form of Horus. You will recall that in Egypt the pharaoh is the earthly representative or the incarnation of the highest god. The first time the pharaoh sleeps with the queen, the moment of the *hieros gamos* in which the new king engenders his first son and successor, the king personifies the god and the queen personifies Isis. The suffering aspect and all that is suppressed by the king (who is the solar principle) is personified by Osiris. Every day, for the twelve hours of the day, one is only one half of oneself. In order to be able to work, we must repress innumerable inner living reactions; one cannot even let them come up to consciousness. As long as conscious activity lasts, only one half of the psyche can constantly express itself, and the other unconscious half is in the situation of the suffering god in the underworld. When, therefore, the pharaoh ages and dies, he becomes, at the moment of death, Osiris. Thus one sees on the inscriptions their names connected as: Unas Osiris, Pepi Osiris. But at this moment the new king has already been reborn, as Horus. We will go into this in more depth later; here I only want to say that the reed is concerned with Horus, with the principle of what comes after. It whispers to us the truth and the anticipation of the future.

The ram has been well interpreted by Erich Neumann, and I think that its meaning is clear to anyone who has ever seen a horoscope. As a zodiacal sign of spring it means aggressive impulsiveness and a temperamental spirit of adventure, a kind of unreflected, naive, masculine initiative. For a woman it naturally represents the animus, but in our case it means an aggressive impulsiveness behind the anima. It would mean that one of the greatest dangers for a man, when he begins to let his anima live, is to fall into an unreflective impulsiveness. It is much more difficult for him to delay a decision than it is for a woman. In Egypt the "ram of Mendes" was always associated with Isis, so that we have here again an allusion to the end of the book. One only needs to look into our newspapers: As soon as there is any kind of difficulty, too much rain, an avalanche, too many cars, and so on, the politicians say, "We must do something; we must have a committee; the state must . . ." Nobody proposes that we wait and see what happens! One must study the origin of these troubles, but one cannot wait. Some women, of course, are also threatened by the ram, but it is more frequent for men. Of course this animal also has a positive aspect. But it is unfavorable for the man who has to realize his anima, for under the influence of the ram he can never realize what she is. Feeling, especially in a man, is generally a slightly delayed reaction. He must be able to wait, to listen to what the feminine side might have to say. If a man overruns that, he will never become conscious of his anima. Whenever we are caught in the temperamental wish for a quick action, we then understand how difficult it is to wait, to patiently let time pass. So Psyche not only has to wait but also has to collect a handful of wool from the ram's hide, to take something from its wool fleece.

The motif of the ram also belongs to the famous story of Phrixos and Hellé: the myth of a brother and his little sister who are both persecuted by a stepmother who wants to kill them. But they hear of it and escape on a ram, which flies with them through the sky. On the way, Hellé bends over and looks down, and falls into the sea, which is how the Hellespont came into existence; the sea of Hellé. Phrixos is saved and is ordered to sacrifice the ram and to hang up the fleece on a tree. Since then, the golden fleece has become the motif of the "unobtainable treasure" of the long journey of the Argonauts; and in later Christian interpretation, this golden fleece hung up on a tree was regarded as the prefiguration of Christ, the sacrificed lamb. This story has been very popular with the Church Fathers, with its amplification of the symbolism of Christ. Even today, among the Knights of the Golden Fleece, those of the highest rank of the Order have a golden chain with a little golden fleece;[12] if they place this on any table, that table has the value of a consecrated altar.

Apuleius alludes here consciously to the story of Phrixos and Hellé. The lock of golden wool is the unobtainable treasure, and this Psyche has to obtain from the rams. Now, every powerful emotion is not only something hot; it is also something which brings light. Generally it is eighty percent destructive fire and twenty percent light. Therefore, if one is overwhelmed or attacked by a terrific emotion, the art is not to let the emotion tear one, but to find out what it could mean. For instance, you may meet someone whom you loathe. Each time you meet that person you become exaggeratedly emotional without any visible reason. That is the reaction of the ram. Now you can either live your emotion out, and then there is catastrophe and failure, or you can repress it, but then you have not learned anything. The third possibility is not to give in to the emotion, but to pluck out its meaning, to ask, Why do I feel like this? What has got into me? Then you have really learned something. Wherever there is a destructive emotion, there is possibly also light, and the art is to perceive this light without getting pulled into the primitiveness of uncontrolled emotion. And that is the meaning of the capacity of being able to wait for the right moment in order to obtain the ram's wool.

7

Psyche's Tasks

The next task for Psyche is to get water in a carved crystal bottle from the ice-cold waterfall of the Styx, something which again surpasses her capacities. At this point again a typical fairy tale motif appears: the eagle of Zeus takes the bottle, fetches the water, and brings it back to her. Merkelbach quite rightly connects the Styx with the water of the Nile. At the end of the novel we will return again to the question of the mystical vessel which contains the water of the Nile; that is *the* unspeakable mystery of Osiris. It is the water of death and at the same time of rebirth, but here it is represented in a Greek context.

Styx is a female goddess, the oldest of all, who rules over all the other gods. Her deadly water destroys any human being as well as every animal and cannot be put into any normal vessel, whether of glass, or lead, not even of gold, for it is even more destructive than the "water" of alchemy, which can be kept only in a golden vessel. Even the gods are terrified of this element, and their most solemn oath is pronounced in the name of Styx. If a god breaks this oath, he will lie dead for an entire year and be banished from Olympus for nine more years. The Styx symbolizes the frightening aspect of the mother archetype and in a certain sense also of the collective unconscious. The fact that we cannot "hold" it in a vessel seems to me to be very meaningful. We cannot indeed entirely grasp or manipulate the collective unconscious. It resembles a wild river of psychic energy which we cannot regulate and which we cannot make use of. The collective unconscious is like a powerful stream of images upon which man has no influence.

The only way to keep some of it, according to myth, is in the hoof of a horse, or the horn of a mythological (in reality nonexisting), one-horned Scythian ass. The horn, a phallic symbol, symbolizes the creative force of the Self,[1] and the horse hoof has also, in a simpler form, the same meaning, because it was believed that horses could stamp springs out of the earth and that the kick of a horse fertilized the earth. So it shows that only the principle of creativeness in the human soul can hold its own against the destructiveness of the water of Styx.

Man never could—and from this mythologem it seems as though he never will—manipulate, voluntarily influence, or possess, even in part, the collective unconscious. This nature principle takes its own course through history. It supports civilizations or nations, or lets them decay, and nothing can prevail against it. One could say that the Roman Empire in the second century after Christ, the time of Apuleius, was already condemned to go under in the water of Styx. In the myth, Styx has also to do with the goddess of Nemesis, the mysterious, revengeful "justice of nature." If an empire or a religion is doomed to extinction because the collective unconscious does not express itself through it anymore, then man is absolutely helpless. The water of Styx governs military defeat or victory; from it stems Nikè ("victory"), this mysterious power of fate, which in battle dooms a civilization or promotes its continuation in life. If we look at the dust of history and consider how many wonderful human achievements have been destroyed again and again by barbaric forces, then we realize the meaning of the water of the Styx. It seems to be an inescapable destiny, the cruel justice of nature which we cannot halt. That is why we cannot hold this water: if Nemesis has decided destruction in the water of Styx, we cannot prevail against it, except with the "hoof of the horse." That is the one comfort we can take from this myth. Nature seems to want to protect its own deepest creative power against everything; and it seems also at times to attach to human creativity a value superior to any other activity. Only if we are in contact with our unconscious psyche can we be creative. Great creative achievements come from the depths of the psyche; if we can keep in contact with the depth of our psyche, we are able to form that which wants to be expressed through it. Sometimes this is a matter of life and death, for we simply do not know if we can bring it into reality. But if we can, then it looks as if nature rewards us with the highest price; and therefore one could say that creative achievement is the only "vessel" which can hold the water of Styx.

Here Psyche is given the vessel as a *present*. She cannot herself approach the water; the separation from Eros makes the solution of the task impossible for her. With him she might manage it, but alone she is up against an impossibility. However, through divine intervention, through the eagle of Zeus, the task is achieved. The eagle represents here intuitive spiritual elation and high-soaring thoughts.

At the moment when the human psyche cannot act by itself, it is supported by a heroic, intuitive spirit which arises from the unconscious. One could call it the mysterious force of hope, for sometimes when one is up against an impossible situation, one has a kind of intuition that things will come right if only one can endure. That is grace. Here, because Psyche courageously makes an honest attempt, she is saved by such an act of grace, by the intuitive vision, which anticipates what she cannot yet do herself.

As the continuation of the story shows, the solution of the problem does not reach the conscious level. One could connect this with the fact that Psyche could not fetch the water of Styx herself. The eagle—an autonomous power—intervenes, as will Eros later, when Psyche will fall into a deathlike sleep after opening the box of beauty. In between these two events, however, Psyche experiences her descent into the underworld.

After she has brought the water of Styx to Venus, Psyche is sent by her into the world of the dead, in order to obtain a certain box with a perfumed beauty cream in it from Persephone, the queen of the underworld, a parallel to the dark face of Isis. In great despair, Psyche wants to kill herself by throwing herself down from a tower, but the tower begins to talk, and it advises her to go down into Hades and then gives her further instructions. The tower, as Neumann interprets it, is a symbol of the Great Mother herself. It is also a symbol of introversion, of withdrawal into one's own inner world, and of contemplation of oneself. It is the withdrawal that allows Psyche to face the tasks which await her.

While crossing the river of the underworld in Charon's boat, a drowning old man, half-dead, begs her to take pity on him. But her task is to not listen to his piteous cries for help. A woman's natural inclination is to mother, to nurse, and to have pity for everything. Wherever there is a wounded being around or anything that touches the natural, feminine, maternal instinct, she wants to support it. To say no to this old cripple is for a woman a more difficult deed than for a man. Not to have any sentimental love for something that is doomed to die and has to go is very hard. This applies also in analysis: a neurotic attitude in the analysand naturally cries out for our pity, but to give in here would mean to keep alive something dying or already dead. To have pity and love, combined with the reckless "cruelty" to allow the condemned thing to die, is very difficult in practical life. It is so much easier to be full of feeling and to give in to one's feminine inclination to sympathize. To have a "knife" in the hand and, without listening to the cries of the patient, to cut off a wrong attitude, this can be very painful for the doctor himself. Naturally the same applies also to the contents of the unconscious which have outlived their time. One should not fall into retrospective sentimentality, but live forward, "letting the dead bury their dead." Psyche succeeds in ignoring this old man who cries for help, and Charon takes her on across the river.

Charon appears here in his usual antique representation, as a miserly, ill-tempered old man who will only take those people over who can pay him. He is, in a sense, the negative personification of what Jung called the "transcendent function."[2] Jung meant by this the faculty of the unconscious for creating symbols. It is "transcendent," for not only does it transcend our conscious grasp, but it is the only thing which, through the help of a symbol, enables man to pass from one psychic state to another. Hence the ferryman! We would be forever stuck in an acquired state of consciousness if this transcendent function of the psyche did not help us over into new attitudes by creating a symbol which shares in both worlds: being associated with the psychic state of the present as well as the future, the symbol helps us over. *"Habentibus symbolum facilis est transitus."*[3] Very often one sees in analysis that somebody has outgrown his old condition but feels lost and confused about the new thing. In this interregnum, or vacuum, one can only hold on to the chain of symbols which the unconscious produces, that is, to one's own dreams, which never let us down, but safely lead us over from an outgrown into a new attitude of life. However, this stage between the two worlds of the conscious and the unconscious has also a quality of being narrowed in, of depression, and of having to cling to small things.

Charon has an Egyptian parallel in the god Acharantos, or Akeru, who, because of a similarity in the sound of the name, was identified with Charon in the syncretistic Graeco-Roman Egyptian religion.[4] But Akeru has a more positive function in Egypt. He is depicted as a simple peasant who sows and reaps wheat, and so is interpreted in many texts of the Egyptian tombs as the agency of resurrection. One could say therefore that the "ferryman," who from the extraverted standpoint is seen as negative—during his appearance there is a certain darkening of consciousness, and only the dreams go on producing symbols leading to the other shore—was seen more positively by the Egyptians, with their more introverted civilization. They saw therein a sowing of the wheat, which disappears in the earth and is awoken again to life. Jesus alludes to the same Osiris mystery of the "resurrection" of the wheat.[5]

The general belief in antiquity that one had to have money

for Charon can also be seen in this light: in most of the tombs of antiquity the dead have under their tongue a penny or a drachma for Charon, who otherwise could leave them on the shore between the two worlds. This shows that the transcendent function requires a minimum of conscious libido. The healing function of the unconscious cannot bring us over "to the other shore" if we do not give it libido, that means conscious attention. One sees this so tragically in people who have dragged on for perhaps twenty years under terrific hidden suffering from a neurotic symptom. Such people have been arrested at the shore for lack of money for Charon. They did not have the right instruction, or they lacked the instinct or the generosity to follow it.

Then Psyche comes to an old man called Ocnus, who again and again winds up a black and white cord and unties it again. Ocnus means hesitation, and to him, also, Psyche must not pay any attention but must walk past and not take notice of what he tells her, otherwise she will get stuck with him. The rope, which also appears in other fairy-tale motifs, refers to a general mythological theme and is interpreted as the alternation of black and white, of day and night, and of other opposites. So one could say that Ocnus—hesitation—occupies himself incessantly with an endless chain of opposites in the unconscious and with the spinning of a yarn from the opposites, so that he never comes to any deed or any breakthrough. This is another classical form of getting stuck in the unconscious: many people realize that everything has a plus and a minus, that everything in the psyche is ambiguous, that everything one undertakes can be naively interpreted as a wonderful deed, but has its dark motivations as well. If one realizes that, then one often becomes unable to do or think anything, and then one falls into Ocnus. Shall I, or shall I not? Everything has a disadvantage, and anything I might do has its absolute counterpart. Such a realization might lame the *élan vital*. The secret is to say, "Oh, well, if it has two aspects, to hell with it, I shall do *this* because this is me, and I am ready to pay for it; everything is half-wrong anyhow, whatever one does!" People with a weak ego-consciousness and a weak feeling function cannot take responsibility for their decisions but get lamed in the face of paradox. In analysis they argue, "You said last time . . . ! But isn't there another aspect?" One replies, "Yes, certainly, but then . . ." Generally they want you to decide for them, and that is the worst of all, for then they could remain infantile. All this sounds simple, but in reality it is terrible and dangerous, one of the real devilries of the unconscious! Ocnus, who is quite rightly represented here as a superdevil, must be avoided!

Next, Psyche has to walk past three old women who are weaving. These, we know from the mythological context, are parallel to the Germanic Norns or the Greek Parkae or Moirae, the weaving goddesses of Fate.[6] Them, too, Psyche must leave alone, which means she must overcome them. Here is a big temptation for women and also for the man's anima: the temptation to plot and help fate along. It is very meaningful that after Ocnus come these three women, because one could say that plotting generally comes after a feeling of hopelessness. For example, if a woman loves a man and there is seemingly no chance for her to conquer him, she will start to plot in order to catch him. Had she the confidence that what is meant to come about will happen, she would not need to plot; but there is the temptation to *corriger la fortune,* to help fate. Here is a particular failing of women. If they happen to give in to the temptation, they destroy, as Jung explains in "Woman in Europe,"[7] their Eros and their creative possibility. But it is also typical for the anima in men. If a man plots, one knows he is still possessed by the anima. To give a kind of blunt primitive example: a man really is only interested in his fiancée's bank account, but that is not allowed to come to consciousness, so he maneuvers himself into feeling that he loves the woman. In reality he wants to have the money but cannot separate this wish from the feeling of uninterested love, and so he keeps himself in a half-dark state, where he makes himself believe that this girl is the right one to marry. There is also perhaps a certain attraction, yet with this other little "thing" in the background: she has a rich father. Psyche escapes this danger in that she walks past the three fate-weavers. Only when one becomes conscious of such unclean, half-unconscious motivations and "walks past them," does not fall into them, can the individuation process continue. Therefore, if a man or a woman cannot desist from this plotting there is no true love, for the two are absolutely incompatible, though they are always close together. Psyche succeeds in escaping from all these dangers.

Psyche's last task is to go down into the underworld and get from Persephone the box which contains divine beauty and to bring it to Venus. Here she is disobedient, opens the box, and falls immediately into a deadly sleep. But by a miracle Eros comes and wakens her back to life. Later, through the intervention of Zeus, Eros and Psyche marry, Venus is reconciled and even dances at the marriage festival. Later Psyche gives birth to a child on Olympus, called Voluptas (Pleasure). Being from the land of death, divine beauty is obviously something poisonous which is kept for the gods and which human beings should not have. One could compare this to the biblical story in which Adam and Eve steal consciousness from God and thus start the tragedy of mankind. But here the sin lies not in the stealing of the knowledge of good and evil, but in the wish to want to participate in divine beauty.

This has to do with the well-known aestheticism of the anima in men. A man's anima whispers to him: what is beautiful is also good, in the Platonic sense of the word (*kalon k'agathon*, "the good and the beautiful go together"). One of man's deepest problems is that he is practically incapable of loving a woman if she is very ugly. He cannot separate his feeling from aestheticism. There is the story of the man who couldn't decide between two women. The one was beautiful, the other ugly but a wonderful singer. After a long struggle the singer won. Then on the first morning of the honeymoon he wakes up, looks at her, and shakes her, saying, "For God's sake, sing!" It is a terrible anima problem, for the man feels that beauty is divine and that it goes with goodness, whereas evil and ugliness belong together.

As Merkelbach has already worked out, Kore, or Persephone, is a variation of Venus-Isis in her underworldly aspect.

But why the problem of beauty? In the story, Psyche naturally opens the box—as in all fairy tales, for nothing has ever been forbidden in a fairy tale which has not been done—and what comes out is a confusion, a soporific mist, which puts her into a deathlike sleep. Thus, she is thrown even deeper into the unconscious. The ointment has a completely negative role in our context, for it was not created for Psyche. It was meant for Venus, who, probably quite legitimately, wanted to heighten her own charms. Venus would not have fallen into sleep if she had opened the box. Therefore we must go into the meaning of ointment.

Oil and many sorts of creamy ointment had, in Egypt, a sacramental or religious function: they represented life substance. The Egyptians bathed and anointed their gods. They brought their statues down to the Nile and washed them regularly and then anointed them with a creamlike substance; the idea behind it was to give them life.[8] They realized, in a projected form at least, that even the gods would be without the slighest life function or importance if men did not give them their psychic substance.

In the Christian tradition the holy oil still plays a great role in Catholic sacraments, representing the Holy Ghost and its gifts. For this reason the king is also anointed. He is the "anointed" one, because he represents the Christian principle on earth and because he fulfills his office with "God's grace." Jesus, the king of kings, is the "anointed" par excellence, but in a more invisible sense than the Egyptian kings.

So one could say that oil and creams represent the life substance of the psyche in its aspect of ultimate spiritual devotion, devotion with complete awe. By anointing the statues, the Egyptians gave their gods the best they could, unconditional devotion and reverence which made them alive.

The ointment has therefore also to do with love, with the reverential awe which a human being can give to a being who is greater than himself. If people try to exploit their dreams for their own purposes, without this loving respect for that which the unconscious conveys to them, then everything turns wrong. It turns dead, and after a relatively good time at the start they begin to doubt the analytical process and their dreams, doubting that they will lead somewhere or further. But they started this wrong way because they did not give unconditioned loving reverence, did not recognize that a living mystery within their own souls has to be kept alive, not for any other purpose than its own sake. Therefore it is right that the ointment should belong to Venus and not to a human girl. Human beings may not steal it; if it is stolen, it creates this soporific effect, which is visible here. Psyche is not killed, but she falls into a complete unconscious state, into the state of the gods, and loses the feeling for her own individuality.

This cream in our story is specifically called Beauty, a beauty cream. We are reminded that the girl to which Psyche later will give birth is called Voluptas, sensuous lust. Here we see clearly that in our context the tale of Eros and Psyche is an anima story. Man's anima today is still very much the same as in late antiquity. To identify the highest values with beauty leads to a kind of aestheticism which is an inadequacy toward life, because life in every respect is a pair of opposites. It is beautiful, but also ugly, and both poles belong to reality, and chasing only beauty and aestheticism, even in their highest form, is a kind of hubris, an inflation, an unreal attitude, but one with which the anima in men especially tries to seduce. Eternal beauty does not exist in nature; it is always varied by gruesomeness and horror, and the same is true for our life. For instance, in the *I Ching*,[9] Hexagram 22 speaks of Grace and Beauty, and there one can read that the great sage Confucius once threw this hexagram and got very depressed, for he realized that aestheticism was not an adequate answer to many of life's questions.

Today we have an overaesthetic attitude about religion. Our churches, our images, and the music played, all must be as beautiful as possible, for only that pleases God. Everything which is dirty, ugly, and out of tune does not belong. This shows how much we are also possessed by that prejudice— then we wonder that some of our youths dance their real religious dances in cellars, sweating in dirt, and have more inner experience there then with sober church beauty!

The Chinese, who, being a people of high culture and great taste, were always threatened by aestheticism, did something compensatory, which was really just a trick, but still seems to me characteristic. In the best time of the Han, Sung, and Ming periods, when the greatest pieces of art were created, if a craftsman made a vase or a bronze vessel, he would make a tiny little mistake on purpose, chip it a bit, or put a little spot of wrong color, so that his work would not be perfect. Something perfect is, in a deeper sense of the word, imperfect. It must contain the opposites, and in order to be complete it must be slightly asymmetrical. But we still identify our highest values with aesthetic values. Only in modern art do the artists try to get away from aestheticism. Their art wants to destroy the false kind of aestheticism and show the "naked truth." One could interpret the cream of beauty, which makes Psyche sink into the unconscious, also as the danger of being fascinated by the divine *otherworldliness* of beauty. It creates an ecstatic condition in which one loses interest in the concrete everyday life. Psyche therefore withdraws into the realm of the gods, into the realm of Venus, and makes no more progress toward the Venus incarnation on earth.

When Jung began to be interested in psychiatry and worked in the Burghölzli psychiatric clinic, he often talked to an ugly old schizophrenic woman. The patient produced interesting material, which he studied and later published. Once Freud visited the ward and exclaimed, "How could you work for such a long time with such an ugly woman!" Jung said that he had not even noticed that she was ugly.

The aestheticism of the anima is always a problem. Even if a woman is beautiful, she may yet get some disease or have to undergo an operation. Women sometimes fear that they may lose their husband's affection after an operation, which shows that the feeling relationship is not quite right. Or they are not rightly married if she fears losing her husband's love for beauty reasons.

In antiquity, aestheticism was a much stronger bond between the sexes. Here, too, Christianity has brought about some change, but the problem has not been developed and needs more understanding. This problem of beautiful form and its connection and disconnection with inner truth is something we are still up against and here is represented for Psyche as the greatest danger. In this ultimate, tragic moment, Eros comes down from Olympus and wakes Psyche, and, with the help of Zeus, a happy ending occurs in the Beyond. On Olympus, Eros may marry Psyche and have her child, and Venus is reconciled. The story ends suddenly with a beautiful festival, a nice party of the gods *on* Olympus. From the human standpoint, Olympus means the unconscious. Thus the whole play of fate disappears. There is a solution, but it disappears; it is in the unconscious and not integrated in the human realm. It remains suspended as an open problem.

Despite the uncertain ending of our story, it is clear that Psyche *had* to open the box, otherwise Eros would not have come to free her. This is basically the same problem as in the story of the Garden of Eden. For if Adam and Eve had not eaten the apple we would still be sitting with long tails, scratching ourselves on trees. Therefore the Catholic Church calls the guilt of Adam and Eve a *felix culpa,* meaning a sin which brought forth the most positive consequences. All such nonallowed deeds in fairy tales and myths are *felices culpae,* for in the end they lead to a higher consciousness. As far as the problem of the beauty ointment in feminine psychology is concerned, I am convinced that this motif does not apply to woman's psychology. Women have other problems. The hairdresser, cosmetics, and all these things indeed play an enormous role in a woman's life, but these have to do with parts of her persona[10] and her conscious social personality and not that which comes at the crucial turning point of a deep process of individuation. I am confirmed in this opinion by the fact that the beauty-box problem does not occur in other folktale parallels, whether old or new. So we are justified in assuming that it is an addition from Apuleius and illustrates specifically an anima problem. However, it is also a problem for women, since the anima attitude of a man influences them. It is instinctual in a woman to wish to appear as the man who loves her would want to see her. There is no conscious calculation here.

It belongs in a certain way to the essence of feminine nature to carry, to a certain extent, the projection of the surroundings, and to act it out quite unconsciously. Certain women are very gifted in this way, and we talk about them in our psychological practice as anima types. It is practiced even by very small girls. A girl wants chocolate, which she does not get from her mother, because it is not good for her teeth. When Papa comes home, she gives him an absolutely melting, beautiful smile and says, "Papa, just this once?" Naturally, he melts, being tired after the office and seeing his little girl only in the evening. So she gets from him all that Mama has forbidden. Little girls of three and four already play perfectly the role of the father's anima. This is an instinctive reaction; but if it becomes a habit, then it produces the classical type of the anima woman. Although a seductive attitude is quite legitimate up to a certain point, sometimes such a woman gives up her personality entirely and only plays the anima. When alone in analysis with another woman, she will collapse into a heap of nothingness, for she is nothing in herself. She does not know who or what she is or what she would be if she did not represent the anima of her partner. She borrows, so to speak, her right to existence through carrying a man's anima projection and is annihilated in her own feminine personality. But then the man misuses this situation, and there comes the occasion when the woman knows that as a human being she has to take a stand and must differentiate herself from the projection of the man who loves her, even with the risk of disappointing him or of a severe disturbance of the relationship. Many women do not have enough love, courage, or honesty for this. It is a marriage problem par excellence and very difficult for women who deeply love their husbands. They do not want to risk the relationship but prefer to continue playing the role, and so deny some instinctual truthfulness they feel within themselves. In that way they keep the man in the unconscious too; for he can never become conscious of his anima, since his wife always represents it. But if she one day does not do that, then the man must say, "She is different from what I thought!"

Jung told us once how he discovered the existence of the anima. A woman in whom he was very interested suddenly behaved differently from what he had expected, and he was deeply disappointed. But instead of running away, as most men do in such a case, he went home and asked himself *why* in hell he had expected her to be different! Then he suddenly realized that he had carried within him an image of the ideal woman, or "how a woman should be." And now this woman in whom he was interested had not behaved in that way. That was for him a step toward becoming conscious of his anima. So if a woman always plays the role of the anima, the image expected of her, she prevents her man from realizing the inner image, his anima. But since women know that as soon as they behave differently from men's feeling expectations, many men will just throw them over, they naturally do not want to take the risk. Such women get into a conflict between their own inner honesty and the risk of the loss of the relationship; then begins the plotting.

The opening of the box was a *felix culpa:* Psyche has to become unconscious and Eros has to rescue her. If you think of Psyche as the archetype of the anima and of Eros as the archetype of the animus, it is a subtle ultimate reversal of role. In the human realm the man normally makes the effort of wooing the woman, otherwise there is a slight shift of normal values. Many mother's boys are too lazy to go after a woman, but are caught themselves by some active woman, which is not usually very successful. Normally it is the man who in the visible world, as an ego, has to actively press his interest in a woman. In the deepest sense, however, in the Beyond realm of animus and anima, it is very often Eros, the highest animus quality of a woman, which is the *logos spermatikos*—the seed spirit of love. The French, who know more about the subtleties of love, have a beautiful way of putting it. They say, "Elle choisit celui qui devra la choisir" ("She chooses the man who shall later choose her"). It can easily happen that on meeting a man for the first time, the woman knows somehow that this is her fate; then she has chosen him. Her active Eros, her inner flame, has touched his sleeping soul, which *he* perhaps discovers five years later, though something in *her* has known it all along. So Eros is that active, invisible principle in woman. Jung has said that if a woman really loves, right to the bottom of her heart, that is, if her Eros really loves—and that is something she cannot bring about with her will or ego, or by plotting—she can get any man. It is something which happens to him as an inner fate.

Psyche falls into a deathlike sleep, and it is then that Eros comes to save her. Eros, as Merkelbach has remarked, is a prefiguration of Osiris, who appears in Lucius-Apuleius's final initiation at the end of the book. The Greeks identified Eros with Osiris; indeed, for the Egyptians, Osiris taught men and women genuine mutual love.[11] Eros and Osiris are both, psychologically, symbols of the Self.

This divine psychic core of the soul, the Self, is activated generally in cases of extreme danger. Eros appears again only when Psyche is at the end of her capacities. But then he takes her away to Olympus, to the world of the gods. This has to do with the fact that Eros appears in this story as an immature youth. It seems as if Lucius had not yet suffered enough to experience the Self inwardly, and as if he were not yet mature enough for the deep religious experience which occurs at the end of the book.

8

Charite, Tlepolemus, and the Chthonic Shadow

We have come to the end of the Psyche-Eros story, to a happy end in the Beyond. Everything has returned into the collective unconscious from which it came, just as the boy savior in the Apocalypse returned to the Beyond, which implies that a realization in consciousness was not yet possible.

One sees similar things on a minor scale in psychological practice. Very often people have numinous dreams, but they are so far from understanding them that even with an analyst who explains the meaning of the symbolism, it does not reach consciousness. Everything happens in the Beyond without being understood. Yet it exists somewhere; in fact, it even has an invisible positive effect.

In our story the positive effect shows as follows: only after Charite and the ass (Lucius) have heard the old woman tell the tale of Psyche and Eros does Lucius decide to run away, and not before. The story must have therefore vivified him somewhere, given him a hope of life, a will to live, even if only unconsciously. Charite has been equally influenced, for she quickly jumps on the back of the ass, when it runs away, in order to escape with it. When the old hag tries to hold both back Lucius gives her a strong kick, which makes her unconscious and they run away.

All that is an unconscious positive effect of the story, though its essential content has passed unnoticed. Only Voluptas and Beauty affect Lucius's consciousness, because he listens to the story and says, "What a beautiful story! If only I had a pencil and could write it all down!" There one can see how aestheticism works. Had Lucius wondered what the story meant, he would have got more out of it. But there is this soporific element. However, the vivifying element is also there so he gives a kick to the old woman and runs away, but Charite ruins it all by wanting to go to the right where her parents live, though Lucius knows they will meet the robbers there and will be caught again. He wants to go to the left. But Charite is a mama's girl; she has been, as the text says, stolen "from her mother's lap." It is this sentimental feeling bond with the mother which ruins their common flight, and makes them fall back into the hands of the robbers.

Afterward, an unknown new robber, Haemus (from *haima*, "blood"; he is the bloody one), appears, and by boasting and shooting his mouth off, he gets accepted by the band as a superrobber. Later we discover that he really is Tlepolemus in disguise, Charite's bridegroom, who has sneaked in among the robbers to free his bride. After catching Lucius and Charite, the robbers decide to punish the couple by killing the ass and taking out his entrails, then sewing the girl into his belly with only her head out. Then they are both to be exposed to the broiling heat of the sun so that she may slowly perish, sewn up in the stinking carcass of the ass. Even this sadistic plan has a strange symbolic meaning if we remember that Lucius should integrate his anima. His problem is that he does not do so, but sees it all from the outside, as beautiful and aesthetically satisfying. He never tries to interiorize the experience. If Charite were sewn up in his belly, that would represent, pictorially, the integration (internalization) of the anima.

It would be interesting to make a study of all the punishments in mythology, for, at least in all that I know, every punishment represents symbolically a form of attainment of individuation, but with a negative turn. For instance, Ixion desired Hera, he wanted to become the bridegroom of a goddess, and as a punishment was bound on a wheel (mandala) in the Greek underworld; or Tantalus, who, hung tied to a tree full of fruits and hanging over a lake, had to die of hunger and thirst; or, finally, Sisyphus, condemned to roll a stone endlessly to the top of a mountain. The wheel, the tree, and the stone are all symbols of the Self. Therefore, all the criminals were tied to the principle of individuation. It is as if the unconscious would say: "If you want to be a god, all right, be a god!" Most punishments and sadistic torture-fantasies are of such mythological character, and the symbols of individuation appear here in a negative, destructive form. It seems as if the process of individuation is an inexorable and inescapable law of nature in man's psyche. If one resists it, then it reaches its goal negatively.[1] These mythological sufferings reveal the deep reasons and meaning of "eternal" torture as it is experienced in neuroses and psychoses.

Since Lucius is not yet able to recognize his anima as something psychologically real inside himself, the sadistic robbers plan to teach him this in their own way. This does not come off, however, because Haemus interrupts their undertaking by proposing instead that they should get money by selling the ass and by selling the girl to a brothel. In that way he saves their two lives. He then makes the robbers fall asleep by giving them a lot of wine with a soporific drug in it, and while they are asleep he ties them up and frees his bride. The robbers are killed later and their den is destroyed. Tlepolemus here achieves what Lucius should have done: he acts. And therefore, seen from the perspective of Lucius the ass, it is still the autonomous, chthonic male shadow who by acting takes over the parts which are not yet integrated by the ego. It all happens in the unconscious, or in a half-unconscious state, and Lucius has therefore no direct profit from it.

Later we hear that the story of Charite and Tlepolemus goes wrong. Another man, Thrasyllus ("the bold," "the daring one," here in the negative sense of the word), falls in love with Charite and wickedly murders Tlepolemus. Merkelbach has rightly pointed out that this episode in which Tlepolemus is killed while hunting a boar is a parallel to the Isis–Osiris story,

where in certain versions Osiris is killed by Seth in the form
of a wild boar. We meet the same motif in the Attis myth.[2] So
here we encounter the mythologem of the death of the *puer
aeternus,* of the mother's son-god, who is destroyed by dark,
brutal, chthonic, masculine powers. Elsewhere, I have commented at length upon the problem of the identification with
the *puer aeternus,*[3] the problem of a man who, because of his
mother complex, is cut off from his chthonic masculinity and
believes himself to be the divine youth. In our story the shadow
of repressed masculinity appears first in the form of the
robbers who are overcome by Tlepolemus, and then in the
form of Thrasyllus. The chthonic masculinity or the capacity
for male action, which Lucius should have, remains in the
unconscious, and there it exercises helpful and also destructive
effects at random. It goes forward and backward without
result. Why on earth did Lucius give in to the beautiful
Charite, even though he knew that her wish to go to the right
was wrong? He lacked the Tlepolemus-Thrasyllus quality; he
just flirted with her and tried to kiss her foot, which was a
waste of time. Thereby the chthonic shadow takes over and
does not function in conscious connection with his ego, so the
whole effort is again in vain. The further fate of both couples
becomes tragic. Charite and Tlepolemus are separated, then
reunited, and finally die violently. Eros and Psyche are reunited, but only in the Beyond. There is also an interesting
fact: in antique gems and pictures Charite is often shown as
Eros's bride. She replaces Psyche, so at that time it must have
been clear to everyone how much the one couple, Charite-
Tlepolemus, represented a replica of the other, Psyche-Eros.
Together they would have constituted a marriage quaternio, an
image of psychic totality. In his work *The Psychology of Transference,* Jung relies upon the engravings of a sixteenth-century
alchemical treatise.[4] Depicted in these engravings are four
persons: the Alchemist and his Soror (his companion, his
mystical "sister") on one side, and the archetypal figures of
the King and the Queen on the other. Here, Charite and
Tlepolemus are likened to Amor and Psyche; Lucius is excluded from the quaternity and the male child is not born: in

such a case, *neither the ego nor the Self are present in the totality.*
The ego, Lucius, has not understood what actually took place.
The drama reaches an acute climax and then everything fades
out again. The last step is missing. In our story, the conscious
ego is so far away from understanding what happens inwardly
that it remains outside the quaternity. If Lucius and Charite
had married, there would have arisen a human couple vis-à-vis
the archetypal divine couple and the totality would have become real. But the fact that Lucius has not integrated Tlepolemus, the man of action, makes the continuance of the process
impossible.

We are confronted here with a problem which is often
overlooked by psychologists, be it by analysts of the Jungian
or another direction. Although the archetype of the Self can
sometimes appear in the initial dream presented by an analysand, one must, as Jung emphasizes, first work out the integration of the shadow. If one does not do this, then the ego is too
weak and does not have enough substance to endure the inner
process. One can compare it to catching a huge fish which one
cannot land, and it disappears together with the hook. The
more shadow aspects the ego can integrate, the more vital,
substantial, and strong it becomes, so that at the decisive
moment it can "land the fish." The moral and ethical qualities
of the ego are decisive, for one cannot lie one's way out. These
are very simple facts which many people cannot accept, so
their individuation is prevented. Life itself, for instance bad
fortune, can help to integrate the shadow and to strengthen
the ego. Being tortured by people in one's surroundings, being
persecuted by them, any kind of pressure, such as poverty,
help to strengthen the ego. I would say that regular work is
the best remedy. Jung speaks of it in his seminars where he
says that work is the means by which to overcome the mother
complex and avoid being overwhelmed by the unconscious.

I remember a very intelligent young man, who had a strong
mother complex, and who entered analysis mainly out of
interest, but he was lazy, which is mankind's greatest passion.
In his inner talks with the anima, who always appeared as a
goddess, he tried to defend himself with a realistic attitude,

but he did not manage very well. When he asked her why she tortured him, she answered that she wanted him to become a man. He replied that she should give him a chance. When she reproached him with being weak, he asked how he could make himself adequate. She answered that he should look at the cornfields behind her and harvest them, and bring in the harvest, and then he would be an adequate man. People who have a weak ego are too lost in the unconscious and cannot work *regularly*. Anybody carried by enthusiasm can work, but the problem of laziness begins when one has to do something which one does not feel like doing. Laziness is the bait by which the Great Mother catches us back; that is her greatest magic charm!

Tlepolemus is the man who endures war and withstands difficulties; Lucius has been forced by fate into conflicts, but involuntarily. In mythology, Ares, the father of Eros in some tales, stands for war. And in the name Tlepolemus there is a hidden allusion to Ares. Charite is secretly one with Psyche, whereas Tlepolemus represents an aspect of the god of war. He is an image of masculine aggressive courage, of endurance and the capacity to withstand conflict and go through it. Men need these qualities when faced with life or with a woman. Men who do not have them are afraid of women, for they feel that at the crucial moment, and instinctively, they will not react in an adequate way. If a man is afraid of women he cannot love them, for you cannot love someone of whom you are afraid, because that would be a question of domination. Real love contains a great amount of trust, and if you are afraid of someone it means that you have no real confidence in them. That is why a mother's boy in relation to women is afraid and leaves them with an uncertain feeling of being cold and distant, for he knows that if the woman really gets aggressive, he will not be up to the situation. He would not be able to take back the bouquet he has brought, slam the door, and say something coarse enough to shut up her animus. In marriage, men who have not assimilated their masculinity become henpecked husbands, just good enough to carry the luggage. If the wife makes a scene, some men go to a friend for advice. Then the friend says he must retain a cool head and take the upper hand; but that does not help because the woman feels that someone else has advised him to do this, and just laughs at him because of that. That defense reaction must come out at the given moment and out of the instinctive basis, and this a man can only achieve if he has integrated his "Tlepolemus." Then he can react at once in a spontaneous way, for he will have the right fantasy and say the right thing. It might even be a joke, if she is sailing around like a dreadnought with her unleashed animus.

After Tlepolemus's death, there is a small strange remark in the book, namely, that Charite worshipped her dead husband in the likeness of Liber, a name for Dionysos. This points to the Dionysos mysteries, which in Apuleius's time had become a part of the Attis and Osiris mysteries. Merkelbach's contention that probably Apuleius thought of these parallels and discreetly alludes to them is therefore justified. So again the sacred marriage, the *hieros gamos,* and the marriage quaternio fall apart. Everything disappears into the realm of death, blotted out without a concrete result, first by the robbers, then by Tlepolemus, as Haemus, and then later by Thrasyllus. If someone has thus missed his chance, his depression will generally then become much worse. This reminds me of the fairytale motif in which a valuable flower blossoms every nine years out of a pond, or the earth, and if one misses this moment, then one must wait another nine years for the next chance. There are those numinous moments of possible realization, and if one misses them then it is over. I remember the story of a man who fell in love with a woman and for conventional, moral reasons did not take up the relationship. His dreams bothered him on and on about it, but he continued to have ethical reasons for not deepening the relationship, till finally one day he woke up from a dream with a voice saying to him, "If one misses certain things at a certain moment, one has missed one's whole life." This frightened him sufficiently to get him to act.

So there are these moments where one knows that if one is now a coward, if one now misses the curve, one will not get the chance again for a very long time. The unconscious generally makes that quite clear, and because things have not reached consciousness we have this terrible comedown afterward.

Out of gratitude, Tlepolemus gives Lucius to a stud farmer with whom he is supposed to have a good life and be happy. But this man, as soon as he is at a good distance from the house of Tlepolemus, uses him as an ass to turn the mill. In antiquity the milling of the corn was done by grinding it between two stones. An animal—cow, horse, or ass—or even a slave or several slaves had to turn the stone. There is still the same system in Egypt for obtaining water. In its negative aspect the motif of milling around means being caught in an emotional complex. When someone is stuck in a neurotic complex, the same problem goes round and round in his head. People cannot get away from the problem, and they tell you the same thing over and over again. But as we have seen, there is also something numinous hidden in the complex, and in the very worst center of the neurosis or psychosis there is generally a symbol of the Self and that causes the fascination and makes people hang on to it. If one contents oneself with the repression of the illness, the symbol of the Self is thereby also repressed, and that is the reason why people often fight against being cured. They have a hunch that the best of themselves lives in their worst suffering, and that is the awful difficulty.

At the basis of neuroses as well as of psychoses one finds generally a symbol of the Self, but it is constellated there in a form which cannot yet be assimilated. So Lucius is bound to the wheel without understanding anything. The picture is especially characteristic since the animals or the slaves mostly had a black bandage tied over their eyes to prevent them from becoming giddy. That is a picture of every neurotic situation: with bound eyes one must drudge in a *circulus vitiosus*, to turn around the psychic center, without being able to "see" something and to understand the meaning of suffering. It is the classical *circumambulatio* of alchemy, but in its negative form.

After this episode, Lucius is sold to a woman and an adolescent boy. The boy uses him to fetch firewood from the mountains. There, being alone with him, he enjoys torturing him sadistically; he also spreads around the village bad stories about him, claiming that Lucius has pursued women and sodomized them, and he thus succeeds in having the ass condemned to be castrated.

This boy represents the most negative version of the *puer aeternus* symbol; he is the shadow of figures such as Attis and Osiris, and also of Lucius himself. The shadow of a young man whose feelings are undeveloped often has the boyish attitude of puberty, like those teenagers who pour kerosene on tramps and set fire to them just to enjoy the reaction. There is a misguided instinct behind it! Youngsters who have been castrated by so-called "good education," those goody-goody mama's darling boys, frequently have a secret longing for what one could call the bloody cruelty of life. It is normal for young men in puberty to develop a certain curiosity about the gruesome and dark sides of life, to go to a morgue to see what corpses look like, or to the backyard of the village butcher to watch the killing of the animals. Such boys instinctively seek shock effects to wake up out of the honey-sweet atmosphere at home in which they have been lulled to sleep. In a way, therefore, a certain amount of curiosity about evil corresponds to a healthy instinct. It means that the young man is seeking the truth of life and yearns to know how things really are. Naturally, if it goes too far it becomes pathological. In our story Lucius is not cruel, not even firm enough with Charite. If he had only said when fleeing, "Shut up now! We'll go where I want to go, we can make love afterward." Or, "You can howl afterward, but now I want to do this or that!" That would have been the man's task, but he missed being cruel with her sentimental nonsense at the right moment. Because of that, his cruel shadow became autonomous and destructive and tortures him now. Lucius is therefore now whipped, castigated, and tortured by this sadistic boy; this means he suffers from a childish self-criticism which leads nowhere. Finally it goes so far that the villagers decide to castrate him, and he only escapes by urinating all over the hostile old woman who intends to burn his genitals.

In alchemical texts urine is an especially productive and

positive substance. *Urina puerorum,* the boy's urine, is, for instance, one of the many names for the *prima materia* of the alchemical stone of the wise. Even in the nineteenth century the poet Gustav Meyrinck, who also secretly practiced alchemy, still believed that. In Prague he paid a lot of money for a very old outhouse and dug round in it for years because he had read so much about urine in old texts. It exploded in his face! In the Canton of Appenzell, the practice of medicine without a doctor's degree is still not forbidden, and it is therefore the canton where a lot of nature healers, good and bad, accumulate. Some of them prescribe that people should drink their own urine, the most marvelous cure for practically every disease. The need to urinate is the only bodily need which we cannot control fully. Even in military service one has the right to step out, and not even the general can forbid it. Urinating is therefore a symbol for expressing one's innermost nature. It is really something of the highest value and so there are so many jokes about it. Even the emperor must go to the *pissoir,* and so on. This urge is the defeat of man's will. He is up against an urge stronger than himself. Sleep and hunger can be repressed for a long time, but not urinating. And because of this impossibility, it is a "god"; in other words, it is stronger than man. It crosses all plans. Very often in analysis, if people do not say truthfully what they should say, or do not confess a transference, or suppress God knows what, they are forced to go out three times during the hour. Jung told a story about a woman who, after she had been sitting with him, was awkward and funny for about five minutes. He felt he had to urinate. He had actually done so just before, but he got up and excused himself, and when he came back she murmured shyly, "I have to go too." And he said, "Damn it, have I even to do that for you?" Frequently in nightmares people wander about with this kind of an urge and cannot find the right place, which always means that they cannot express their true nature. Therefore, if Lucius here escapes with the help of urinating, this means that at the last minute he returns to a completely natural, genuine expression of himself and by that he saves his own life. It shows that his innermost genuineness is not broken, and if completely cornered it will still come forth against his will. So the principle of individuation manifests in this rather elementary form.

With the death of Tlepolemus and Charite there is an end to any normal love life in the novel; from here on there is nothing but adultery, homosexuality, and sodomy, with the exception of the last chapter. The themes of the novel are now perversion, crime, and torture. First, the sadistic boy is killed by a bear; after that, his mother has an outburst of rage against the ass, whom she accuses of being responsible for the boy's death. This accusation is not without symbolic meaning: the bear is a mother symbol and one of Artemis's animals. In American Indian tradition it is connected, as it is in Greece, with madness as well as with healing powers.

In the Greek language the word *arktos,* for "bear," is feminine. In reality, therefore, the sadistic boy is killed by the same destructive, devouring mother who threatens Lucius. The negative elements destroy each other, something which at the end enables Lucius to escape. What attitude would be needed in consciousness for this to happen? In fairy tales the hero often meets three giants who quarrel, and the hero acts as judge. The giants kill each other, and the hero gets the magical object which is the source of the conflict. For the opposites to eat each other up is an ideal situation; but one needs detachment, since the ego must stand the conflict and not identify with either party. If the ego does not identify, then the opposites will eat each other up. If one is involved in a conflict, the inner opposites will always try to pull one in; but if one succeeds in staying "outside," which means staying objective, they may destroy each other, as here the bear and the sadistic boy do.

From now on the story becomes somewhat tedious. One disgusting affair follows another. But psychologically this tiring repetition is not accidental. Often something similar happens within analysis. There is generally a phase where the neuroses becomes rather stabilized and the process is less fluid than hitherto. It is as if the neurosis builds up a defense mechanism. One feels that a part of life is excluded, for the same kind of bad experience is continually repeated. Every time one hopes that something may change, but nothing results, and so the great emotion which would sweep away all the neurotic fixation cannot break through. This long period of being stuck in such a neurotic situation is depicted in this part of the book. I do not know of a general solution for such cases. One has the feeling that the analysis should be able to break through the blockage and force a decision, but one cannot reach the nucleus of the personality. The temptation is then to give up and to send the case to a colleague. The other possibility is to struggle further, even if it means working for two or three years, hoping that one day the unconscious will have accumulated enough energy for a breakthrough. This is what happens finally in our story. Only after a long adverse stagnation does the big breakthrough come in the eleventh chapter. As our diagram shows, much has happened above and below the line, but from now on there will be only nonsense for a long while, little happens above or below, and one wonders where the psychic energy is.

At the end of this tedious part there follows the wonderful appearance of the goddess Isis. So, after the event it becomes clear what actually happened before: while you were plowing through the dirty nonsense, all of the life energy was accumulating in the deeper layers of the unconscious until the healing archetypal content could break through. Before, nature had tried over and over to get through, but now it seems it had to wait until enough explosive force had been accumulated. Admittedly, this is also dangerous, because the energy then returns in a too-powerful way. It is a dangerous moment, because then the energy comes in a brutal form. In such a case you may come to a shock solution, or a catastrophe, for nature does not care which. It can also happen that, if the resistance is insurmountable, inner realization may come only on the deathbed; for example, a cancer can manifest itself and the interior unity is not realized until the last hour.

At any rate, there is here a quiet period when nature accumulates her forces. This is hinted at by the description of the dragon episode: the ass and its master walk past a dragon which is devouring everything. This seemingly meaningless episode, and the fact that no fight takes place with the dragon, conveys that the "devouring mother" has now taken on her deepest, coldest, and most destructive form and has disappeared into the bowels of the earth. The mother complex has become a completely destructive force. Nothing happens anymore on the level of consciousness. The god Seth, the enemy of Osiris, was represented sometimes by the figure of a crocodile or a snake (but in Greek the word *drakon* means both "dragon" and "snake"). It is, as it were, *he* who now rules the whole unconscious level. If an archetype takes on the form of a snake or a dragon, it means it is in such deep layers that it can manifest only in the psychosomatic area, in the sympathetic nervous system. Then the conflict has taken on a form which can not be assimilated into consciousness: there will not even be any more important dreams. It is the stillness before the storm.

The tragic end of Tlepolemus and Charite, who disappear into the underworld, is told to us in a side story and is not

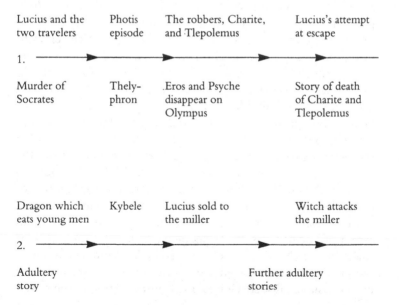

reported as an episode of the main narrative. This is a decisive point, at which all events, which till now occurred on the level of consciousness, fall down into the unconscious, where they take their course in the form of inserted stories. They disappear into Hades, the land of death.

Both Olympus and Hades are ruled by Zeus. One couple of the novel disappears in the former, the other into the latter, but both sink into realms of the unconscious which have no connection with human life. In a way, the marriage quaternity is united again, but in the Beyond, in a place we know nothing about. Only at the end comes a positive development, which runs in the opposite direction: Isis comes up from the realm of the underworld gods. In this way, the death of Charite and Tlepolemus connects with Lucius's process of rebirth through Isis at the end of the story.

During the period when he is running away, Lucius, at an inn, hears the story of a slave who loves a free woman and whose wife is so unhappy that she kills herself and her child. The master of the house hears about this and has the slave tied to a tree and his body smeared with honey so that the ants will eat him. Honey, as I mentioned earlier, is a substance which plays an important role in the mysteries and mother cults, so the slave is covered with "mother substance," which serves to bring the ants. One could compare ants to the dissolving effect of the mother complex. What could be a most unifying experience becomes here dissociating, a being lost in mass ecstasy, for the individual element, the anima, has gone into Hades. The personal feeling would be the filter to humanize the religious experience, but it is gone. Swarms of ants often represent a process of disintegration. For instance, before the Emperor Nero went mad, and after he had killed his mother, he had a dream in which his horse was attacked by a swarm of flying ants. There his latent psychosis became manifest.

The slave who loves the free woman personifies again an aspect of Lucius himself. As people nowadays still project their shadow onto the maid or servants, so in the Rome of antiquity, the upper classes projected their common and lower reactions onto the slaves. Robert Graves, in his introduction to the novel, considers this to be one of the most important aspects of the book.[5]

We know that if a man has a mother complex he is to a certain extent cut off from chthonic masculinity, in other words, from his low and "common" reactions. The pedagogic animus of his mother has endeavored to cut him off from such reactions because they contain that virile power which could separate the adolescent boy from the mother. Therefore the castrating effect of the mother's animus[6] cuts off not only his sexuality, but also all other low, primitive reactions. Nowadays one might think that such cases are the result of a Christian education, which is true, for that also reinforces the rejection of the animal element, but the problem already existed before Christianity. There has always been a tendency in the West to cut off this part in order to reach a more highly differentiated level of consciousness. If this is achieved in a wrong way, a split results and the person has no basis of fertile, primitive earthiness anymore.

I would like to mention an example. A man who had very noble and particularly Christian ideas and a gentlemanly attitude got married. Everything seemed to be quite all right until his wife had an affair with another man. When I saw the husband the first time, I expected to hear a song all about his jealousy, and so on. But he was not jealous! He said that they had agreed to allow each other complete freedom, as he thought it mean to be conventionally minded. I said that that was quite all right, but that somewhere one has a primitive reaction. But he was so idealistic that he did not feel any other reaction. In his dream, however, the whole cellar was on fire and an apelike man raved about, beside himself with rage. Naturally, the patient had the normal reaction! But it was completely repressed and therefore much more destructive than if he had noticed it. Those are the slave reactions in us, where one is neither noble nor reasonable.

We are the victims of our passions and greed. We are "slaves," the passive victims of events in life of which one has to take notice. But if there is a schizophrenic split, these emotions are not only not let out, they are not even noticed.

There are pros and cons for that, whether one lets them out, but in either case it is necessary to be aware of, and feel, and experience one's primitive reactions. Some people are so identified with their ideals that they succeed in completely cutting off their emotional reactions and can honestly say that they do not feel anything of the kind. But "the cellar is on fire" and there, naturally, are the vulgar, or basic, or primitive, or animal reactions, in which one is not free but bound by one's passions, which are usually projected onto the lower classes or political opponents.

I knew a well-bred man of good family, a true type of *fin de siècle* nobility, who, probably even when he goes to the toilet or blows his nose, thinks that he does this differently from ordinary people. Every night he dreamed that the Communists were breaking into his beautiful villa. Ordinary men broke in and smashed all the beautiful things he inherited from his ancestors. Not being in analysis, he saw it as a mediumistic prediction of what was to come in outer reality. He thought the Communists would devastate Europe and did not see that the dream had a very personal meaning. He had repressed "the man in the street" within himself and had projected him onto the Communists. Anyone split in that way is secretly fascinated by the Communists, and behind his own back he will help the spread of Communism, because part of himself is behind the Iron Curtain and even hopes that the Communists will invade Europe. People who have the most to fear from the Communists support them in this way and sympathize with their ideas, though they would be the first to fall into despair under their regime. Thus, the Communists often carry the projection of the common, collective man who has not been integrated.

We all have a common man, or a common woman, within us with the reactions of the man in the street, and the strangest thing about it is that this can even be an aspect of the Self—the Self being the highest and lowest at the same time. Christ, too, is called in the Bible both the king of kings and a slave. He was crucified as a slave. It is a paradox. People who do not know much of Jungian psychology think it is something esoteric and aristocratic. They do not realize that the process of individuation always moves in two opposite directions: on the one hand, one becomes more individual and less identical with the mass emotions; but, on the other hand, one also goes "down" in order to integrate "the man in the street." The process encompasses an expansion of the personality in both directions. The most common and the most humble qualities have to be integrated, for otherwise a kind of elitist individualism creeps in which must not be confused with real individuation. The higher a tree grows, the deeper its roots must reach, and the more one develops consciously, the greater becomes the need to accept the general human reactions with humility and simplicity. So the slave symbolizes another of Lucius's shadow figures, which longs for freedom. But this slave seeks freedom in an egoistic way: he acts out of himself, without waiting for a sign from the gods; and furthermore he neglects his wife and child. That is why he cannot reach the goal. The forces of the unconscious destroy him. Only when Isis, the redeemer, and Osiris appear on the threshold of Lucius's consciousness can a true liberation of his slave side be possible.

In this and some other stories which follow there is nothing magical or numinous. To remind oneself: the first and the second stories deal with witchcraft and the third is a magic story. But after the marriage quaternity breaks up and Charite—the personification of Lucius's feeling life—disappears into the underworld and becomes completely split off, the inserted stories degenerate. What remains is just human dirt. It is feeling which decides whether something is valuable or not; therefore, if their feeling function is suppressed, people no longer know what is important and what is just banal. Everything becomes flattened into undifferentiated human dirt. Sometimes in an analysis, for weeks or months, there is nothing but gossip and the "washing of dirty linen." Nothing archetypal or numinous is constellated, and nothing much happens. One just has to plod on in human dirt.

9
The
Ass in
the Service
of Many Masters

The ass is now brought to market and bought by an old homosexual man, the chief priest of a band that goes around carrying an image of the Syrian goddess Kybele. The old man, Philebus, is a lover of youths. The members of this band behave like certain dancing dervishes in the Orient; at the end of their dances they fall down, wound themselves in masochistic ecstasy, and afterward collect money from the onlookers. Furthermore, in the case of this band they indulge in homosexuality and sodomistic pleasures. These people buy the ass, and Lucius has to carry the image of the goddess and some of their goods. Apuleius describes how they dance and how one of them suddenly begins to sigh deeply, pretending to be filled with the heavenly breath of the goddess, and prophesies in a state of ecstasy. Then there comes a sentence which shows why Apuleius wrote about this episode. He says the dancer pretends to be in a manic state, "as though human beings would become weak and ill through the presence of the gods, and not better than they were before." Here he points out that this kind of connection with the divine does not have a curative effect, but represents a morbid religiosity.

If one believes that Apuleius inserted this description consciously, that could explain the description of the great goddess Kybele as a wonderful counterimage to the Isis mysteries at the end of the book: first we have in front of us ecstasy and religious experience in their destructive aspect, and then Lucius becomes possessed by the goddess, because he does not *serve* her. Then follows, at the end of the novel, the positive counterimage of a genuine religious attitude toward the mother goddess. Whenever an archetype is pressing for realization, this realization can take place positively or negatively. If one accepts and turns toward it, it becomes a healing experience; but if one runs away from the archetype, it becomes negative and possessive, and one falls into the grip of it. Here the homosexual old man is possessed by the mother archetype, and through that has only a pseudoreligious experience. Many homosexuals seem to have a rich inner psychological life, an artistic and religious side, but if one looks closer, something has a wrong twist. The religious attitude of the homosexual is difficult to define. It is a question of feeling. But though it is admirable and gives a certain depth and dimension to life, one feels, as a woman at least, as if something were lacking. It lacks substance. It is not quite convincing, not quite real somewhere. Naturally this is not true of all homosexuals.

In the description there is another aspect which in our time, too, is a great problem: the wild dances which today take the place of conventional dance. Our situation is parallel to that of the Roman Empire in so many ways! What children are offered today in the way of religion is often insufficient and does not reach the emotional depths any longer. So, naturally, they have a longing to be ecstatically gripped and to experience moments in life where one is lifted out of one's miserable existence. Because they do not get the wine of the Holy Ghost, they drink the dirty water of the street instead. They turn to wild music and dances, and become drug addicts and even criminals. Even the political demonstrations en masse are not political activities for many youngsters; rather they spring from a longing for ecstatic experience. Because they do not experience the ecstasy in religion, they turn to political mass movements, which afford a morbid, pseudoreligious ecstasy. This shows a degeneration of the religious function; the more the religious problem is neglected, the more we have such compensatory substitutes. Therefore, too, the great attraction of homosexuality in this kind of movement. It all belongs together.

The ass now gets into further danger. The company stays that night near a rich household from whose kitchen a dog has stolen and eaten "the side of a fat bucke," which was to have been roasted for the evening meal. The cook is in despair and about to hang himself, when his wife prevents him, advising him to secretly kill the ass of the strangers in order to use one of its sides as a substitute. Nobody would notice the difference when it was roasted and served with a good sauce. The poor ass in his deadly terror breaks his halter and runs into the parlor, where he upsets all the company by throwing all the food and drink off the table onto the floor. The master of the house says he should be locked up. At this moment a boy arrives with the news that there is a mad dog in the town which has bitten a lot of animals and people, and everyone is frightened that the ass has rabies and they all want to kill him immediately, but he saves himself by running into the master's bedroom. There he is locked in, so he lays himself on the bed, sleeps the whole night like a human being, and awakes much refreshed. The people peep through the door and, seeing him standing there, quiet and peaceful, debate what they should do. One suggests offering him water, so as to prove whether he has rabies or not, and the ass proves his sanity by drinking greedily. He is therefore laden again with the statue of the goddess of Syria and other trumpery, and driven away. Having escaped being eaten, he continues with the dancing Kybele priests.

In this last story the ass begins for the first time to become more human again. For a short time in the bedroom he behaves like a human being. It is interesting that the people around interpret his humanness as madness. This has a parallel in the analytical process, for if a patient begins to be more healthy, sometimes the people in his vicinity think him more crazy than ever and do all they can to force him back in his illness. The return to normality is shocking to those around. It is always crippling to an ordinary group to have to take back to themselves the projection of the illness, which before was thrown onto the "other." If the other person becomes normal, the equilibrium of the group is disturbed. Therefore there is an unconscious tendency in the group to prevent the healing process in the sick person.

I had once a sad experience when visiting a big hospital in the States. An analyst of our group had selected a few patients and taken them into personal analysis. Among others, he had selected a fifteen-year-old girl who had been raped by her father, a drunkard, and brought to the hospital and diagnosed as schizophrenic. She was catatonic. The analyst had treated her and got her onto a better level. In a moment when the girl felt much better, she went into the kitchen and stole a big chocolate cake. She did not eat it herself, but took it to the children's ward and distributed it, and they had a wonderful feast and everything was covered with chocolate. The head nurse appeared in a flaming rage, saying that the girl must be shut up again, that she was completely mad, that the psychotherapy was doing her a lot of harm, and that she must be isolated and given shock treatment, and so on. It was an impressive example of a dreadnought animus. But the doctor said, "Don't you see that this is an improvement, that she had feeling for the other children and had established contact with them?" But the household was disturbed, so the nurse thought she must be mad and must have shock treatment again. When people who begin to become normal again have a transitional stage in which they are socially a nuisance, for they are neither mad nor normally adapted, people in the vicinity get excited, for they do not like things to be changed. Here the ass is becoming a little human, and it is interpreted as "rabies."

Then follows the inserted story of a carpenter who returns home unexpectedly one morning when his wife's lover is there. The wife hides the man under a tub and scolds her husband for wandering about doing nothing while she has to work so hard. But he says that, on the contrary, he has been busy and has succeeded in selling for some money the tub, which simply clutters up their place. The woman thereupon says that she has done better than that and has sold it for more money. "The man willing to buy it is just now inspecting it." The lover then shows himself and says the tub is dirty so that he cannot tell whether it is cracked or not, and the husband should bring a light. The unsuspecting husband fetches a lamp and says he will clean the tub himself, which he does while the other two, hidden by the tub, continue to make love, and are not found out.

The story has neither magical nor supernatural elements in it, but is a plain story of adultery. Whereas earlier the stories above the horizontal line of consciousness of our diagram were realistic, and those below the line were numinous, now the latter are banal, and in Lucius's conscious life there is the wrong kind of ecstasy. This is typical where there is a wrong relationship with the divine: the ego intoxicates itself in a false ecstasy, while the unconscious becomes more and more banal. The anima, who should be the mediator to the deeper layers of the soul, no longer fulfills her function. The marriage does not work, and this adultery is nothing more than a purely sexual distraction without feeling or love. The anima has fallen into an undifferentiated, immoral state.

Later the priests of the Syrian goddess are caught and accused of theft. The ass is sold once again, this time to a baker, whose mill it has to turn. The description of the mill which follows throws a light on the social situation of the time. Lucius sees the poor slaves, carrying sacks, in miserable condition, and others marked by the irons which had burnt their heads. The faces of some are blackened by smoke and others full of wounds. The horses, too, are old and weak and covered with scars. They cough continually, their sides worn bare with the harness and their ribs broken with beating. It is a dreadful sight, and Lucius reflects sorrowfully on his own past behavior. His only consolation in his present evil situation is that he can hear and understand what goes on around him, for nobody fears or suspects him of being human. He remembers how Homer describes "him to be a wise man who travelled divers countries and nations," and gives thanks to his ass shape for these unusual experiences.

If one admires the monuments in Greece and Rome and the tourist guide relates how superior the civilization of that time was, it is time to remember that these cultures were flowers of the swamps. There is an uncanny analogy to our civilization, where a small group strives for intellectual and moral differentiation, while the mass remains undifferentiated. After a time, what has not been differentiated washes away what has been built up. Basically this is the problem of the inferior function:[1] If single individuals, instead of overdifferentiating their main function, would work on other parts of themselves and bring them at least to a certain level, then such a split would not happen—individually or collectively. In our times we are confronted with the same split within and without. It is shown in the horrible display of social egoism which threatens our culture.

Naturally there were in antiquity a few exceptions who had compassion for the slaves, such as Seneca, the Stoic philosopher, but the majority of the other philosophers shut their eyes to the fact that many people had to live as slaves under dreadful conditions. Seneca taught that slaves should be treated as humanly as possible, for one's own sake, for you could not enjoy your food if you were served by an unhappy, hungry slave! However, such ideas did not touch most of the Romans, and therefore the late Roman Empire—as Jung pointed out— was filled with a strange kind of melancholy, which actually was the longing of the slaves for redemption. The upper classes (as exemplified by Horace and his friend Maecenas) were deeply depressed, but they did not know why. Then came the Christian message, which gave a "new" symbolic meaning to life. Once more we are in the same situation as the Roman Empire; we too have to give up some of our intellectual and technical achievements in order to heal our outer and inner psychic dissociation, which threatens to destroy us, because otherwise the dark swamp of mob psychology will sweep away the cultural flower which has grown out of it.

In the mill the ass hears a few other stories of adultery, which we know that Apuleius borrowed from an earlier novel. Apuleius-Lucius relates that the baker was an honest and sober man, but his wife "the most pestilent woman in all the world" who "abandones her body with continual whoredom." An old woman, "a messenger of mischiefe," who haunts her house daily, tells the wife the following story:

Barbarus, a senator of the town (whom the people also called Scorpion, for the severity of his manners), being jealous and wanting to keep watch over the chastity of his wife, leaves her in the charge of the slave Myrmex ("the ant"). He threatens him with death if any man does but touch her with his finger as he passes by. Myrmex, therefore, does not allow her to go out and even sits beside her when she spins, and accompanies her to the baths. But a certain Philesiterus, whom the old woman who tells the story recommends as a lover for the baker's wife, is enamored of her and tempts Myrmex with money, a part of which is to be for him and a part for the wife. At first Myrmex refuses, but then he asks the wife, who, greedy for money, consents. Myrmex brings Philesiterus, disguised, to his mistress. But about midnight the husband returns unexpectedly. Myrmex delays in opening the door, and Philesiterus makes his escape, but he forgets his slippers, which the husband discovers the next morning. He suspects Myrmex and has him bound, and on their way to court for trial, when passing through the marketplace, they meet Philesiterus. Terrified that the whole story may come out, Philesiterus beats Myrmex about the head, accusing him of having stolen his slippers at the baths. So both are saved.

The story does not need much comment. It has sunk to the level of people who have insects' names and sheer, cruel, instinctive animal reactions. With insects we are dealing with reactions of the sympathetic nervous system with all its coldness, brutality, and lust. There is nothing human left. Remember also that in Greek myth the ant is a symbol of the aboriginal man. It overcomes the scorpion, which could be interpreted as the personification of evil.[2] Thus we do have here a slight progress: the autochthonous real man is saved and the true evil is outwitted.

Hearing this story, the baker's wife then decides to make Philesiterus her lover and prepares an especially good supper with lots of wine. He is scarcely seated when the husband comes home, and the wife just manages to hide him under a tub. The husband, who does not suspect anything, tells his wife of a neighbor who hid her lover under a wicker basket which served for bleaching the clothes hung across it. It stank of sulphur vapor and, when all of the occupants of the house were at the table, the hidden man had to sneeze. First the husband thought that it was his wife who sneezed, but when it happened again, he became suspicious, found the lover and would have killed him if he, the baker, had not prevented him from doing so.

The baker's wife cannot insult the other woman enough, but, remembering her own lover, she tries to convince her husband to go to bed. However, he wants to eat first, and she is forced to offer him the food which was prepared for the other. The ass, disgusted by her conduct, treads on the fingers of the young man which are sticking out beyond the tub and takes all the skin off. The young man screams, and the husband discovers him and punishes him by locking his wife in the bedroom and raping him homosexually in his own room. Next morning he has him thrashed and driven from the house. He then divorces his wife, who goes to an enchantress for help. But, as none of her spells will reconcile the baker, the latter sends the spectre of an old woman to his house. Pretending to have a secret, she takes him into a room with her. As the baker does not reappear, the servants break open the door and find he has hanged himself. But the dead baker returns as a ghost to his daughter, with the cord round his neck, and tells her what happened to him; he explains the circumstances of his death and how "by enchantment he was descended into hell."

Bake shops, like mills, were often types of brothels in antiquity. Moreover, bakers were looked on as being servants of the goddess of grain, Demeter.[3] Here, our baker is destroyed by the Great Mother in her witch aspect. And here, for the first time, these stories of adultery become less banal, and the dark, divine element comes in again, though in an uncanny form which shows that the problem has fallen to such a low level that, in practical terms, it cannot be integrated. The old woman who lures the man to suicide represents the killed feeling function, that part of the anima which is in the underworld of ghosts. Charite has committed suicide and is in the ghost world. When the man is lured to suicide by the anima, it becomes more and more dangerous, for it has become a drive toward death: a power which lures the man to self-destruction. But there is still a positive aspect as well, for at least the supernatural appears again. Therefore one can say that the dark mother powers have come back, though in an uncanny, ghostlike form.

The ass is now sold to a poor gardener. This gardener gives a night's shelter to an honest and rich man of the next village, who, to reward him, takes him later to his house, where the gardener is served a wonderful meal. While he is eating, a hen produces a chicken instead of laying an egg, the earth under the table opens and spews out blood, and in the wine cellar the wine is boiling in the casks. Then a weasel is seen pulling a dead serpent into the house, and a live frog jumps out of the mouth of a sheepdog, and immediately afterward a ram kills the dog. While everyone is terrified at these happenings, a message arrives to say that the rich man's three sons are all dead. The good man is so upset by these terrible tidings that he cuts his own throat. So the gardener returns with the ass to his house. On his way he is attacked by a soldier who demands his ass. The gardener tries to dissuade him, but when the soldier will not listen, the gardener knocks him down, leaves him seemingly dead, and runs away. He asks a friend in the next village to hide him from the police, who are pursuing him for murder. The friend hides him in an upper story of the house, but inadvertently the ass puts his head out of the window and one of the soldiers sees his shadow. Both ass and gardener are discovered, and the latter is imprisoned.

The important thing in this story is that Lucius cooperates unconsciously with evil and helps to destroy his master, who is a good person. This he does by "showing his shadow." This is meaningful if one recollects the fact that the book was written by a Neoplatonist philosopher. The Neoplatonists believed in the supremacy of good, and that evil was only a kind of ignorance and misunderstanding. Upheld by this sort of illegitimate optimism, Plato tried to meddle with politics in Sicily and, as is known, suffered shipwreck; he was even sold as a slave. Toward the end of his life Plato had therefore to correct his too-optimistic views and work over his theories, for his bitter experiences had shown him that evil did exist and that the real world did not match his ideal picture. This theme, too, is represented in our novel, and it shows how reality appears to a Neoplatonic philosopher. Hitherto the stories have been concerned with the problem of relationship, but from now on come forth the problem of good and evil and a clear tendency to pessimism. The evil forces predominate, and the ass is even cooperating with them involuntarily. In our culture, too, there still exists this problem. Many Christians have too optimistic an idea of evil. The more we are one-sidedly idealistic and wish to do good and the right thing, the more we involuntarily cooperate on the side of evil. On the contrary, if one takes trouble to take into account the dark side as well, one can better avoid evil suddenly forcing itself into the foreground in too strong a way. To do good may still be one's aim, but one becomes more modest, for one knows that if one is too good, one constellates the compensatory destructive side. It is more realistic not to do good in an unreal way, thereby with one's left hand increasing the weight of evil without noticing it, and afterward justifying it by saying that one did not know.

This problem is especially acute for those who want to become analysts. Again and again analysts with the best intentions are too good to the analysands, and have bad effects without noticing them. They do not realize that they can harm an analysand, who is telephoning in despair, through too much sympathy. If one gives too much, either in feeling or in cooperation, one makes the analysand childishly dependent, even if it may not be the intention. That is only one example of how the best intentions can lead to wrongdoing if one is not skeptical enough about oneself and is not conscious of one's own shadow. If one stresses the right, the left appears.

Christian morality is derived to a great extent from Neoplatonism and the Stoics, and has the false idealistic tendency or coloring which is unhealthy and which builds up involuntary destructiveness.

"Good intentions" can therefore be very dubious and can even become extremely dangerous. But what to do? What can guide one? Only dreams can show us what is happening and what our motivation really looks like. The balance and healthiness of the analyst are therefore of much greater importance than his dubious good intentions. After the problem of evil there arises at the end of our novel also the problem of psychic healthiness. From the tenth chapter on, the problem of our book becomes a medical one, having to do with illness and medicine.

The next story is that of a stepmother who wrongly accuses her stepson of incest. (Here we may remember that Apuleius was a lawyer.) Briefly, the story runs as follows. The ass is taken over by the soldier whom the gardener had beaten up. They come to a little town where the ass hears the story of a young man and his stepmother. She is in love with her stepson and so tormented by her feelings that she sends for him to come to her room. The young man acts warily, saying that they should wait for a convenient time when his father is away. The woman persuades her husband to go on a journey and then bothers the young man, who always makes excuses, until she realizes that he does not care about her, whereupon her love turns into hate, and she and a servant plan to kill him. The servant buys poison, but by mischance her son, and not her stepson, drinks it and falls down dead. The woman sends for her husband and tells him that her son has been poisoned by his stepbrother, and the father sees he is going to lose both sons. As soon as her son's funeral is over, the father denounces his son, saying that he killed his stepbrother and threatened his stepmother, which is what the woman had said. The senators and counselors are called together; the accuser and "offender" are produced and commanded to have their advocates plead their causes. The servant is also called and falsely accuses the woman's stepson. So the young man is sentenced to be sewn in a skin with a dog, a cock, a snake, and an ape, according to the law.

In this moment a physician comes forward and states that the servant had offered him a hundred crowns for some poison. He shows the hundred crowns and at the same time he states that he became suspicious and had not given poison but a drink of mandragora, which puts one to sleep only temporarily. Therefore the woman's son would be found not to be dead. The stone of the sepulcher is removed and the son is found alive. Sentence is then pronounced: the woman is exiled and the slave hanged.

Everybody at the trial was first in favor of condemning the stepson. If the old physician had not appeared, the whole thing would have gone wrong. Today, too, the problem of good and evil has become so subtle and difficult that it goes far beyond the categories of good and evil in jurisprudence. In many cases it has become a question of psychic health or disease. This is experienced again and again, for the person with the best intentions, if neurotic, will have a destructive effect. So the problem of good and evil is linked with psychic health, which is often more important than following the letter of the law.

Again, we have a similarity with Roman civilization, inasmuch as at that time people began to think that civilization was a question of paragraphs of the law. But the psychological health of the individual matters much more. Therefore, with Apuleius, it is a medical doctor who settles the problem and not the lawyers, who would have given the wrong verdict. We, too, suffer from the fact that many of our leading politicians are neurotic; here we see how burning the problem still is. In primitive tribes, if there is a case of theft, they do not call in a lawyer, but the medicine man, who has to right the situation and must be the judge of good and evil. In our culture the field of law and health is split too much. I believe that only decentralization to a certain extent can help, for in a smaller group everyone knows if the village mayor is "neurotic." His wife will talk about him, and so on. In village communities everyone still knows everyone and has a better feeling about whether the other is psychologically healthy or neurotic.

Merkelbach has convincingly interpreted this story by relating it to the mysteries of Osiris.[4] In his view, the two brothers represent Osiris and Seth: the truth and the lie. The resurrection of the innocent stepson recalls the resurrection of Osiris. The wise doctor is an image alluding to Thoth-Hermes. According to Plutarch, Thoth is the cosmic Logos and the wise doctor.[5] In these inconspicuous images, there is already being prepared the revelation of great symbols of the initiation mystery at the end of the book. For nearly the first time, the positive element, truth, carries the victory over the forces of evil. Imperceptibly, something shifts in the psychic process, leading to a return of positive elements.

Then Lucius is again sold on the marketplace. This time he is lucky, for his new masters are a cook and a baker. The two are in the service of a rich man, and bring home with them all kinds of meats, sweets, and pastries. The ass, Lucius, discovers this food and steals from it, and the two wonder how things disappear. They finally suspect Lucius and, watching what he does, catch him in the act. They call their master to see this strange ass who eats human food. He is thereafter made to sit at table with a napkin around his neck. As an ass he has to be careful not to betray that he is really human, and so pretends to learn slowly how to eat like a human being. The people are delighted with his intelligence and teach him also how to dance and answer questions.

The owner of the two slaves has the interesting name of Thiasus, which is the name of the orgiastic reunions in the Dionysian mysteries. Dionysos was at this time completely identified with Osiris. So the work of rehumanizing the ass relates to the Dionysian mysteries. This is meaningful. If one looks upon orgiastic cults from a superficial angle, then their intention seems to be to bestialize man through ecstasy. But, looked at in another way, they served to humanize the animal in man. Apuleius here alludes to their secret meaning. The mysteries did not serve to release the beast, but to bring that side of man into an acceptable form in which it could be integrated. Thiasus therefore personifies something divine, which helps the ass to come back toward a human level.

Finally, a rich matron falls in love with the intelligent ass and wants to sleep with him. And the rather shocking story of how she sleeps with the ass is told. If one understands this symbolically, it shows that the anima attempts to rehumanize Lucius, who has fallen down to a level below the human. Though it is an anima figure which tries to heal him, this effort at redemption is not wholly successful because it is on the level of sexual pleasure. But there are signs that the situation is improving: the masters of the ass are less cruel, and a human being even "loves" him. So the process of a rehumanization starts from all sides. The *enantiodromia*, the turning over to the opposite, has set in.[6]

In a personal analysis this is a dangerous moment. When the first symptoms of a positive change appear, there is the greatest danger that the analysand will commit suicide. This is rarely the case when the analysand is undergoing his worst times, but when he is at the point where there is the first indication of an *enantiodromia*, then generally one must reckon with a last outburst of destructiveness. At the moment when the devil and the destructive forces are beginning to lose the game, one must expect them to make a last attack. The same thing happens in exorcism: the devils do something awful at the last moment. They explode the lamps in the church, or go off leaving a dreadful stench of sulphur behind. The devils never go quietly, but give a last display of their destructive power. This is a psychological truth. Therefore, one must be very aware of that dangerous moment when an improvement first begins to set in.

Lucius Returns to Himself

A fter a slow deterioration, the last story leads to a negative climax: in a circus Lucius is supposed to have a union in public with an inferior, criminal woman. She has poisoned a number of people and is the worst creature in the whole novel. Lucius is utterly repulsed by the idea of having intercourse in public with such a woman. Here, for the first time, he definitely refuses to be caught by the entanglements of the negative feminine. He stands up for himself and insists upon his own feeling attitude. In a moment of general confusion he escapes from the circus through the streets of the town. He goes along to the seashore to Cenchris, a famous harbor town, and then, to avoid the crowds of people, he goes to "a secret place of the seacoast," where, exhausted, he lays down and falls into a sound sleep.

The fact that he goes to the seashore and, avoiding people, goes to a lonely place is meaningful. If we remember our diagram, we can see that this corresponds to the deepest place: he has reached the bottom of his misery. In his bitter experiences he has gone through personal tragedy and now finds himself at the sea, the border of the collective unconscious. For the first time, Lucius, rejecting involvement with people, seeks to be himself, to endure his own misery and his loneliness, and in this state he falls asleep. Apuleius reports through Lucius:

> When midnight came I had slept my first sleepe, I awaked with suddaine feare, and saw the Moon shining bright, as when she is at the full, and seeming as though she leaped out of the sea.[1]

He wakes and sees the full moon over the sea, a most holy experience. He thinks of the mother goddess, Ceres-Demeter, and associates her with the moon, for it is at the moment of the full moon that the goddess has her greatest power. People assumed at that time that everything pertaining to vegetative and animal life depended on the moon, as well as the whole rhythm of nature, death, and life.

> And I considered that all the bodies in the heavens, the earth and the seas, be by her increasing motions increased, and by her diminishing motions diminished: as weary of all my cruel fortune and calamity, I found good hope and sovereign remedy though it were very late, to be delivered from all my misery, by invocation and prayer, to the excellent beauty of this powerful Goddess. Wherefore shaking off my drowsy sleep I arose with a joyful face, and moved by a great affection to purify myself, I plunged my head seven times into the water of the sea; which number of seven is convenable and agreeable to holy and divine things, as the worthy and sage philosopher Pythagoras hath declared. Then very lively and joyfully, though with a weeping countenance, I made this oration to the puissant Goddess:
> "O blessed queen of heaven, whether Thou be the Dame Ceres which are the original and motherly nurse of all fruitful things in the earth, who, after the finding of Thy daughter Proserpine, through the great joy which Thou didst presently conceive, didst utterly take away and abolish the food of them of old time, the acorn, and madest the barren and unfruitful ground of Eleusis to be ploughed and sown, and now givest men a more better and milder food; or whether Thou be the celestial Venus, who, in the beginning of the world, didst couple together male and female with an engendered love, and didst so make an eternal propagation of human kind, being now worshipped within the temples of the Isle Paphos; or whether Thou be the sister of the God Phoebus, who has saved so many people

by lightening and lessening with thy medicines the pangs of travail and art now adored at the sacred places of Ephesus; or whether Thou be called terrible Proserpine, by reason of the deadly howlings which Thou yieldest, that has power with triple face to stop and put away the invasion of hags and ghosts which appear unto men, and to keep them down in the closures of the Earth, which dost wander in sundry groves and art worshipped in divers manners; Thou, which dost luminate all the cities of the earth by Thy feminine light; Thou, which nourishest all the seeds of the world by Thy damp heat, giving Thy changing light according to the wanderings, near or far, of the sun: by whatsoever name or fashion or shape it is lawful to call upon Thee, I pray Thee to end my great travail and misery and raise up my fallen hopes, and deliver me from the wretched fortune which so long time pursued me. Grant peace and rest, if it please Thee, to my adversities, for I have endured enough labour and peril. Remove from the hateful shape of mine ass, and render me to mine own self:[2] and if I have offended in any point Thy divine majesty, let me rather die if I may not live."

When I ended this oration, discovering my plaints to the Goddess, I fortuned to fall asleep again. . . .[3]

Lucius invokes the great goddess in the four names of Demeter, Venus, Artemis, and the underworld goddess, Proserpina: three light aspects of the great cosmic goddess of nature and a fourth, dark aspect. He has now fulfilled the whole cycle of his mother complex. He has experienced all the aspects of this great archetype, and that he can invoke her in four ways means that he has become fully conscious of most of the essential paradoxical aspects of this great unknown power which has ruled his life. He knows that the bad fortune which has pursued him is this goddess, and that only the goddess who is the cause of his misfortunes is able to turn them. For the first time, he does not even ask to go on living. He is weary of life, not even caring whether she grants him a continuation of life or releases him through death. The only thing he asks is that *she give him back to himself.* This attitude is the most important thing in individuation; the ego must take it when it is confronted with fate: not to want this or that; to give up the ego-will which would like this or that or the other; to want neither to live nor to die, or no longer to suffer. Lucius has been worn down so much that he has realized that nothing is more important anymore than to be able to be himself.

Here Lucius, for the first time, turns directly to the unconscious. This is so infinitely simple and yet the most difficult deed in the everyday psychological situation: when one is gripped by something and made to turn toward it, rather than being possessed by it from behind. This turn, which one could also call reflection, needs an inner quietness, a keeping still, stopping and looking at the situation in which one is driven, asking what it is that drives one, what is behind it. This is infinitely simple and infinitely difficult at the same time. But having gone through so much unhappiness, Lucius has reached this stage. He then bathes in the sea.

Then comes the famous prayer which begins with the words "Regina coeli, O blessed Queen of Heaven." This invocation has been partly taken over by the Church in the cult of the Virgin Mary and has been used as a model and inspiration for numbers of prayers and litanies to the Madonna. After these opening words comes something which may seem a bit artificial, a mentioning of various goddesses, but here we must remember that the time is that of late antiquity, when many of the more educated people were impressed by the fact that all the different nations worshipped similar types of gods, and had begun to discover the archetype behind these different names. Lucius means that there is only *one* great mother goddess and that different people call her by different names and worship her differently. He directs his attention to the absolute essence behind all regional goddesses. He addresses the archetype of the Great Mother itself. We would say that he recognizes one transcendental power behind all these different goddesses. Therefore he says:

> . . . whether Thou be the Dame Ceres which art the original and motherly nurse of all fruitful things in the earth, who, after the finding of Thy daughter, Proserpine, through the great joy which thou didst presently conceive, didst utterly take away and

abolish the food of them of old time, the acorn, and madest the barren and unfruitful ground of Eleusis to be ploughed and sown. . . .[4]

He alludes there to the Eleusinian mysteries, in which the secret cult is based on the myth that Proserpina, the daughter of Demeter, was abducted by Hades, and her mother went to look for her, and so the great cult of Demeter's search and the reunion with her daughter was established. Lucius alludes secretly also to the cult of Venus-Aphrodite when he says, ". . . or whether Thou be the celestial Venus, who through her son Eros has united all people. . . ." He addresses the goddess as the mother of Eros, ". . . being now worshipped in the temples of the Isle Paphos; or whether Thou be the sister of the God Phoebus . . ."—that would be Artemis—". . . that has power with triple face to stop and put away the invasion of hags and ghosts which appear unto men, and to keep them down in the closures of the Earth."[5] Persephone is the goddess of death. Lucius gives the Great Mother four names: Ceres-Demeter; Diana-Artemis; Venus-Aphrodite; Proserpina-Hecate (the underworld goddess). Proserpina is the dark, underworld aspect, ruler of death and of the ghosts, but also protectress of the living against the ghosts.

He gives the goddess no more and no less than an involuntary *quaternio*[6] of aspects, which represents a totality in a female form. He exhorts at this moment the mother-anima figure as being identical with the Self. This identity appears often in the beginning phase of the development of the Self. In a series of dreams on which Jung has commented in *Psychology and Alchemy*,[7] there are, for instance, dreams in which a woman appears with a round object which shines like the sun, and Jung says that there the anima and the Self are still identical.

Later Lucius realizes that the goddess is only a guide, a mediatrix who will help him to find Osiris, the real symbol of the Self.[8] Only at the end of our book does the direct realization of the Self appear. But in the present moment it appears to him through the mediation of the goddess, indicated by her fourfold aspect. She is for him the totality of the psyche in its female aspect. The anima personifies here his overwhelming religious emotion. If we think back to his sensual attitude and his cynical intellectual attitude, we can see this new attitude as an astonishing change. Even the style of writing, the tone, has changed (though some mannerisms remain), which has even caused certain philologists to assume that this part of the novel has been added by another author. When Apuleius, however, ceases to be ironic and mocking, it is a tremendous achievement, for he now gives himself naively to the inner experience. It is an experience of the totality of the godhead, conveyed through the anima, revealing what was really behind all the experiences through which Lucius had passed.

Proserpina-Hecate especially personifies the magical aspect of the mother goddess. She transforms her lovers into beasts. Lucius suffered from the magical aspect of the feminine in his experience with Photis, but everything he has gone through has been along the lines of personal involvement; now, at last, the archetypal meaning has become clear to him.

At the end of the prayer Lucius reaches an attitude in which wanting to live or to die are no longer important; what is important for him is to be himself. There is an analogy between this text and that of the conversation in *The World-Weary Man and His Ba,* an old Egyptian text studied by Helmuth Jacobsohn.[9] The Ba in this text personifies the soul or the Self of a man who wants to commit suicide. It says to the desperate man that it is a minor problem whether one returns to life or kills oneself. The only important thing is the man's relation to his innermost soul, the Ba-Osiris, that is, to be one with the Self. The realization of the Self is an experience of eternity and conveys the feeling of being beyond life or death. To live or to die becomes secondary in the light of an experience which transcends the ego and our way of attributing importance to time and space. People who have had such an experience can die, as some primitives still do, with dignity and calm and without the struggle of the ego which does not want to submit to its fate.

After this prayer there follows the revelation of the goddess.

Lucius falls asleep and dreams that the goddess appears to him in a personal form.

> . . . and by and by (for mine eyes were but newly closed) appeared to me from the midst of the sea a divine and venerable face, worshipped even of the Gods themselves. Then, by little and little, I seemed to see the whole figure of her body, bright and mounting out of the sea and standing before me: wherefore I purpose to describe her divine semblance, if the poverty of my human speech will suffer me, or her divine power of eloquence rich enough to express it. First she had a great abundance of hair, flowing and curling, dispersed and scattered about her divine neck; on the crown of her head she bare many garlands interlaced with flowers, and in the middle of her forehead was a plan circlet in fashion of a mirror, or rather resembling the moon by the light that it gave forth [Helm: "picture of the moon"]; and this was borne up on either side by serpents that seemed to rise from the furrows of the earth, and above it were blades of corn set out. Her vestment was of finest linen yielding divers colours, somewhere white and shining, somewhere yellow like the crocus flower, somewhere rosy red, somewhere flaming; and (which troubled my sight and spirit sore) her cloak was utterly dark and obscure covered with shining black, and being wrapped round her from under her left arm to her right shoulder in manner of a shield, part of it fell down, pleated in a most subtle fashion, to the skirts of her garment so that the welts appeared comely. Here and there upon the edge thereof and throughout its surface the stars glimpsed, and in the middle of them was placed the moon in mid-month, which shown like a flame of fire; and round about the whole length of the border of that goodly robe was a crown or garland wreathing unbroken, made with all flowers and all fruits.[10]

Here we have four colors, and before there were four names. The goddess wears a black garment with stars and a full moon on it. She emits a wonderful perfume, and she speaks to him.

There are a few details in this description of the goddess which need discussing. She wears a moonlike mirror in her hair, something like the third eye. The mirror would symbolize seeing oneself by reflection, for a mirror throws our image back at us. Just as we cannot see ourselves physically, except to a limited extent and never in full, and are unconscious of our own form, we need the outer thing to reflect us. So the mirror as a symbol gives us the possibility of seeing ourselves objectively. It gives one a shock when one suddenly sees oneself in a mirror or hears one's voice on a tape recorder for the first time. All such experiences show how little knowledge we have of our inner and outer appearance.

If, through analysis, one has gained a certain amount of objective knowledge and then hears or reads the honest attempts of people who have not had such an experience, but who want to better and reflect upon themselves, one realizes that what they have done is extremely restricted, for these people seek to understand themselves only with the ego and without the help of the reflecting unconscious, in other words, without dreams. The Godhead, the Self, is that which reflects us *objectively,* as without it we could not see ourselves. In Saint Paul's letter (1 Corinthians 13:12) it is said: "Now I know in part; but then shall I know even as also I am known." This means God knows us before we recognize Him, and He sees us before we see ourselves. Expressed psychologically, this is about reflection and having insight into our innermost being. We can only get reflected knowledge of ourselves from dreams, just as we need a relationship to others to know more about ourselves. So the goddess carries potential insight, the round mirror, as a symbol of the Self which gives Lucius objective Self-knowledge.[11]

The poet Lucianus interprets the moon itself as a huge mirror, and moonlight is a symbol of the diffuse light of the unconscious, contrasted with the more focused light of consciousness. In our example, the mirror is surrounded by snakes, the symbol of the deep unconscious and of the wisdom of the goddess.[12]

Now we come to the motif of the many colors: the garment of the goddess shimmers sometimes white, sometimes yellowish, sometimes reddish, and covering it all is a robe of black. The black would correspond to the *nigredo* of the alchemists, followed by the *albedo,* the whitening, then by the *rubedo,* the reddening which transcends the opposites, and finally the *citrinitas*, the yellow of gold as the fourth color.[13] All these colors were also ascribed in antiquity to the underworld. They were the colors of the Beyond, and from there stems their correspondence with the four stages of the alchemical process in which the idea of totality is associated with the goddess who contains within herself the four stages. Black is the first color that one encounters in the decomposition of the *prima materia*, the so-called *nigredo*, when one enters deeply into the unconscious and discovers one's shadow. This is also the case for Lucius, for until now he has only experienced the *nigredo*, a state of depression and folly. Even the garlands of flowers and fruits are found in the texts of alchemy. In the intermediary stage between the *nigredo* and the *albedo* there appeared generally a stage of varied colors, an experience of the world of plants and animals.

Black, white, and red are not only the typical colors in the alchemical process. They were used long before in the decoration of coffins and everything which had to do with the cult of the dead. In the Graeco-Roman, as well as in the Egyptian epochs, they were the colors of the Beyond. Black and white are in a way no colors, therefore one can really say that they refer to the Beyond. They are the most extreme opposites outside the spectrum of "life's color game." In old Sparta, for instance, white was the color of mourning and death, just as black is with us. In China also, white is the color of death. So black and white, all over the world, are associated with the Beyond, with everything that lies outside the visible, earthly human life, while red was looked on more as a symbol of the essence of life. One finds red colors in Egyptian tombs, and even earlier, in prehistoric times, the corpses or the whole insides of coffins were colored or smeared with red, which was meant to symbolize the secret continuation of life in the Beyond and the idea that the dead are not dead but still have a life of their own.

These four colors of alchemy have been compared by Jung to the typical stages of modern's man descent into the unconscious, in which blackness would correspond to the first realization of the unconscious, of the shadow, where one's former conscious attitude is blackened out. This is a stage where mostly the shadow problem comes up. The shadow at this stage represents the whole unconscious and everything that has remained "in the shadow" as a result of the former conscious attitude. Very often, therefore, the first meeting with the unconscious brings deep depression, a feeling of confusion, of being lost in the dark, and the undoing of the former conscious attitude. Then comes the green aspect with its flowers and animals, which would mean that after having worked through the stage of the impact with the shadow, life begins to return.

But this is only a transitory aspect. Then comes the next step, the problem of the realization of animus and anima, in which one is taken far away from outer reality. The integration of these two powers means hard work on oneself for years. In this stage, one is still, so to speak, in the land of death. One can only work the anima or the animus problem out by a period of great introversion. Even if it should come into one's life in the form of a transference, that is, in a projected form, the only part one can work on is the subjective inner aspect. It is therefore a stage which teaches one detachment from outer reality, and where one has to keep the retort of one's own inner work closed, and completely reflect, in the literal sense of the word, upon oneself.

In the black and white stage in alchemy, the alchemist has to work hard, and in analysis the analysand has to work hard. The opus, the work, consists in trying to become conscious of these powers. However, after this part is done the alchemists say, the hard work is over. Afterward one has only to go on and to warm one's substance with a mild and gentle fire, without any more effort. Then the *rubedo,* the red color, appears by itself. When this appears, one can open the retort and—expressed in alchemical language—the sun or the philosopher's stone comes out and takes over the ruling of the world.

In less poetical language this would mean the beginning of the realization of the Self, which at this moment takes over the process so that the ego no longer has to work. Close reflective introversion can now be loosened up, for in the realization of the Self, it is equally important to know whether or not one should take outer steps in order to obey the Self. One becomes the servant of a principle which oscillates, manifesting itself sometimes in an introverted form and sometimes in an extraverted form. One may have an order from the Self to do something in the outer world, or an order to realize something within oneself. The retort has, therefore, become superfluous, because the Self is not something which falls apart: the solidity of the vessel has now become the solidity of the "philosopher's stone," in other words, a permanent inner experience of the Self, which gives the personality innermost consistency, making any outer artificial solidity or solidification superfluous.[14] In many alchemical texts, the vessel and what is cooked in it, the philosopher's stone, are one and the same thing. It is a symbol of the solid nucleus of the inner personality. This is not identical with the ego; rather, the ego realizes itself in a serving function. Hence, the philosopher's stone in alchemy is called the king, the new ruler, who far exceeds the ego complex in power.

In the garment of Isis, all these possibilities are hinted at in its three-colored beauty, and she for the moment has indeed taken over the continuation of the process. Though one reads frequently in many summaries of Jung's ideas that the process of individuation is first a realization of the shadow, then behind that the realization of the anima or animus, and then of the Self, this is only true *grosso modo*. Actually, one first meets the *whole* unconscious, the Self, with animus or anima in the shadow, because the shadow is generally all that people are capable of realizing out of the entire impact of what they receive. It is the only thing close enough to their grasp, the only thing one can make clear and real. The rest generally remains purely abstract; only after work on the shadow does one begin to differentiate further. A man would then see some feminine element behind what he now knows as an unconscious part of his personality, and the woman would realize certain typically masculine elements. In this stage one realizes the feminine or masculine contrasexual aspect of one's unconscious personality, but the animus and anima figures again contain the whole unconscious, so that here with Lucius it is a meeting with the archetypal anima absolutely contaminated with the Self.

We shall see that only after Lucius-Apuleius has gone through his initiation into the Isis mysteries, and lived a certain time in Rome as a lawyer, in a normal way, feeling himself to be the servant of the goddess Isis, that he is called a second time through dreams into a new initiation. This time he is to experience the god Osiris, or that aspect of the unconscious which reveals itself as the nucleus of the total personality: the Self. But for the moment Isis is the Self and the anima in one. She personifies for the time being the totality of the unconscious. All the future possibilities of development of Lucius are contained in her, so she quite rightly tells him that he must serve her in an unconditional way.

Later, as mentioned, Lucius is initiated into the cult of Osiris. Since Isis and Osiris represent the feminine and masculine aspects of the totality, this would correspond to the experiencing of the *rubedo*. After the Isis initiation he returns to Rome and becomes a lawyer, fulfilling the role of a lay priest in the mysteries. During his service for the goddess Isis, he remains a *katochos,* in other words, he lives within an enclosure, also being enclosed into himself; only when the "inner enclosure" has become solid enough is there no longer any need for this outer imprisonment. One now has an inner solidity against the impact of the outer world, so one can return to life in a seemingly unreflected way.

The alchemists make very strange references to the fourth or yellow stage, calling it *multiplicatio* and comparing it to the grain of corn which multiplies by thousands and thousands. With the philosopher's stone one can turn any ignoble metal into gold. The *lapis* has a transforming emanation which even goes into the cosmos. In symbolic form this would mean: with the realization of the Self, one is in complete harmony with the whole world, in a synchronistic correspondence with the inner and the outer universe. This is a stage which most people can reach only for a few moments and which the Chinese describe as being one with the Tao.

This reminds me of the famous Zen Buddhist series of "Ten Oxherding Pictures,"[15] in which the Chinese painter represented the inner course of development in symbolic form. First comes the releasing, then the catching, and then the taming of the ox. This would correspond to the *nigredo* and belongs to the "animal" stage of self-education and its problems. Then comes the picture of the full moon and the adept praying to it. He has forgotten the ox and also the whip with which he should tame it, the whole animal problem has disappeared. The next picture is the round disc of the moon, the stage of enlightenment without polarity which is no longer an ego experience. This enlightenment is "Buddha." Nothing can be added anymore. And then a branch of a cherry tree in flower appears. One does not quite understand what it portends, only that it probably has to do with a return to life. The last picture shows an old man with a fat, hanging belly, walking along, smiling. His servant boy is with him carrying a begging bowl, and a few branches of cherry blossom are before him. He is going to the market, begging, and the text says: "He has forgotten the ox; he has forgotten his own big experience; he has even forgotten himself, but wherever he goes the cherry tree blossoms." That would correspond to the yellow or gold stage of alchemy. There is then a union with the cosmos. It appears to be a stage of complete unconsciousness, but in reality it has to do with the opposite. In this connection I must refer you to the last two chapters of Jung's *Mysterium Coniunctionis* on the *unus mundus,* where the same experience is described in alchemical and psychological terms.

In our text the Goddess holds a sistrum and brass timbrel in her right hand, an instrument used in the Isis cult to chase away evil demons and ghosts.[16] It could be compared to the bell used by the Catholic Church during mass, the ringing of which concentrates the attention of the believers onto the holy moment and also has the function of keeping away all that is unholy. That bell has its origin in the cults of Isis and Mithra. In her left hand Isis carries a golden bowl, which is the most

central and important symbol, its meaning corresponding to
the vessel mentioned earlier in connection with the waters of
Styx. This golden bowl resembles a jug. It is, as we will see
later, a symbol of Osiris. In Roman cults, everything to do
with underworld gods was associated with the left hand. It was
always the left hand which sprinkled the flour over the sacred
sacrificial animals when they were consecrated to the gods of
Hades. Contrary to that, everything which had to do with the
upper gods was connected with the right hand. For Apuleius,
the goddess is holding something in her hand which symbolically announces the next step in the process, which is still
unconscious: the realization of the Self, which goes beyond
the realization of the anima. It resembles a mysterious veil over
something which one does not yet know. She carries the
potentiality for the realization of Osiris in her hand and says:

> Behold, Lucius, I am come; thy weeping and prayer hath moved
> me to succour thee. I am she that is the natural mother of all
> things, mistress and governess of all the elements, the initial
> progeny of worlds, chief of the powers divine, queen of all that
> are in hell, the principal of them that dwell in heaven, manifested
> alone and under one form of all the Gods and Goddesses. At my
> will the planets of the sky, the wholesome winds of the seas,
> and the lamentable silences of hell be disposed; my name, my
> divinity is adored throughout all the world, in divers manners,
> in variable customs, and by many names. For the Phrygians
> that are the first of all men call me the Mother of the Gods at
> Pessinus; the Athenians, which are sprung from their own soil,
> Cecropian Minerva; the Cyprians, which are girt about by the
> sea, Paphian Venus; the Cretans which bear arrows, Dictynnian
> Diana; the Sicilians, which speak three tongues, infernal Pros-
> erpine; the Eleusinians, their ancient Goddess Ceres; some Juno,
> other Bellona, other Hecate, other Rhamnusia, and principally
> both sort of the Ethiopians which dwell in the Orient and are
> enlightened by the morning rays of the sun, and the Egyptians
> which are excellent in all kind of ancient doctrine, and by their
> proper ceremonies accustom to worship me, do call me by my
> true name, Queen Isis. Behold I am come to take pity of thy
> fortune and tribulation; behold I am present to favour and aid
> thee; leave off thy weeping and lamentation; put away all thy

sorrow, for behold the healthful day which is ordained by my providence. Therefore be ready and attentive to my commandment; the day which shall come after this night is dedicated to my service by an eternal religion; my priests and ministers do accustom, after the wintry and stormy tempests of the sea be ceased and the billows of his waves are still, to offer in my name a new ship, as a first-fruit of their navigation; and for this must thou wait, and not profane or despise the sacrifice in any wise. For the great priest shall carry this day following in procession, by my exhortation, a garland of roses next to the timbrel of his right hand; delay not, but, trusting to my will, follow that my procession passing amongst the crowd of people, and when thou comest to the priest, make as though thou wouldst kiss his hand, but snatch at the roses and thereby put away the skin and shape of an ass, which kind of beast I have long time abhorred and despised. But above all things beware thou doubt not nor fear of any of those my things as hard and difficult to be brought to pass; for in this same hour that I am come to thee, I am present there also, and I command the priest by a vision what he shall do, as here followeth; and all the people by my commandment shall be compelled to give thee place and say nothing.[17]

The Isis procession with its dates and meaning are part of the Graeco-Roman tidal calendar, and a part of the great calendar year which existed in Egypt[18] from oldest times, and which one could parallel with our Church Year. Certain periods of the year have their holy association, so that Time is also psychologically involved in the religious cult. In the winter the boats at the Mediterranean were brought ashore, practically all navigation ceased, and at a certain date in spring it was resumed with a procession of the whole population to the sea, which has to do with the festival, described here (March 5).

The goddess Isis was the protectress of navigation and seamen, as the Virgin Mary still is in Catholic countries. As the *stella maris,* the Virgin Mary has inherited the function and title from Isis. During this procession the goddess promises that Lucius will find the roses which he needs for his redemption. But there is still a double danger; when he tries to eat the roses held by the priest he could either be beaten away by horrified people or, after being turned back to human shape, he would stand there naked. However, Isis has even foreseen these difficulties and has instructed the priest in a dream that Lucius should quickly be given garments and thus there would be no fuss or scandal about the strange transformation which is to take place in public.

II
The
Goddess Isis

We cannot rationally understand the whole greatness of the goddess Isis and what she means in all these connections, for one can never say or exhaust what an archetype contains. But one can to a certain extent circumambulate it by showing its different aspects and functions within the psychic situation. I therefore want to describe briefly the role of the goddess Isis and show why, and in what connections, she suddenly became so tremendously important in the late Graeco-Roman period of antiquity.

For this it is necessary to briefly outline the history of the Egyptian religion. Though I want to assume responsibility for my ideas, I have in the main been inspired by the themes and amplifications of Helmuth Jacobsohn.[1] What he has beautifully worked out is the principle of the divine trinity and the trinitarian idea of God, as well as the problem of the fourth divine aspect in the Egyptian religion.[2] In Egypt there were two gods named Horus, Horus the elder and Horus the younger. In later times these two were mixed up with each other, but in their nature they were two very different gods. The elder Horus was a kind of pantheistic godhead who included the whole cosmos, matter, spirit, the world, the totality of nature and life; the younger Horus was the reborn Osiris, the new sun.

The Egyptian religion probably originated from, and was more influenced by, African rather than Mediterranean or European sources. It very likely had its very essence in African tribes along the sources of the Nile, and then slowly wandered down the Nile into Egypt.[3] Whoever has visited this country has definitely been struck by the absolutely non-European strangeness of the early Egyptian religion. It was truly African, which, to my mind, gives it its special value. Horus the Elder would, therefore, be an African cosmic nature principle. In classical times, however, this god no longer played a great role, but was replaced by a trinitarian representation of the god Ré or Ra.

The pharaoh was, so to speak, the incarnated representative of the sun god Ra, and in innumerable invocations and titles is represented as such. But he was not only an earthly personification of the god, he *was* the god. For instance, when the pharaoh for the first time entered the bedroom of the queen and generated for the first time his successor, his eldest son, he was then invoked in the text as the supreme god, Amoun, visiting the goddess Isis, and generating his son with the help of the *Ka-mutef,* which means "the bull of his mother." Therefore, this first union of the king and queen in which a successor was conceived—in other words, the new sun god was generated—became a *hieros gamos* between mother and son. The queen is at the same time mother, wife, and sister of the king. Jacobsohn rightly points out that, in a way, the *Ka-mutef* plays the same role as the Holy Ghost in the Christian trinity. He mediates between Father and Son and generates the Son from the Father.

Quite generally, however, the *Ka-mutef* was *the* generating power, namely, that which kept man and cattle fertile; it was the dynamism of the godhead which spread through the whole empire. But the fourth was missing, and this invisible fourth, which was excluded from the light, solar, trinitarian principle, was in Egypt the goddess Isis, symbolizing matter. Or it was Osiris, who in this framework of the two older empires represents that which was not included in the upper solar trinity; the passive principle in nature, the suffering, that which is sacrificed and excluded. Osiris is the irrational element that was lacking in the conscious order of the Egyptian civilization. Therefore, Osiris became the secret ruler of the underworld. One could call him the personification of the collective unconscious, all that existed in the collective unconscious psyche, but which was not included in the conscious religious forms of that time.[4] The sun principle in its trinitarian form is visibly associated with a conscious order of the world. Its worship coincides with the invention of the measuring of fields and the invention of writing, the fixing of definite boundaries on the surface of the earth, the settling of all the territories of wandering tribes and neighbors into a fixed order which was guaranteed by the king and his polis. This was at that time one of the great advances toward a higher consciousness in mankind. Another great advance took place at the same time; namely, the invention of hieroglyphs and the establishment of archives fixing possession and the law.

For the first time in this oldest Egyptian empire, there was thus established a continuous conscious order which was not constantly obliterated or corrupted by invasions of the unconscious. Osiris, however, was still not included; for the more rigid and continuous, firm and systematic consciousness becomes, the more the other aspects of the psyche, the irrational aspects, are relegated and fall into the unconscious. The irrational element which was excluded became more differentiated in time. It became possible to distinguish another trinity in relationship to the first (see diagram on p. 190).

Osiris, the suffering king and god-man, was, according to the legend, a good king and a great musician and artist, but he was brutally murdered by his enemy, Seth. One could see Seth as the aspect of evil which has been excluded from the conscious order. The color red is attributed to Seth, and in the Egyptian language "doing red things" means doing evil. Seth stood for emotionality, for murder and brutality. Osiris was represented by the black or green color. "To do green things" meant to act according to Osiris. In superficial books on the Egyptian religion, Osiris is characterized as a vegetation god. This is seen too simply, although he was associated with

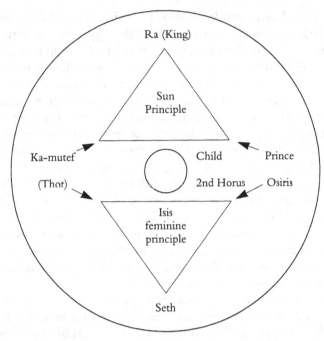

vegetation, with the wheat growing in the spring or after the Nile floods. But in his deeper meaning he is the symbol of greenness in the form of resurrection. As Jacobsohn has beautifully worked out, he is associated with vegetation because he represents the passive plant life, that living and irrational element which does nothing evil and, on the other hand, is the great sufferer from the beginning of the world. Every animal, every louse, every ant eats up the vegetation, and it silently grows again. Osiris is this life principle, this evergreen life in the human psyche—that which continues to live after innumerable deaths. Seth was really evil, and that is why I have put Seth at the bottom of the lower triad, for he disrupted the civilized behavior of the Egyptians. Seth is the great counterplayer, the darkest point in the lower principle against the upper trinity.

The chthonic, the earthly or nature mediator between the two opposites, is, in most texts, Thot, the baboon god, the god of medical art, spirit, and wisdom. He is connected not only with the sun principle, like the *Ka-mutef,* but also with material nature itself. Thot is the Egyptian forerunner and partly the model for the alchemical spirit, Mercurius. He personifies the nature wisdom of the unconscious. Taken in this way, Thot would belong to the lower trinity. The upper triangle in the diagram represents all aspects of the solar principle, and the lower triangle the aspects of the passive principle of Isis. One could say that the whole lower triangle belongs to the Isis principle.

After Osiris was killed by Seth, Isis flew down in the form of a hawk onto his corpse and was able to extract some semen from his penis, so that she became pregnant after his death and was able to give birth to him again.

She gave him birth in the form of the Horus child, often called Harpokrates; he is the "divine child" of all the late Egyptian mysteries and is generally represented as a little boy holding his finger to his mouth (the gesture of a baby), but it was interpreted in later times that he points to the great secret of the Egyptian mysteries. He is quite aptly called Horus, because he is really the restored cosmic wholeness, the restored totality in all its aspects. I have, therefore, put him in the center, between the two opposing triangles. He contains *in nuce* all the different aspects of the other gods: he is the new sun god, the renewed sun principle, and the divine child, who renews all life on earth. He is the secret spiritual goal which comes from the goddess Isis. When Isis reveals herself to Lucius, she brings to him the promise of spiritual renewal. She presents herself to him as Mother of the Cosmos—one of the names, *domina rerum,* given also the Virgin Mary. "I am the ruler of all nature: I am the highest of all the Gods and Goddesses; I am the queen of the ancestral ghosts (Manium)." She is the ruler of the ghost world.

In later Greece and in Egypt there was a strong tendency toward monotheism, which culminated in the worship of the goddess Isis, or Nut. In Egypt the heavenly sky was the *one* all-embracing divinity, Nut, and all other gods were stars in it; their polytheism is the internal multiple aspect of the One.

From the psychological perspective, monotheism tends toward a strengthening of consciousness and a unification of the personality and a movement away from the stage of possession. We inherit character traits and have contradictory ancestral elements in us, which drag us from one psychic condition to another and which the ego cannot quite bring together.[5] Education and self-will try all they can to form us into one unity, but they can have no success without the help of the Self. This unity, individuality, can only be attained with the help of the transcendent function,[6] expressed particularly in dreams, and which was personified in late antiquity by the god Hermes-Thot.

Isis, the ruler over ancestral spirits, is a symbol of psychic wholeness, the Self in a feminine form. She governs human society through dreams. For instance, she gives instructions to Lucius and to the priests in their sleep, and synchronistic events accompany the dream. In our case she appears to Lucius and to the priest for the first time the same night, so that two people come together, through the principle of synchronicity, to perform what is necessary for Lucius's transformation.[7] Later the same thing will happen when they have to fix the moment of his initiation.

From now on Lucius acts entirely under the guidance of dreams, even in connection to the amount of money that he needs for his initiation. If, in our times, a minimum fee is fixed for analytic sessions and if the therapist dreams that he must take a patient for less, what is he to do? I would do it, but insurance and professional rules prohibit most therapists from doing so. Intervention into the social order by the gods is destroyed by all kinds of bureaucracy or totalitarianism. Therefore, only a minimum organization is desirable in a society, for otherwise it kills the spontaneous spirit and destroys the secret work of the transcendent function. A too intensive organization and too many laws exclude the secret play of the gods and prevent the appearance of something irrational, which can be the germ of transformation. One believes in norms and that plans must be established, and by doing so one inhibits the possibility of a much greater spontaneous *psychic* event. If such a thing happens, it is either not noticed, pushed aside, or devalued. Thus the *natural* human community is disrupted and replaced by an artificial one.

One speaks of "coming closer together," one believes that one works toward it by "organizing" human relationships, while suppressing the one thing that will be effective: the irrational play of dreams. Mystery cults were secret communities formed by those who were "one" in spirit, wherein the irrational play could move freely. In the same way, there was a vibrant spirit in the primitive churches, a spiritual impulse which was neither utilitarian nor "reasonable." Yet there everything was organized by the gods. It was and still is the "invisible church."[8]

Above all, Lucius must recover his human form. The Goddess commands him to take part in a procession which is arranged in her honor the next day, and says to him:

> Moreover, think not that amongst so far and joyful ceremonies, and in so good company, that any person shall abhor thy ill-favoured and deformed figure, or that any man shall be so hardy as to blame and reprove thy sudden restoration to human shape, whereby they should gather or conceive any sinister opinion of thee; and know thou this of certainty, that the residue of thy life until the hour of death shall be bound and subject to me; and think it not an injury to be always serviceable towards me whilst thou shalt live, since as by my mean and benefit thou shalt return again to be a man. Thou shalt live blessed in this world, thou shalt live glorious by my guide and protection, and when after thine allotted space of life thou descendest to hell, there thou shalt see me in that subterranean firmament shining (as thou seest me now) in the darkness of Acheron, and reigning in the deep profundity of Styx, and thou shalt worship me as one that hath been favourable to thee. And if I perceive that thou art obedient to my commandment and addict to my religion, meriting by thy constant chastity my divine grace, know thou that I alone may prolong thy days above the time that the fates have appointed and ordained.[9]

When the divine Isis has spoken these words, she vanishes away. This is important. The Goddess demands that Lucius wholly accept his interior obligation with his feeling: he must be engaged, bound to his religious experience, for without this total engagement it is as though there were no religious experience at all. There are many people who have some great experience which somehow is swept away again. They have not recognized and accepted it, or realized that they had to do so. The moral obligations of gratitude do not only apply to our society but also to that of the gods. The inner factors also have the right to the human attitude of gratitude and loyalty, and of abiding by the experience. People lose that in moods and extraversion and do not feel the obligation. They eat the fruits of paradise, but then the experience is lost in the adversities of life, for they have not drawn the consequences of their experience. That is the alchemical task of *keeping the fire going!*

On the other hand, one should ask why an event so numinous and impressive as the transformation of the ass-Lucius into a human being should happen in such a shocking way, in public. One aspect which has simply been omitted in Adlington's translation, a detail which many translators omit, is the very last sentence of the book where Lucius, speaking to the priest of Isis, says this:

> . . . he chose me to enter the college of the Pastophores,[10] nay he allotted me to be one of his decurions and quinquennial priests: wherefore I executed mine office in great joy with a shaven crown in that most ancient college which was set up in the time of Sylla, not covering or hiding the tonsure of my head, but shewing it openly to all persons.[11]

The *tonsura*, the shaven crown, points to the consecration to the service of Isis, for all her priests and initiates had shaven heads, just as the monks of the Catholic Church do. The sentence continues, and many translators omit it: ". . . without being ashamed." This detail furnishes the answer to our question of why the transformation has to happen in public. The tonsure has the meaning of the *sacrificium intellectus*. Some of one's own self-willed thoughts are sacrificed to a higher principle. It is also a symbol of spiritual rebirth, and therefore he has, like a newborn child, a bald head. It is just as the myths say, when Jonah came out of the whale in which he experienced the great mystery, he became *quasi modo genitus,* again reborn. For from the heat of the whale's inside he had lost his hair. That is very often a symbol for being a reborn child, a *renatus in novam infantiam,* which is another aspect of baldness, of having sacrificed oneself and one's intellectual thoughts, of having gone through a process of rebirth through the underworld, and of being now and forever the sun child of the goddess. By that Lucius-Apuleius really becomes Horus, the reborn child, son, partner, and bridegroom of Isis. That is what he shows by his tonsure, and he has to stick to that in every aspect. The other transformation, during the procession, illustrates another awkward situation. He must eat those roses and stand there naked, and the priest has to get a shirt to cover him up, for everybody will wonder who that is and what is happening. I think the reason for this goes partly along the same lines as the reason for the tonsure, but beyond that it implies that he has to take the full force of the mockery in the open daylight of human life, of the fact of having been an ass, and of having become a human being again. Jung once wrote: "We owe mankind not only our good, but also our inferior side." Mankind has a claim on that too. We owe that to it, so if we have an inferior side and realize it, then we have to accept it and the humiliation of taking it as such. But then, as Lucius would otherwise not have experienced, the redeeming grace lies in the fact that, to an amazing extent, other human beings then generally become charitable. It is a positive experience for the human beings around you to see you once in your weakness, and through that for you to see them becoming charitable. If you are always top dog, always the one who swings the situation, always the one who behaves right according to your conscience, you become a stone of offense to everybody else, because you give them feelings of inferiority. You never get into the animus or anima; your shadow never gets you; you are always right. So everybody else feels absolutely outdone. Therefore, it is really a worthwhile experience to have to once face the fact that you have done everything all wrong, and that you are just at the bottom of the pit, and then to find that even jealous colleagues suddenly become human, because you are not up but down. One could say that when you are on the top of the mountain, the water of life always flows away, but if you are at the bottom of the pit, then it flows toward you and you are given back to humanity. You are just one of those many poor devils who has struggled, fallen down, and got up again, and that is a tremendous feeling experience. Think how lonely clever Lucius-Apuleius, the philosopher, was!

A religious experience means a total experience in which nothing must be excluded. For a mocking intellectual and coward like Lucius, it would be the greatest act of courage to stick to his inner religious feelings and his transformation in front of the public, even when confronted with the mockery of the educated Roman society to which he belonged; he must remain faithful in front of a frivolous collective attitude, of which he had formerly been a part. Thus he makes his inner experience into something whole, by excluding himself in this way from social vanity and intellectualism.

Apuleius was loyal to his inner experience, but he never revealed its real religious secret. In the Bible it is said that the man who finds "the pearl" (the kingdom of heaven) hastens to conceal it.[12] The pearl *must* be hidden, and it has no value unless one keeps it secretly within oneself, not taking pride in declaring it publicly or by trying to convert others and founding a new sect. Apuleius does not even say exactly what he experienced during his descent into the underworld. He finishes with three little sentences: "He descended into the underworld; he saw the midnight sun; he returned to the threshold of the upper world." He maintains an almost total silence about his experience during the initiation, and that is right. This is the hiding of the "pearl," the treasure, which one must not show to anyone unless on the basis of an inner command. This does not necessarily mean that one must no longer join collective social activities. One must only adhere firmly to one's own inner experience, without exteriorizing it uselessly, and also without denying it. If this numinous experience is accepted with sincerity, genuineness, and courage, it will bring forth a conversion, a "metamorphosis," a profound transformation of one's entire being. This will then indirectly affect one's behavior and will thus have repercussions in one's social life.[13]

Two attitudes are thus to be avoided. First is the desire to tell one's experience to everyone, whatever the costs, at the risk of suffering misunderstanding and making a fool of oneself. This is frequently the result of an inflation, wanting out of vanity to impress others, which makes one lose the experience completely. The second attitude to avoid is the desire to guard everything for oneself, pretending that one is the same old intellectual or pious Pharisee, or whatever one was before.

One can, as much as possible, hide the numinous experience under the veil of the *persona;*[14] but if, by an interior command, one is told to unveil the experience, one must have the courage to do so. One may have to say: "I am not going to do anything tomorrow." There is evidently no need to say that one acts so because of a dream, or to give an inner reason. But it can also happen that one has an interior command to stand up now and to say what one thinks, even if that means some kind of persecution. For instance, one may be led to go against a collective opinion, though without taking oneself to be the wise sage whose mission is to enlighten others, or by playing the martyr. Naturally the introvert will always be tempted to keep it too much to himself, and the extravert to blurt it out.[15] Both are wrong. The oscillation between these two rhythms belongs to the work of the Self, if the inner experience has been understood rightly. In general, dreams indicate clearly how one must act. The Self determines when one should expose the secret and when one should hide it.

It is very meaningful that Lucius-Apuleius, who was shy about standing up for naive feeling experience, should have to be exposed before Roman society, where all the nice mocking grins and pointed remarks of the others would certainly be directed toward him. They would mock at his shaven crown saying, "Ah, he has been initiated into the Isis mysteries," and they would drill into that. Previously, mockery, intellectualism, and aestheticism were all part of Apuleius's ego defense mechanism, and so to stand openly would be for him the test of total acceptance. His experience is not just a new small thrill which he can keep for himself, carrying on with his old outer life as before. Isis knows what she is doing when she imposes upon him the public confession. It is not what happens normally, but doing that fits his problem and his pattern.

The question arises why Lucius's redemption comes about through the intermediary of an *Egyptian* mystery cult and why the Isis-Osiris cult has such redeeming power over him. Why not the Christian or the Mithraic? We have knowledge of the fact that Apuleius knew much about other mystery cults and must have had therefore a personal reason for being more attracted and moved by the Egyptian. Because of his mother complex, a purely patriarchal mystical cult in which the masculine archetype of the god image was in the foreground would not have meant much to him. At the beginning it might have been of use to him by reinforcing his masculinity. If instead of falling into the hands of robbers he had gone into a masculine cult such as Mithraism, it would have been a better way to find his masculinity. But now it is a question of getting to the bottom of the mother complex and realizing its deepest meaning. Here the Mithraic cult or the Christian religion, both of which have a patriarchal character, would have been out of the question. For it was only in the third century that the cult of the Virgin Mary began to take on life and form, particularly in Ephesus. In the age of Apuleius, and later as well, that devotion was not very widespread, or was only locally recognized. Another reason, which may have played a certain role, was the fact that Apuleius came from North Africa and that the whole of the African civilization was under the domination of Egypt at that time. Therefore, when the cult out of the unconscious appears in this Egyptian symbolic form, all his native earth returns to him. His earliest childhood memories are connected with this experience. They are his "roots"—to suggest more modern examples.

In order to understand more clearly the problem of Apuleius-Lucius, we must consider the role and the meaning of the Isis and Osiris cult, in which the goddess always played an important part, in the late Egyptian religion. It is only at the end of antiquity that the absolute domination of Isis and Osiris came to the fore.[16]

Helmuth Jacobsohn, in his excellent article,[17] developed the idea that through the three thousand years of the development of this religion there is a further step, which seems to complete itself within the Christian civilization. After having emphasized the analogy between the Egyptian trinity and the Christian Trinity, Jacobsohn remarks that one can distinguish two basic rhythms in the emanation of a god and his becoming conscious. The first rhythm would be the phase of emanation and creation, and the second the phase of going back and gathering together what had been dispersed. The rhythm of Brahman, for example, could be compared to the diastole, while Atman would correspond to the return, or systole, symbolized in India by the sacrifice of the horse, or sometimes by a spider which, after having spun its web, consumes it again. The god loses himself into his own creation, and, in an opposite process, takes himself back again and becomes conscious of himself. Osiris's progressively increasing role in the later Egyptian religion follows such a systolic movement: retiring from the multiplicity of his creation, the god condenses again and becomes conscious. But while in the Indian myth this movement is cyclic and extends over billions of years, the Egyptian myth contains a new element of progression and evolution, for the return of the god is not like his first appearance: it is not a simple repetition. If one were to diagram this movement, it would be a spiral and not a circle; its new quality consists in this: Osiris, when he is reborn, resembles the Ba, the human soul. He has acquired by his death and resurrection that mystical something which is human individuality, which adds something, an otherness, to the divinity.

The process repeats itself with the coming of each new sun-king. When the pharaoh died, he became Osiris. Then came the figure of his son, who had to lead all the sacrificial rites and take over the role of the Sem priest; with the iron hook, he opened the mouth of the dead, so that the dead could eat and drink and speak in the Beyond.

What would that mean psychologically? Let us compare this

myth with what happens in a human being. A man identifies with the principle of consciousness and makes its meaning his own: he knows how to bridle his own impulses, he can work, propagate; in short, he becomes a socially adapted ego. On a smaller scale, he represents the development of the sun-divinity. He feels "I am," "I think." He believes himself to be the owner of his thoughts and considers himself a small sun. When in the midlife crisis he falls into a depression, it is as though the sun descended below the horizon: all conscious values have disappeared, he no longer knows what he thinks and even doubts his own identity. This would correspond to the death of the sun-king in Egypt. This state is represented by the death of the king, though not the actual death. In a situation of this type the psychotherapist would try above all to help him carry on; instinctively he would feel like dropping everything and becoming completely passive, and, to a certain extent, this is wise. But one cannot simply remain in this state and await return: something in the person must assure continuity. A certain interior attitude is necessary during this time. I would compare Horus the younger with that attitude: he is the image of the consciousness which lives in death and which works on the corpse of the king. It is that which "brings about the redemption of his father."[18]

In the process of individuation, the young Horus would thus be that psychological attitude which keeps up enough ego activity to say, "I will write down my dreams (the opening of the mouth), for the depression must convey to me what it is." While you are attending to a deep depression, you are looking after yourself in a dead state, nursing and serving yourself, your greater Self. It is Horus, I think, who represents this psychological attitude at the moment of complete darkness. In predynastic days in Egypt, when the king died, everybody could steal and murder for three days. There were no laws. Everyone waited till the king died! You can imagine what happened. But later in dynastic times in the interregnum, madness did not break out because Horus stood on guard. This was a very long time before dynastic Egypt. Therefore, Horus represents the psychological semiconsciousness which caries on while one is knocked out and then becomes the new principle of consciousness.

The god Thot, too, took part in the process of the renewal of consciousness, but since Apuleius mentioned neither Thot nor Anubis, I do not want to go into their meaning. But I must mention that Seth, who was first a murderer, later also played a positive role in the resurrection of the king, when he was linked with the upper light and killed the Apophis serpent every night. Since he was thus cooperating with the sun god, he represented rather integrated aggression, instead of simply the autonomy and the brutality of aggression.

This development of the Egyptian solar religion appears to us as a projection, a process of integration of the psychic totality. It is what we would call today the process of individuation,[19] but here the process is projected onto mythical images and dramas of gods and fates of kings. One can say that in the course of this process "the god" became conscious, step by step, in the human being. At first, it was assumed that only the pharaoh went through this process of death and resurrection that lead to immortality, but later it spread to the masses and was no longer considered a royal prerogative.

At the same time, toward the end of the old Empire, probably around the year 2500 B.C., the unconscious began to revive the myth of the feminine principle. (One could compare this end phase to the time of Christianity, in which the Pope, Pius XII, exalted the feminine principle and declared as a dogma the corporeal assumption of the Virgin Mary.) At that time (2200 B.C.), when the problem of restoring the inner totality of man became urgent, the one divinity which kept its unity and was never split into many figures was Isis. That is why it must be Isis who leads Lucius to wholeness. In the myth, Isis collects the bones of the dead Osiris and performs the rites of his resurrection. She is the instrument of his rebirth, hence Egyptian coffins often represented the dead resting in the arms of the mother goddess, Nut or Isis. The coffin and the lid carried her image; the dead await rebirth in her arms. Interpreted psychologically, Isis would represent the emotional and feeling experience of the totality which leads the way.

Later one may also realize the process in thoughts, but *she* is the element of the religious *feeling* experience.

But the Isis myth also means something else. In the case of a man who, like Apuleius, repressed his feelings through a negative mother complex, the anima often appears as a prostitute, and in the dream this is generally interpreted as sexuality or sexual fantasies on a relatively impersonal level. It often does have this meaning, but I have seen people in whom such figures had nothing to do with sexual fantasies but had the meaning of a mental prostitution, namely, that such a man was not loyal to an idea or a mental image, but flirted and misused his ideas, the way he might misuse a prostitute, paying the money and walking out. Such men are not capable of recognizing a truth and abiding by it, for they have no feeling for it. To them, intellectual and mental processes are a sort of amusement or game or a means of gaining prestige. If they think that they can have success with it, they will stand for something, even if they do not believe in it themselves. Spiritual life becomes for them an instrument for prestige and for the furtherance of personal vanity.

Such men pursue an idea not out of conviction, but only in order to show off their own intelligence. An enormous intellectual output is produced by such methods with nothing behind it. This is mental prostitution, and often called so in dreams. The anima, or soul, of such a man is a whore who flirts with all kinds of philosophical ideas or political theories, but does not marry any, and has no children, so that his ideas remain sterile. John Dee, an alchemist of the seventeenth century, often held conversations with God. One day God attacked him, accusing him of whoring. Poor Dee could not explain what this was supposed to mean; he thought of all his sins and sexual fantasies and found nothing to correspond to the insult. But as Jung emphasized, his whoredom lay in the fact that he did not stick to what he realized to be true and was not loyal to his spiritual task.

Apuleius, too, flirted with practically every philosophical system and every mystical cult, without taking a stand. One can judge this behavior from the aspect of his sexual instability and the degeneration of his feeling function in relation to women, but it is equally a mental prostitution. This persisted until he had the vision of Isis that he describes in his book, where it is said in the words of Lucius that he is "going unashamed with shaven head." He had finally decided to be loyal to his inner truth.

Apuleius probably was not aware of all these deep truths as we have discussed them here. But one wonders how the Isis mysteries could have had such a redeeming effect, that from then on he felt that he had found his place within, his relation to the divine, and the meaning of his own life? I think that one can see how much this motif belonged to Apuleius, if one remembers all the adventures through which his Lucius went. As long as he was a purely intellectually interested, idealistic Neoplatonist philosopher, Apuleius-Lucius was identified with the sun god Ra. That is literally so, because the idea of the good and the beautiful really dominated the Platonic ideas, like the sun in heaven in the center of all the stars.

Seen from this new perspective, the story of the murder of Socrates, discussed earlier, is also comparable to a story in Egyptian mythology. When the sun god Ra aged, Isis wanted to have his power and therefore created a huge snake, which lay in his path and bit the god, so that he suffered but, being a god, could not die. So Isis offered to cure him if he would tell her his secret name. In order to be cured, he had to sacrifice his power. The philosophical principle which has aged—the old king, the petrified conscious principle, which is unable to act—is overpowered by a dark mother figure, the image of the unconscious.

The transformation of Lucius into an ass corresponds in mythology to the killing of Osiris by Seth. His human side is covered by the ass or the asinine principle, comparable to the moment in which Seth kills Osiris. But Osiris survives within him, insofar as he suffers being an ass: Lucius, through all his experiences as an ass, is never really an ass, for he always suffers as a human being. One can say that in this case the divine in the human being is overwhelmed by the shadow, acting together with sexuality and all brutal impulses. Lucius's

humanness is drowned in the ass. His conscious personality is
still there, but its fate can be compared to that of the dismembered Osiris. Then Isis appears, and in the Egyptian myth it is
she who recollects the dispersed parts of Osiris and helps to
bring about his rebirth and resurrection. She always does what
has to be done. She does the negative thing in order to dissolve
consciousness, then the positive thing in order to bring forth
the process of individuation. As the destructive and at the same
time redeeming Great Mother she is everywhere. She is the
feminine principle which furthers the inner transformation. In
the world of Ra she is the divine mother and eternal, and
therefore we can say that when she wants to care for Lucius
she wants to develop the Osiris quality in him. What she really
cares for is his divine inner Self. She is that feeling experience
which is meant to give birth to the higher inner personality of
Lucius and can heal his inner split. Therefore, through the
initiation in the mysteries, he experiences the inner feeling that
his fate is comparable to that of Osiris. He recognizes the
deeper meaning of what has happened to him. To suffer from
neurotic complications, without knowing their meaning, is the
worst that a person can experience; but to realize the deeper
meaning behind them is already half healing. Then one can see
one's difficulties as part of a meaningful process, which helps
one to accept and transform them. Isis solves for Lucius the
problem of the opposites, the problem of Seth and Osiris. In
Christianity the Virgin Mary does the same. Jung has pointed
out that the new title of the Virgin Mary is *domina rerum* and
regina coeli, which lays emphasis on her role in the Catholic
world and expresses mankind's longing to heal the split which
our civilization has brought us. It seems as if there were
tendencies in our civilization parallel to the end phase of the
Egyptian development.

The Isis cult is described by Apuleius with poetic emotion,
but he says practically nothing of his later experience in the
Osiris cult. The experience of Isis was an emotional one and
could be conveyed in poetic language. But about the other he
clearly could not talk, for it was even more important and a
real mystery.

But what happened to the mother goddess archetype when Christianity followed on the dying Roman Empire? Mary was given the title of Theotokos (Mother of God) and Sophia (Wisdom), and played a certain role in the Eastern Church, but in the Western Catholic Church she had to step into the background. Naturally, there were survivals in legends and local cults, so when I say that with Isis the archetypal image of the Great Mother disappeared, this must be understood only relatively. But in the official Christian Church there was a strong tendency not to take the problem of the feminine seriously, for the cult of the Virgin Mary was not a center of attention. In the Western Church she was actually replaced by the image of the institution of the Church, so that a part of her mystical quality was projected onto the institution of the Church, the Mater Ecclesia. Jung discusses this problem in *Psychological Types* when he comments on the book *The Shepherd* of Hermas,[20] in which the author writes of his conversion to Christianity. The book was probably composed from elements of Jewish, Oriental, and Greek material. Hermas has made it into a pamphlet of early Christian propaganda, describing his visions and the inner experiences which led to his conversion to the Catholic Church.

To Hermas there appears in a vision an old woman whom he calls Domina, the goddess, or mistress, who gives him advice and shows him the vision of a tower which is the Church.

This vision is probably not all genuine, for much conscious material has been added to it. But the idea of his being initiated into the Catholic Church by an old woman, a dark figure, is certainly genuine and shows where the goddess continued to live. She had been transformed into the Ecclesia, the mother Church, so that a motherly quality was projected onto the institution of the Church, which replaced the figure of Isis.

Two aspects got lost through this development: First, the human-personal aspect of the goddess (an institution is never very human) and, second, the relationship to matter. For Isis was also an image for cosmic matter, and this aspect is not contained in the institution of the Church. There is, however, a certain concretism which compensates negatively for the lack of matter: the Pope represents God on earth, and matter is somehow contained in the Church, insofar as it is a concrete organization. But matter in our modern view is also a divine cosmic principle, as modern physics might discover soon. In the Middle Ages, however, these two aspects disappeared from the general consciousness, while some other aspects survived in the institution. If one has Catholic priests in analysis, one sees that their anima is projected into the Church. She is the carrier of the mother anima figure and partly replaces the real woman. The priest experiences the Church as mother-bride not only allegorically, but quite concretely. On the other hand the priest is the bride of Christ, he is therefore "feminine" and wears feminine clothes. He is thus simultaneously male and female. If he understands what he is doing, this could offer him the possibility of an experience of psychic totality, reached by the painful sacrifice of sexual life. On the other hand, the fact that a human institution replaces a divine power obviously creates a great problem.

This situation has also led to other consequences. If the human and material aspects of divinity—certain elements of an archetype—fade away from the conscious field of attention, we must expect them to reappear in the form of obsessions. When something essential disappears from conscious life, it will appear somewhere else more strongly. One sees this later in the persecution of the witches, upon whom the shadow of the vanished Great Mother was projected. Another obsession that is typical of the entire Christian theology, and which I believe is important, expresses itself in a certain *concretism of ideas,* as I would like to call it. The Christian teaching with all its dogmas suffers from it. If we try to compare the forms of thought of psychology with those of theology—and it does not matter whether Catholic, Protestant, or Jewish—there is always the same argument of the theologians, an objection often repeated, which must be respected, for it is extremely important: "God," the theologians say, "is not only an image in the human soul or in the collective unconscious. All your psychological interpretations of the Trinity are 'only psychological'; the Trinity must also have a metaphysical reality, and we, the theologians, are talking about that and not about the psychological aspect." There is the implication that this "metaphysical reality" is the real thing. All theologians can agree with us if we tell them that there is somewhere a metaphysical space in which God and Christ exist, and that we are only speaking about their psychological mirroring in the soul. If we say that, the theologian is pacified. What he does is subdivide the cosmos in the old Platonic way, into one world which is "only" an analogy to the other, or an experimentally observable psychological world, and, beyond that, a second cosmos which is called "metaphysical reality," and there God is as He is absolutely, and Christ as he is absolutely. Yet there the theologians speak of God as if He were describable! In analysis we can experience God in our own souls. The theologians know God, not by psychological truth, but through revelation, which is in the Bible, but God ceased publication two thousand years ago. Our God is an image in the soul, but the other is God from revelation. If you argue that the Bible was written by people, you come to the main complex, and then comes the difficulty. After all, the revelation somehow reached us through the human psyche!

If you look at it without emotion, then you see that it is a subdivision of the idea of reality. There is something like a metaphysical or transcendental reality which is concretely real, and what flows into that is the suppressed matter aspect of Isis. That creates a kind of idealistic materialism. Theologians are generally caught in this mental materialism through what they call a "metaphysical fact." It is a name obsession which exists in most theologians, and one cannot switch them out of that projection. The great mother goddess has been taken into the institution of the Church and has not been recognized as matter, *so there is a compensatory unconscious materialization of ideas*. Christian theology is much too mental. It is a patriarchal institution, and the mother aspect gets them from behind, and thus they are convinced that their ideas are somehow materially real. Our hypothesis, on the contrary, is that there is a living *x* behind the archetypes. We have not made the separation; matter and the collective unconscious are not two separate dimensions for us.

What strikes one so much in the Egyptian religion and was recognized by the Greeks and the Romans is also the strange concretism of what we would call an idea. There was, for instance, a belief in immortality attained through *chemical treatment of the corpse*—an incredible, primitive-magic concretism! In the museum of Cairo there is a papyrus[21] with the prescription for the embalming of the corpse: "See that the head does not fall back; remove the intestines, which will decay. . . ." It is a complete description of what should happen with the corpse, together with the exact words, the liturgy, and the texts, which had to be repeated during the execution of the work. Words and work went together. Everything was done concretely in such a way as to make the human being actually chemically immortal.

This concretism only apparently disappeared; it emerged secretly again in Christianity as the concretistic "reality of metaphysical facts." The old primitive concretism, therefore, makes it quite impossible for many people to discuss facts in an objective empirical way. It provokes a kind of fanatical obsession of ideas inspired by the anima which much too often blocks every scientific understanding. There is always the hope that "somewhere" the ideas must have an absolute reality, but this does not allow any psychological discussion. Psychology is treated as "nothing but" psychology, a minor reality in relation to the "absolute truth." This is where the depreciation of the feminine Goddess has led!

In the Jewish religion this very same concretism appears in the Law. In certain circles of Orthodox Jews at one time it was an important legal problem whether an electric light might be lit on the Sabbath, since it is forbidden to kindle a fire on that day; this was a matter of serious discussion. The mother goddess is not officially recognized in the Jewish religion. So she is hidden in the material aspect of the Law and in the idea that the announced kingdom of the Messiah will be *on this earth,* in other words, material.

All totalitarian political views, regardless of their orientation, proceed along the same lines. They preach beliefs that are completely concretistic, namely that the "kingdom of heaven" must be established here, and only here, on the earth, at any cost. For them, blessings, happiness, and psychic equilibrium are to be attained solely on earth. If one believes in such a Marxist, Fascist, or any other such ideology, one is saved, and if not, one is killed. Here the concretism of ideas reaches its climax.

However, in our day, this one-sided materialism has become obsolete, for modern physics has recognized that one must give up attempting to describe matter *in itself* and be content with creating mathematical models, in other words, psychic ideas about it. In fact, as Jung remarked, the psyche is the only reality that we can know through immediate experience. The names "material" or "spiritual" are no more than formal distinctions that we give to our *psychic* experiences; the first concerns those experiences that come to us from outside and from our bodies; the second are the inner experiences. This duality of perception is inherent in the structure of our conscious ego, but in the domain of the unconscious it does not seem to exist. As Jung formulated, outside this duality of our perception the world is probably one, an *unus mundus*,[22] which transcends our conscious awareness. Rightly then, modern physics begins to be interested in parapsychological phenomena.[23] On the higher coil of the spiral we are found therewith at a point in time which corresponds to the period in which the curiosity *(curiositas)* of Lucius-Apuleius toward the occult was awakened!

Although the secret of matter was recognized only a little in the Christian-Catholic Church and not at all in the Protestant, it survived in concealed form in alchemy, whose whole attempt consisted in finding "the divine soul in the *prima materia*." Jung has elaborated on this in *Psychology and Alchemy*[24] and in *Mysterium Coniunctionis* and has tried to bring back to our consciousness the relation to the "goddess" of matter, appearing in alchemy as the mother goddess Materia, or as a feminine *anima mundi,* as the soul in cosmic matter, and in other texts as Mater Alchemia, or even directly as Isis.

The second aspect of the goddess, mentioned before, which got lost as soon as she was interpreted as Ecclesia, was her aspect as a personal human being. Thus, the Eros principle— that is, the individual relation and warmth—was substituted by an organization, consisting of laws and hierarchies. This loss has become today so obvious and severe that we do not need to discuss it at length. It is the human problem of our time par excellence.

12
Matter
and the Feminine

T he next morning, on a beautiful spring day, the procession toward the sea in honor of the goddess Isis begins. The festival is celebrated after winter, when the ships and boats go to sea again, and the people carry lamps and lights down to the sea in order to launch the first ship. In the procession the priests of the mystery cult carry different symbols of the goddess,[1] which all have a deep symbolic meaning.

One of the priests carries a golden lamp in the form of a ship, indicating that the light of the goddess carries one across the waters of the unconscious. Other priests carry small altars with gods on them, corresponding to the Egyptian custom of bathing the statues of the gods and then returning them to the temple. One carries the caduceus of Mercury, and the symbol of justice is alluded to by the left hand of Isis, carried by another priest. This custom goes back to a time more ancient than the Egyptian civilization, for the left hand is a very ancient apotropaic talisman. In Islam it later became the hand of Fatima, the daughter of Mohammed, which today still protects one against the evil eye.

Another object, carried by the priests, is a golden vessel in the form of a breast, a symbol of the mother goddess, dispenser of milk and nourishment. A libation of milk was always poured on the tomb of Osiris, for milk was supposed to have the power to nourish and revive the dead.[2] From a historical perspective, it is interesting that Zosimos of Panopolis, the Graeco-Egyptian alchemist whose visions Jung has analyzed,[3] writes at some length in a treatise about this "vessel in the form of a breast," which the alchemists used in their work. He says that this breastlike vessel was a holy "secret of the art," so here there is an immediate and factual connection between a symbol of the Isis mysteries and one of the earliest alchemical documents.[4] There is actually a tremendous amount of connection between these two worlds. Zosimos, as an Egyptian, was certainly acquainted with the Isis mysteries and therefore used the vessels and instruments of her cult in an alchemical way. The next object carried is a golden basket for corn. This is also a symbol for Osiris, who dies and is resurrected like the corn. In the museum at Cairo there is a corn mummy in the form of Osiris, which was covered with linen and watered and kept damp so that corn grew on it. This was part of the resurrection ritual.

After this there follow in the procession a vessel which is not described and then a priest with the statue of Anubis. He is the one who is responsible for the whole ritual of mummification in Egypt, for Anubis, the god with a jackal's head, according to the myth, found the bones of the dead Osiris and put them together again.

All the objects which are carried in the procession have a specific meaning. Some point to Isis and others to Osiris. But then the text emphasizes an especially holy symbol: a small round shining gold jar, covered with hieroglyphs, with a mouthpiece on one side, and a broad handle on which is a coiled serpent on the other. Apuleius does not give the deeper significance of this jar, but he says that it is "incredibly holy" and that one "must honour it in deep silence." This round golden vessel reminds us first of all of the holy mystical vessel in alchemy, which was considered as a symbol of cosmic totality. Zosimos, for instance, says of the alchemical vessel that it is a round cup which represents the totality of the cosmos and in which the holy alchemical process takes place.[5] In alchemy it represents the all-embracing principle and the concept (*concipere*, "to conceive") of the contained thing; that is, the psychological attitude, or the approach toward matter, toward the mystery in alchemy. This symbolizes self-concentration and the absolutely essential introversion needed for this proper approach toward matter and the mystery of the cosmos. All this is symbolized by the vessel, and some alchemical philosophers even say that the *lapis philosophorum*, the philosopher's stone, in the vessel and the vessel itself are the same thing, a different aspect of the same mystery. For Apuleius the vessel probably represents Osiris. I was delighted to find that Merkelbach comes to the same conclusion. Innumerable jars and vessels have been found in Egypt with human heads on them representing Osiris. He was also very often represented just by a vessel filled with Nile water. That was the holiest symbol, the unspeakable symbol; in its meaning it would correspond to the transubstantiated host, the great mystery in the Catholic Church.

Like other symbols, this vessel symbol, too, has its very deep primitive roots originating in Central Africa and has come down the Nile into Egypt. Leo Frobenius found tribes on the Upper Nile which had the following burial custom: when the chief died (the chief was the carrier of divine mana, the divine power, which was incarnated in him), his corpse was put in a hut by itself and placed over a kind of grid. Underneath that a vessel was put, into which the secretions of the corpse slowly dripped. After a while the corpse became dried out, and in the vessel appeared an unappetizing kind of juice, usually full of worms and larvae. This was put into a separate vessel because it was the soul which had left the body through these liquids. The vessel was then closed, except for one hole into which a little bamboo stick was placed as an opening. This was watched day and night, and when a worm or insect came out, it was believed that now the soul had come out. The vessel was then closed completely, and the dried-out corpse and the vessel were placed separately in a cave. Here the vessel with the liquid in it represents the spiritual soul essence of the dead king. It was believed that the soul, which left the vessel as an insect, went into the successor who then became the representative of the divine principle. (In Egypt the insect is the scarab.) In some other tribes there are somewhat divergent customs, but the idea is always of the transmission of the soul and spirit essence of the dead king into the continuing series of kings, or chiefs, of the tribe.

So the vessel contains the psychic essence of the god-king during his transformation from death to rebirth. According to Egyptian mythology, it would represent Osiris in the process of his transformation into Horus.[6] When Osiris is dead Isis holds the vessel of his soul substance.[7] Later he is reborn from there as Horus, the new sun god, the sun child. Seen psychologically, it is the mysterious moment of the transformation, when our conscious idea of the god is "dead" and is reborn in the unconscious. The mystery of the vessel represents for the Egyptians the secret of the death and the rebirth of the sun god. This vessel of the Isis mysteries continued in the mystery of the Holy Grail, which is a close parallel. According to the legend, Christ appeared to Joseph of Aramathea and gave him a vessel containing the blood from his wounded side, confiding it to him as the secret of the Grail tradition. So there again is the living substance of the dead god, the hidden secret which guarantees his life on earth. When Christ died he took his body with him. He left no relics of his earthly life except his blood, which the early Christian mystics interpreted as his psychic life, the *anima Christi*, which lived on in the Grail vessel.

That is how the story of the Grail tradition started in the Middle Ages. It is the mystery of the vessel containing the secret of the death and rebirth of the god image, the numinous possibility of the rebirth of the Horus child, of the god symbol, the symbol of the Self, which is no longer a partial principle but again comprises the totality of existence. Horus is identical with the reborn Osiris when he leaves the vessel. After that comes the sunrise. Primitive tribes make gestures of worship not to the sun, but to that *numinous moment when the sun rises*.[8] When the sun is a bit over the horizon it is no longer divine.

Sunrise, the *aurora consurgens,*[9] is the moment when the realization of the Self appears out of the vessel of the unconscious psyche. It can perhaps be best described, or amplified, by modern African material whence this Egyptian and Grail symbolism mostly comes.

In Abomey, Nigeria, there lived natives who worshipped the oracle god called Gbaadu. He personified the truth which expresses itself in oracles.[10] It was said that Gbaadu represented the *highest degree of self-knowledge that a human being can attain.* A parallel is the god Fa. Fa's names consist also of an entire African sentence: "The sun rises and the walls become rose-colored." And an old medicine man added: "When one understands the truth, it is as if the sun rises and the gray walls become rose-colored." This is Horus-Osiris, when he comes out of the vessel!

The ass Lucius sees the procession pass by and, following his own dream, searches for the eyes of the priest who carries a wreath of roses. As soon as he sees him, he presses through the crowd. The priest, having been ordered in a dream to do so, stretches the roses toward the ass, who succeeds in eating them. As soon as Lucius eats the flowers he loses his ass form, which falls off like a coat, and he stands there as a naked man. The priest calls to someone to bring him a linen garment and then addresses Lucius in front of everybody, telling that now he is free and saved by the great goddess Isis and must therefore become her servant. Everyone is amazed, and the people acclaim the goddess. Then the procession continues:

> I was not deceived of the promise made onto me: for my deform and assy face abated, and first the rugged hair of my body fell off, my thick skin waxed soft and tender, my fat belly became thin, the hoofs of my feet changed into toes, my hands were no more feet but returned again to the work of a man that walks upright, my neck grew short, my head and mouth became round, my long ears were made little, my great and stony teeth waxed less, like the teeth of men, and my tail, which before cumbered me most, appeared nowhere. Then the people began to marvel, and the religious honoured the Goddess for so evident a miracle, which was foreshadowed by the visions which they

saw in the night, and the facility of my reformation, whereby they lifted their hands to heaven and with one voice rendered testimony of so great a benefit which I received of the Goddess. [11]

In antiquity, roses were sacred to Aphrodite-Venus and to Dionysos and symbolized *eros*. One found wreaths of roses in sepulchers, where they probably represented the "victory wreath" that the dead received after their resurrection. [12]

Then the text relates that Lucius turns back to the beloved figure of the goddess and settles down in a house inside her holy area *(temenos)* where he lives for a long time before receiving his initiation:

> I went again before the face of the Goddess, and hired me a house within the cloister of the temple, since I had been set apart for the service of the Goddess that hitherto had been kept private from me, so that I might ordinarily frequent the company of the priests, whereby I would wholly become devout to the Goddess, and an inseparable worshipper of her divine name: nor was there any night nor sleep but that the Goddess appeared to me, persuading and commanding me to take the order of her religion whereto I had been long since foreordained. But I, although I was endued with a desirous goodwill, yet the reverend fear of the same held me back, considering that as I had learned by diligent enquiry her obeisance was hard, the chastity of the priests difficult to keep, and the whole life of them, because it is set about with many chances, to be watched and guarded very carefully. Being thus in doubt, I refrained myself from all those things seeming impossible, although in truth I was hastening towards them. [13]

This passage refers to an institution widespread in antiquity called *katoché*. The *katochoi* were people who, gripped and possessed by a god or a goddess, dedicated themselves to their service and lived within the walls or courtyard of the temple over months or even years. These people were exempt from taxes and, if condemned to prison, could not be taken from the temple. Therefore, some interpreters assumed that all this had nothing to do with ecstatic possession by the divinity, but simply that these people took refuge in the sanctuary only to escape the police or anyone else who was after them. From the psychological viewpoint, however, quarrels about this subject are sterile. One could say simply that it means to be under the domination of an archetype, or in the service of an archetypal figure, in a state of trance or inner transformation. The *katachos* submitted himself voluntarily to captivity which could last for years and withdrew from the outer world. A criminal also who would find refuge in the temple was virtually imprisoned; for if he put a foot outside he was caught; if he had committed some misdemeanor, he had the choice of a secular or a religious prison—in either case it was a prison.

About thirty years ago a papyrus was found written by a man named Ptolemaios, who lived in the *katoché* of a Serapis temple in Egypt. He wrote down his dreams, which was obligatory, and it seems as though the priests had interpreted them. If one read Artemidoros's dream book, one would think that people dreamed differently then, dreaming only of synchronistic events, and that they had only "big dreams." But, this is not true. It is just that in the scientific dream literature of antiquity, only such dreams were recorded. But in this papyrus of Ptolemaios the dreams of an ordinary man were preserved, and they are quite ordinary. He dreamed of his family, of money problems, and so on. These dreams are not understandable for us, because we do not have the personal associations, but at least we know through them that those people dreamed exactly as we do, though the rest of the literature recounts in detail only the archetypal dreams. In the *temenos* or the *katoché* around the temple there were even priests who specialized in the interpretation of dreams.[14] So those in the *katoché* were actually "in analysis." The procedure was the same as today except that the conclusions drawn from the dreams were somewhat different. So the *katoché* was a voluntary state of complete introversion and concentration on one's dream life.[15]

During this time the following dream comes to Lucius:

On a night the great priest appeared unto me in a dream presenting his lap full of treasure, and when I demanded what it signified, he answered that this portion[16] was sent me from the country of Thessaly, and that a servant of mine named Candidus was thence arrived likewise. When I was awaked, I mused in myself what this vision should portend, considering I never had any servant called by that name: but whatsoever it did signify, this I verily thought, that such offering of gifts was a foreshew of gain and prosperous chance. While I was thus anxious and astonished at my coming prosperity, I went to the temple, and tarried there till the opening of the gates in the morning: then I went in, and when the white curtains were drawn aside, I began to pray before the face of the Goddess, while the priest prepared and set the divine things on every altar with solemn supplications, and fetched out of the sanctuary the holy water for the libation. When all things were duly performed, the religious began to sing the matins of the morning, testifying thereby the hour of prime. By and by behold arrived my servants which I had left at Hypata, when Photis entangled me in my maze of miserable wanderings, who had heard my tale as it seemed, and brought with them even my horse, which they had recovered through certain signs and tokens which he had upon his back. Then I perceived the interpretation of my dream, by reason that beside the promise of gain, my white horse was restored to me, which was signified by the argument of my servant Candidus.[17]

In accordance with the classical view of dream interpretation, Candidus is seen as the servant that had been announced. The rest of the dream is not interpreted, as for Apuleius-Lucius only the synchronistic event is important; for he takes it as a "sign" that the goddess is looking after him and that he is on the right path. One could say more about this dream, though I think that the old interpretation is valid on that level. For instance, the priest offers Lucius parts of a meal sent from Thessaly, the country of his mother, the place where he learned about witchcraft and became an ass. One could say: everything Lucius experienced hitherto was negative, but now a turning point has been reached, and he receives from the Mother Earth inner nourishment, which helps him find human contact again. All this announces the transformation of his negative mother complex. From Thessaly now comes the possibility of relatedness, communion, and nourishment from the unconscious, and finally Lucius even finds his white horse again.

We said in the beginning that the horse belongs mythologically to the sun hero, it represents that aspect of our libido which carries us towards the spiritual and not the chthonic. Lucius had lost his light horse a long time ago and moved completely into the darkness. Now the light and a movement towards consciousness, which had been denied, comes back. *Candidus* in Latin means "white," innocent in the sense of being uncomplicated and spontaneous, the virginal white. One could say therefore that Lucius returns to an unsophisticated, spontaneous attitude. Most neurotics, especially men with a negative mother complex, have great difficulty being spontaneous, as their feeling is hurt and sensitive. Such a man does not dare to be open, for he fears in every woman the "terrible mother." If he assumes an innocent, spontaneous, and candid attitude, any woman can hurt him. We can conclude from this that Lucius discovers again his feeling and idealistic side, previously so badly hurt by the negative mother and lost in the moment of invasion by darkness, and that this innocence has been found in a new form.

We can assume that his most pure and spontaneous feelings now belong to the mystery cult of Isis, where his heart can come alive again. The white garment which he receives at the transformation would indicate this. The white garment was also used by Christians at baptism to illustrate the new attitude where all sinfulness fell off and a new beginning could be made. The Christian interpretation was more connected with the idea of ethics and sin. But one could say that any kind of unconscious contamination means not being at one with and true to oneself. When one is true to oneself one finds a new attitude and a new impulse towards life, a return to spontaneity and naturalness. The dream shows us that Thessaly, where Lucius was bewitched, now stands for something positive. It is the archetype of the mother which after all the developments now shows its other side. Seen in this light, even the two witches who murdered Socrates at the beginning of the story were a form of the goddess Isis.

It is the great goddess under her double aspect who dominates the life of Lucius. After the negative form of the archetype had been exhausted, the *enantiodromia* to the positive aspect has set in.

Lucius grows very impatient while waiting to become one of Isis's initiates, but the text says that the priest checks him, speaking to him in a friendly way, "just as parents reply to the immature wishes of their children." (One can compare this to the behavior of patients who, after three weeks of analysis, want to become analysts themselves!) But the priest advises him to be patient:

> But he, which was a man of gravity and well-renowned in the order of priesthood, very gently and kindly deferred my affection from day to day with comfort of better hope, as parents commonly bridle the desires of their children when they attempt or endeavor any unprofitable thing, saying that the day when any one should be admitted into their order is appointed by the Goddess, the priest which should minister the sacrifice is chosen by her providence, and the necessary charge of the ceremonies is allotted by her commandment; all of which things he willed me to attend with marvellous patience; and that I should beware both of too much forwardness, and of stubborn obstinacy, avoiding either danger, that if being called I should delay, or not called I should be hasty.[18]

All haste, the priest tells him, is dangerous:

> . . . considering that it was in her power both to damn and to save all persons, and that the taking of such orders was like to a voluntary death and a difficult recovery to health.[19]

Later Lucius has another dream informing him about the day and the place of the initiation, as well as the name of the initiator, the great priest Mithras, because he "is related to him through a divine conjunction of stars." In the morning, when Lucius relates his dream to his priest, he finds out that the priest himself has also been told in a dream that he should be the initiator, and all is arranged for the ceremony.

That the priest is called "Mithras"[20] and that there is an accordance in the horoscopes of both, points to a psychological "kinship," just as there often exists an alchemical "affinity" or soul kinship between analyst and analysand, so that the right relationship establishes itself. One would not want to analyze a person one found revolting, although if there is a very negative feeling perhaps there is also a kinship.

Lucius is instructed from the holy texts, some of which are in hieroglyphs drawn in a spiral. Such drawings of texts written in a circular manner exist and are also to be found in some early alchemical texts. The writing begins at the outer end of the spiral and moves towards the center. Alchemical prescriptions and magic formulas were sometimes written in such a mandala form, which shows once again the close relationship between alchemy and the mystery cults. Again Lucius-Apuleius says almost nothing of the content of these instructions, remembering the respect due to the mysteries:

> I would tell thee if it were lawful for me to tell, thou wouldest know if it were convenient for thee to hear; but both thy ears and my tongue should incur the like pain of rash curiosity.[21]

Even in cases of Christian propaganda against the mysteries, the real contents were never given away, which shows how numinous they were, for even where the initiate turned later to another religion, they had been so deeply touched that they could not betray the mystery. Only a few meager references were made to the mysteries by the early Christian Fathers. Lucius himself says:

> I approached near unto hell, even to the gates of Proserpine, and after that I was ravished throughout all the elements, I returned to my proper place: about midnight I saw the sun brightly shine, I saw likewise the gods celestial and the gods infernal, before whom I presented myself and worshipped them.[22]

That is all we know about this part of the initiation: a vision of the midnight sun, in other words, an illumination that comes from below, and the realization of the upper and lower gods. According to Egyptian cosmography, Ra crosses the heavens in daytime and then goes down over the West. During the night he sails by boat through the underworld. The god Seth kills the Apophis snake every night, then Ra reappears as Khepera, the scarab, in the East, after which begins again his daily journey across the sky.

In a funerary text, Isis is called "mistress of light in the realm of darkness."[23] Initiations into the mysteries of Isis and Osiris were underworld cults with a chthonic aspect; therefore Lucius worships the midnight sun. The initiation is a descent to the underworld and an illumination by a principle of consciousness which comes from the unconscious, in contrast to the doctrines of collective consciousness. (You can be illuminated by the latter, but that would be the sunshine of the day.) Lucius experiences this in some kind of symbolic form, and worships all the gods according to the different hours of the day and the night which are the various personifications of the sun god. The initiate goes through the whole night, and then:

> When morning came and that the solemnities were finished, I came forth sanctified with twelve stoles and in a religious habit, whereof I am not forbidden to speak, considering that many persons saw me at that time. There I was commanded to stand upon a pulpit of wood which stood in the middle of the temple, before the figure and remembrance of the Goddess; my vestment was of fine linen, covered and embroidered with flowers; I had a precious cape upon my shoulders, hanging down behind me to the ground, whereon were beasts wrought of divers colours, as Indian dragons, and Hyperborean griffins, whom in form of birds the other part of the world doth engender: the priests commonly call such a habit an Olympian stole. In my right hand I carried a lighted torch, and a garland of flowers was upon my head, with white palm-leaves sprouting out on every side like rays; thus I was adorned like unto the sun, and made in fashion of an image, when the curtains were drawn aside and all the people compassed about to behold me. Then they began to solemnise the feast, the nativity of my holy order, with sumptuous banquets and pleasant meats.[24]

This ending indicates that, during his initiation, Lucius has not only gone the way of the sun god, but that he has been assimilated into the Sun at the end. In the morning he has himself become the new sun god. This was also practiced in the Mithraic mysteries, and is connected with the famous *solificatio* to which the alchemical texts allude.[25] In these, the moment of realization of the work is often described as the appearance of the sun rising over the horizon, signifying that a new form of consciousness is born after a descent into the unconscious. Psychologically, the *solificatio* corresponds to the completion of the individuation process.

Later, having said his farewells to the great priest Mithra, "his father," Lucius returns to Rome:

> I departed from him straight to visit my parents and friends, after that I had been so long absent. And so within a short while after, by the exhortation of the Goddess I made up my packet and took shipping towards the city of Rome. . . . And the greatest desire which I had there was daily to make my prayers to the sovereign Goddess Isis, who, by reason of the place where her temple was builded, was called Campensis, and continually is adored of the people of Rome. When now the sun had passed through all the signs of heaven and the year was ended, and that the Goddess warned me again in my sleep to receive a new order and consecration, I marvelled greatly what it should signify and what should happen, considering that I was most fully an initiate and sacred person already. But it fortuned that while I partly reasoned with myself, and partly examined *the perplexity* of my conscience with the priests and bishops, there came a new and marvellous thought to my mind: that is to say, that I was only religious to the Goddess Isis, but not yet sacred to the religion of great Osiris, the sovereign father of the gods.[26]

We have seen that Osiris, after having gone through the underworld, in the end rises over the horizon as an immortal star, and is assimilated into the new sun god. This is the path followed by all initiates into the mysteries. In some form every dead person was assimilated to this total cosmic god.

Christianity teaches the transformation of man into an immortal being after death and the last judgment. Thus immortality is a hope, or a promise, and hence a content of faith. In the antique mystery cults, on the contrary, there was a kind of symbolic ritual, which was supposed to bring about this transformation into immortality while one was still in the earthly life. The same idea existed also in alchemy, where the texts frequently said that the production of the "stone of the philosophers" meant at the same time producing the incorruptible body of resurrection. According to the Christian idea, at the last judgment we are supposed to be recreated in a new form and enter eternal life; the alchemists, on the other hand, thought of it as an inner experience which happened during one's life time; the immortal or glorified body should be produced through meditation or through an alchemical process, just as the "diamond body" is created in this life, according to the Eastern cultures. Out of the mortal body, an immortal nucleus is extracted with a breathlike quality. The same idea lives in the antique mystery cults: the eternal personality is already established in this life and is not projected into a postmortal sphere.

Unfortunately, I am not able to go into the whole problem of alchemy, which I should since it is here that alchemy begins. Alchemy contained the germs of ideas which the Christian doctrine rejected but which reappeared in the Renaissance and even earlier in the Arabic sphere. They appeared also in some movements in Western civilization which repenetrated Europe at the time of the Crusades when the Templars got in touch with Arabic traditions. Also, in the legends of the Holy Grail, the Arab and antique mystery symbolism survived to a great extent and suddenly came up again at the time of the Crusades; but it was never officially recognized by the Church.

Afterward, Apuleius-Lucius returns to Rome and lives a normal profane life until another dream heralds that now he should be initiated into the mystery cult of Osiris. At first he is surprised, because he had thought that they were the same as the Isis mysteries, but the dreams say that there are even higher regions, which he does not yet know. Everything happens as it did the first time:

> . . . for in the night after appeared unto me one of that order, covered with linen robes, holding in his hands spears wrapped

in ivy, and other things not convenient to declare, which he left in my chamber, and sitting in my seat, recited to me such things as were necessary for the sumptuous banquet of my religious entry. And to the end I might know him again, he shewed me a certain sign, to wit, how the heel of his left foot was somewhat maimed, which caused him a little to halt. After that I did manifestly thus know the will of the gods, and all shadow of doubtfulness was taken away, when matins was ended I went diligently from one to another to find if there were any of the priests which had the halting mark of his foot, according as I learned by my vision. At length I found it true; for I perceived one of the company of the Pastophores who had not only the token of his foot but the stature and habit of his body resembling in every point as he appeared in the night, and he was called Asinius Marcellus, a name not much disagreeing from my transformation. By and by I went to him, which knew well enough all the matter, as being admonished by like percept to give me the orders; for it seemed to him the night before, as he dressed the flowers and garlands about the head of the great god Osiris, he understood by the mouth of his image, which told the predestinations of all men, how he did send to him a certain poor man of Madaura, to whom he should straight away minister his sacraments, whereby through his divine providence the one should receive glory for his virtuous studies, and the other, being the priest himself, a great reward. When I saw myself thus deputed and promised unto religion, my desire was stopped by reason of poverty; for I had spent a great part of my patrimony, which was not very large, in travel and peregrinations, but most of all my charges in the city of Rome were by far greater than in the provinces. Thereby my low estate withdrew me a great while, so that I was in much distress betwixt the victim and the knife (as the old proverb hath it), and yet I was not seldom urged and pressed on by that same god. In the end, being oftentimes stirred forward and at last commanded, and not without great trouble of mind, I was constrained to sell my poor robe for a little money; howbeit, I scraped up sufficient for all my affairs.[27]

This time Lucius is not only called to be an initiate of Osiris, but also one of his priests, a *pastophore*. *Pastophoroi* were the priests who carried the holy barges in the procession. Osiris appeared to him in a dream summoning him to be his priest:

Not very much after I was again called and admonished by the
marvellous commands of gods, which I did very little expect,
to receive a third order of religion. Then I was greatly astonished, and I pondered doubtfully in my mind, because I could
not tell what this new vision signified, or what the intent of the
celestial gods was, or how anything could remain yet lacking,
seeing that twice already I had entered the holy orders.

After this sort the divine majesty persuaded me in my sleep
what should be to my profit. Whereupon I forgot not nor
delayed the matter at all, but by and by I went towards the priest
and declared all that which I had seen.[28]

Lucius, having made ritual preparation for his ordination, adds:

And verily I did nothing repent of the pain which I had taken
and of the charges which I was at, considering that the divine
providence had given me such an order that I gained much
money in pleading of causes. Finally after a few days the great
god Osiris appeared in my sleep, which is the more powerful
god of the great gods, the highest of the greater, the greatest of
the highest, and the ruler of the greatest, to me in me in the
night, not disguised in any other form, but in his own essence
and speaking to me with his own venerable voice, commanding
me that I should not get me great glory by being an advocate in
the court, and that I should not fear the slander and envy of ill
persons, which bare me stomach and grudge by reason of my
doctrine which I had gotten by much labour. Moreover, he
would not that I should serve his mysteries mixed with the rest
of the number of his priests, but he chose me to enter the college
of the Pastophores, nay he allotted me to be one of his decurions
and quinquennial priests: wherefore I executed mine office in
great joy with a shaven crown in that most ancient college which
was set up in the time of Sylla. . . .[29]

Osiris is the divine son, husband, and brother of Isis, hence
this new initiation means that Lucius has now become the
divine husband and son of the great mother goddess. Previously he was negatively possessed by the *puer aeternus* god, but
now the development has reached its goal so that he realizes
consciously that he is the god himself, the eternal son of the
Great Mother. The divine aspect of the individual is realized

here in its symbolic form. Lucius becomes conscious of his greater divine inner being.[30] This is what Jung calls the realization of the Self. The symbolism in the cult of Isis means a realization of the anima, but now follows the realization of the Self, of his own divine inner nature. The value of the experience, through which he has a positive relation to the goddess, can now be seen in his life. After this last initiation, Lucius realizes himself as being a god and also a servant of the divine principle; he is both, master and servant at once.

It has been mentioned already that there is an analogy in Christianity to the myth of Osiris in the cycle of the legends of the Holy Grail.[31] After his death on the cross, Christ was buried in a tomb covered with a stone. When the women came to anoint the corpse with unguents, an angel told them that Christ was no longer there but had resurrected. According to a legend of the second or third century, Joseph of Arimathea had a vision of the resurrected Christ, who gave him a jar filled with his blood, and said that he had chosen him, Joseph, to carry on the secret tradition and the cult of his grave. Here again, as in the Osiris cult, the symbol of the dead god is a vessel, in which his blood, that is to say, his life substance, is contained. Later the legend was altered, and one assumed that the jar was lost, crossed the sea, and landed in a fig tree in Marseilles, where it was discovered and was brought to the cloister of Fécamp. That was how the Holy Grail came to France.

Here again we have an analogy to the Osiris myth, in the vessel containing the god-essence. It is the archetypal motif of the incarnated god, who, after a short human life, is killed and then continues to live in the form of his essential soul substance preserved as a relic in a jar, out of which his spirit emanates invisibly. According to the legend, sometimes a voice is heard from the holy vessel and helps the knights in their task. Why, one might ask, was there need for such a relic in order to fulfill the exigencies of the Christian faith? If we consider the history of religions more generally, we see that in many religions there are phases in which the religious symbols, originally experienced individually, have passed over onto institutions and collectively recognized rituals and litanies. Christ himself was first *experienced* as the divine God-man by the small circle of his apostles. Saint Paul experienced him in his vision.[32] The fact that Christianity spread so quickly was due to a great extent to the dreams and visions of the individuals. The description of the lives of monks, martyrs, and saints report, for example, a figure clothed in light, wearing a crown of roses on his head, or of an oversized shepherd. Such dreams often do not specify that they concern Christ, but every masculine divine figure was immediately interpreted as such, which then for men became the carrier of all visions of the Self, or, for the women, the positive animus.[33]

In this way Christ was still a living archetype, with whom many individuals were connected through a personal inner experience. Christ for them was a divine being that could be experienced, someone who lived amongst them, circulated at the heart of the community, and had influence on their lives. Later, the living symbol faded, it lost its emotional quality and numinosity, which means more and more people knew only from what their grandmothers taught them that there was such a god, but they themselves had no longer a feeling of relationship to him. They still prayed in the old form, because they had been taught to do so, but they could not speak of a personal religious experience. That is why Nietzsche, in a crucial moment of his life, said that "God is dead." However, he is not dead, only his life has become invisible, returned to the womb from which he was born, in his unconscious archetypal original form; in this state he is the god contained in the jar.

One can thus say that the round vessel symbolizes the secret of the human psyche, containing the living god substance, in other words, an imperishable divine reality which is eternal. Although man sometimes worships God and sometimes does not believe in him, yet there subsists always in the psyche an eternal essence of God which cannot die. The figure of Christ is today in danger of becoming a dead god, but as far as he personifies an archetype his figure is eternal. He embodies the experience of an archetypal reality and in this sense he is immortal. He survives his own death through a return into the womb of the unconscious human psyche, from which he came. The vessel and the god substance therein are the symbol of a psychological attitude and experience, in which everything religious is experienced within the individual, and nothing is seen any more in outer forms. Nothing is projected any longer in pictures and rituals, or in an institution. It has again become the personal, numinous experience of the individual human being. That is the moment when the dead god is returned to the vessel, out of which he comes again as that which he has always been: an eternal psychic reality. That is why the Egyptian symbol of the jar with the essence of the god has survived even in late Christianity. When certain doubts arose about the figure of Christ, suddenly all those legends came to life which circled around the idea of the Holy Grail, from which a new orientation could take place. The Church saw in the Grail material a certain danger, because of the individual element in it. Therefore, for a time it fought these ideas and called them heretical. But the ideas continued to live in alchemy and in the secret societies of the *fedeli d'amore,* a group to which Petrarch and probably also Dante belonged. But how far, in that time, was it understood that the Grail vessel symbolized the unconscious psyche of the individual or the individual as a vessel of the divinity? How far did one understand that every individual is really the vessel that contains the god? We cannot judge this. But at least the poets had some notion about this, as one can see from some of their writings.

The secret paths of the world of the courtly love, which carried further the psychic experience of the antique mysteries, disappeared almost completely in the seventeenth century. They were superseded by the Enlightenment, the rationalism and scientific and technical development with which we live today. But since archetypal values cannot die, in our day they reappear everywhere in the proliferation of sects, in drugs, in an infatuation for the esoteric in all its thinkable forms.

At the same time these irrational values, which nowadays have disappeared from collective consciousness, live again in an unexpected form in Jungian psychology. By being willing to descend into himself and to confront himself with the unconscious forces ("to worship the lower and upper gods"), Jung has shown us a way of dealing with these forces. It takes a strong consciousness, which is flexible and modest enough, to be able to accept what the unconscious—the gods—has to say to us, and to realize the will of the gods, of the god who manifests himself in us, and to put us into his service, without forgetting the individual limits of our human nature.

It is not for nothing that Jung inscribed over the door of his home in Küsnacht the words of the ancient oracle: *Vocatus atque non vocatus deus aderit*—"Called or not called, the God will be there." Even if we are unconscious of it, the god survives his death in the vessel of our soul, as in the jar of Osiris, or of the Grail.[34] It is up to us to pay attention and to allow the development of that which within us seeks to fulfill itself.

For the people of antiquity it was easier to find this way than it is for us today, because—as we see in the example of our novel—mankind still had the mystery cults, which imparted to him the experience of the unconscious and of the Self. We no longer have these images and are therefore less protected in our confrontation with the forces of the unconscious.

I hope that these attempts at a psychological interpretation, which are often only tentative suggestions, have conveyed to the reader the following: that this novel of Apuleius is a highly important *document humain* which one can even put next to Goethe's *Faust*. It leads into the deepest problems of Western man and points symbolically to developments which today we still have not realized in consciousness.

NOTES

Introduction

1. Apuleius, *The Golden Ass,* translated by W. Adlington, revised by S. Gaselee. A bibliography of Apuleius has been compiled by C. C. Shlam in *World,* no. 64, pp. 285–309.

2. For bibliography and further details, see Rudolf Helm, "Das Märchen von Amor und Psyche," pp. 188ff. See also R. Reitzenstein, "Das Märchen von Amor und Psyche bei Apuleius," pp. 88ff.

3. For the literary form, see Bruno Lacagnini, *Il significato ed il valore del Romanzo di Apuleio,* p. 19.

4. We owe this term to Pierre Janet, who referred to a diminished state of conscious attention which allows unconscious contents to manifest themselves.

5. John Gwyn Griffiths offers the same theory and has compiled as complete a bibliography as this author knows, in *Apuleius of Madaura: The Isis Book.*

6. Karl Kerényi, *Die griechisch-orientalische Romanliteratur in religionsgeschichtlicher Beleuchtung.*

7. Reinhold Merkelbach, *Roman und Mysterium in der Antike.*

8. See chapter 9 of the present work.

9. Cf. Griffiths, *Apuleius of Madaura,* pp. 13f.

10. Cf. Georg Henrici, "Zur Geschichte der Psyche" (On the History of the Psyche), pp. 390–417.

11. Cf. the Acts of the Apostles, 9:1–19, and Saint Augustine, *Confessions.*

12. The first relationship between the child and its mother influences its psychic structure and its relationship with the world. On the

subject of the positive and the negative mother complex, see C. G. Jung, "Psychological Aspects of the Mother Archetype," pp. 75–110.

13. Cf. C. G. Jung, "Answer to Job."

Chapter 1. The Life and Times of Apuleius

1. Cf. Griffiths, *Apuleius of Madaura*, p. 10.
2. See Serge Lancel, "Curiosités et préoccupations spirituelles chez Apulée," pp. 25ff. For further details cf. Griffiths, *Apuleius of Madaura*, pp. 5, 408ff.; his attitude was probably rather anti-Christian.
3. Apuleius, *L'Apologie*. Cf. the detailed adaptation by A. Abt, *Die Apologie des Apuleius von Madaura und die antike Zauberei* (The Apology of Apuleius of Madaura and Antique Witchcraft).
4. Cf. Griffiths, *Apuleius of Madaura*, p. 10.
5. Cf. Griffiths, *Apuleius of Madaura*, p. 61.
6. Plinius Minor, *Epistulae*, p. 316f.
7. We also have fragments of other works by Apuleius and excerpts from his most famous lectures, which, however, are not very relevant for the present study. Cf. *Florides* and *Opuscules et Fragments Philosophiques*.
8. Cf. Frank Regen, *Apuleius Philosophicus Platonicus*. The author considers all the material without, however, taking Apuleius seriously enough.
9. Jane C. Nitzsche, *The Genius Figure in Antiquity and the Middle Ages*, chapter 1.

Chapter 2. The Two Companions and the Tale of Aristomenes

1. The question of whether or not Apuleius called himself Lucius, as tradition has it, is discussed by modern critics.
2. By the term *shadow*, Jung means the unconscious, repressed, and less differentiated aspects of the personality. See his *Aion*, para. 13ff.
3. The "Self," in Jungian terminology, is the center of the psychic totality of the personality; its realization is the goal of the individuation process. It is superordinate to the ego and different from it. Cf. Jung, "The Relations between the Ego and the Unconscious," paras. 404ff.; and *Psychology and Alchemy*, paras. 126ff.

4. Marie-Louise von Franz, *Puer Aeternus.*
5. Karl Wyss, "Die Milch im Kultus der Griechen und Römer," chap. 7 and 8.
6. Griffiths, *Apuleius of Madaura,* p. 154.
7. Apuleius, *The Golden Ass,* book I, p. 15.
8. Cf. Georg Luck, *Hexen und Zauberei in der römischen Dichtung.*
9. The *anima* is the "personification of the feminine nature of a man's unconscious" (C. G. Jung, *Memories, Dreams, Reflections,* p. 279). See also Jung, *Psychological Types,* under "soul image"; and Jung, *The Archetypes and the Collective Unconscious,* paras. 111ff. The anima personifies a man's Eros, his unconscious moods, and his irrational feelings and fantasies.
10. Cf. Charles Seltmann, *The Olympians and Their Guests.*

Chapter 3. Lucius Meets Byrrhena, Photis, and Goatskins

1. Apuleius, *The Golden Ass,* book II, p. 49.
2. See Griffiths, *Apuleius of Madaura,* pp. 29f. Riefsthal and Scobie have pointed out the relationship between the scene in this bas-relief and the Isis theme without, however, grasping its most profound implications.
3. Apuleius, *The Golden Ass,* book II, xxv–xxvi, p. 87.
4. Cf. 1 Samuel 28:7–10.
5. Cf. Theodor Hopfner, *Griechisch-ägyptischer Offenbarungszauber.*
6. K. Preisendanz, *Papyri Graecae Magicae.*
7. Cf. Matti Hako, "Das Wiesel in der europäischen Volksüberlieferung," in particular pp. 33ff.
8. These meanings are more than uncertain. Cf. Griffiths, *Apuleius of Madaura,* p. 351.
9. Cf. Apuleius, *The Golden Ass,* book III, xviii, p. 127.
10. The transpersonal nucleus of the personality.

Chapter 4. The Ass

1. See Hermann Diels, *Doxographi Graeci,* fragment 15.
2. Cf. Hopfner, *Griechisch-ägyptischer Offenbarungszauber,* vol. 1, pp. 235ff.
3. As mentioned before, by *shadow* Jung means the inferior aspect of the ego, which is mostly unconscious.
4. Pp. 63ff.

5. Mircea Eliade, *Rites and Symbols of Initiation*.

6. Cf. Merkelbach, *Roman und Mysterium,* passim. Whereas certain commentators have not discerned the profound relationship between this tale and the story of Lucius taken together, others, though less numerous, have recognized its link with the intitiation mysteries that occur at the end of the novel. The attempt has always been made to interpret the book not only as an entertaining novel, but in part as mirroring a mystery, but Merkelbach only alludes to the story of Amor and Psyche, and to the shrewd doctor who gave evidence in the case of the young wife, who due to her unrequited love for her son-in-law accused the latter of poisoning his brother. He gives an interpretation by linking it with the mystery cult, and mystery tradition of antiquity, but does not analyze the whole novel throughout. He disregards the rest of the story as being profane, or as not belonging. I agree with practically everything he says along those lines, but, as far as I know the literature, I think that what has not ever been understood is that one cannot pick out a few stories and ascribe a deeper meaning only to them. The whole story is consistent. Naturally, not knowing the psychology of the unconscious, Merkelbach tends to describe the novel as if Apuleius had consciously woven in all those meanings, something which I definitely doubt. I think Apuleius thought a lot about it, and wove quite a lot into it consciously, but that quite a lot more has also flowed out of his pen without his quite realizing how well it fitted, which means that, probably, like every genuine piece of art, it arose out of a collaboration of both aspects of his personality. Merkelbach's book, however, I can warmly recommend.

7. C. G. Jung, "The Psychology of the Transference," paras. 437f.

8. Jean-Valentin Andreae, *Les Noces chymiques de Christian Rosencreutz*.

9. Para. 134.

Chapter 5. Amor and Psyche I

1. Erich Neumann, *Amor and Psyche*. Jung was of the opinion that the tale deals to a large extent with anima psychology, but that Neumann's attempt to interpret it from the feminine aspect could be accepted just as well since femininity in a man is not completely different from the femininity of a woman.

2. Two years after the first edition of this present work, James Hillman published an essay in *The Myth of Analysis* in which, basing his interpretation on Neumann's study, he develops some interesting

ideas about the myth of Eros and Psyche and its importance for our epoch. His point of view differs, however, from mine, in that he interprets the tale apart from the rest of the novel. We also have a psychoanalytic interpretation, which ignores the religious element but otherwise is thorough, in F. E. Hoevels, *Märchen und Magie in den Metamorphosen des Apuleius von Madaura* (Fairy Tales and Magic in the Metamorphoses of Apuleius of Madura).

3. Cf. G. Binder and R. Merkelbach, "Amor und Psyche," which contains a complete collection of works concerning this type of story.

4. R. Reitzenstein, "Das Märchen von Amor und Psyche bei Apuleius."

5. Reitzenstein, ibid.

6. Plato, *Symposium*, 202c and d.

7. Translated by K. Preisendanz, *Papyri Grecae Magicae*, "Le glaive de Dardanos" and "Prière à Eros," p. 129.

8. Cf. Pierre Solié, *Médicines initiatiques*. See also C. A. Meier, *Ancient Incubation and Modern Psychotherapy*.

9. Concerning the psychological aspect of the Kore figure, see Jung, *The Archetypes and the Collective Unconscious*, paras. 306ff.

10. For details, see Jan Bergmann, "Ich bin Isis," p. 33.

11. Cf. Jung, *Aion*, paras. 20ff.

12. Epistle to the Philippians 11:7.

13. Cf. also Ludwig Friedländer, "Das Märchen von Amor und Psyche," pp. 16ff.

14. A collection of almost all of the popular versions of this story has been assembled by J. Svahn in *The Tale of Cupid and Psyche*.

15. Karl Kerényi and C. G. Jung, *Essays on a Science of Mythology*.

16. A method of Jung's, in which one speaks with figures of the unconscious in a waking fantasy.

17. Cf. Jung, *Aion*, chap. 3.

18. Cf. Michael Maier, *Atalanta Fugiens*. Engraving 30 represents two figures, the sun and the moon, accompanied by a cock and hen.

Chapter 6. Amor and Psyche II

1. Cf. Saint Irenaeus, *Adversus haereses*, I, pp. 4ff. A beautiful presentation is to be found in Hans Leisegang's *Die Gnosis*, p. 379.

2. Cf. Jung, "The Philosophical Tree," para. 452.

3. Reitzenstein was the first to recognize the relationship between the gnostic Sophia and Psyche. Cf. Reitzenstein, "Das Märchen von Amor und Psyche," pp. 105ff.

4. The reborn son god Horus, too, is often represented in Egyptian funeral texts as being surrounded by a snake.
5. Cf. "The Singing, Soaring Lark," in The *Complete Grimm's Fairy Tales*.
6. Erich Neumann, *Amor and Psyche*, pp. 76ff., 85.
7. Jung, "Answer to Job."
8. The word is from the Sanskrit, meaning "magic circle." For Jung it is a symbol of the center, the goal, and of the Self as psychic totality. In Lamaism and Tantric yoga it is an instrument of contemplation. Cf. Jung, *Memories, Dreams, Reflections*, p. 384; and Jung, *Psychology and Alchemy*, paras. 122ff.
9. Erich Neumann interprets the seeds as "sexual promiscuity." Cf. his *Amor and Psyche*, pp. 94–96.
10. Cf. Angelo de Gubernatis, *Zoological Mythology*, volume 2, p. 50.
11. Cf. Neumann, *Amor and Psyche*, p. 95; and Kerényi, "Urmensch und Mysterien," pp. 56f.
12. Cf. the renowned portrait in the Museum of Dijon of Philippe le Bon, Duke of Bourgogne by Roger van der Weyden. Philippe le Bon created the order of the Toison d'Or in Bruges in 1429.

Chapter 7. Psyche's Tasks

1. Cf. Jung, *Psychology and Alchemy*, paras. 518ff.
2. Cf. Jung, *Psychological Types*, paras. 828, 883ff.
3. "For those who possess the symbol, the passage is easy."—A saying of the alchemists.
4. He appears in an alchemical work as Acharantos or Achaab. Cf. M. Berthelot, *Collection des Anciens Alchimistes Grecs*, Vol. 1, pp. 30–32, "La prophétesse Isis à son fils."
5. "Except a grain of wheat fall into the ground and die, it abideth alone; but if it die, it bringeth forth much fruit."—John 12:24.
6. Merkelbach interprets them as symbols of the uninitiated. See his *Roman und Mysterium in der Antike*, p. 46. I prefer the general meaning.
7. Cf. Jung, "Woman in Europe," paras. 236ff.
8. Cf. Philippe Hofmeister, *Die heiligen Oele in der morgen- und abendländischen Kirche*.
9. Hexagram 22: *Pi*, "Grace."
10. Her social role or mask.
11. Cf. Theodor Hopfner, *Plutarch: über Isis und Osiris*, vol. 1, pp. 30–31, 33, 36.

Chapter 8. *Charitie, Tlepolemus, and the Chthonic Shadow*

1. As a Latin proverb says, "Fata volentes ducunt, nolentes trahunt"—
   "Fate leads those who are willing and drags those who resist."
2. Cf. H. Hepding, *Attis, seine Mythen und sein Kult*, pp. 10f.
3. Cf. Marie-Louise von Franz, *Puer Aeternus*.
4. Jung, *The Practice of Psychotherapy*.
5. Apuleius, *The Golden Ass*. Translated by Robert Graves.
6. The animus is the unconscious masculine part of the soul of a
   woman.

Chapter 9. *The Ass in the Service of Many Masters*

1. In Jung's typology, the conscious ego has four functions: thinking
   and feeling, and intuition and sensation, each pair opposed to the
   other. An "inferior" function is, in effect, an undifferentiated
   function.
2. Cf. Luigi Aurigemma, *Le signe zodiacal du scorpion dans les traditions
   occidentales*. This beautiful study on the symbolism of the scorpion
   contains a remarkable iconography.
3. Cf. W. Danckert, *Unehrliche Leute*, pp. 138ff.
4. Merkelbach, *Roman und Mysterium*, pp. 82ff.
5. Hopfner, *Plutarch*, p. 54. The mandragora the doctor gives the
   servant is again an image of Osiris "without a head" *(akephalos)*;
   cf. also Merkelbach, *Roman und Mysterium*, p. 85.
6. For Heraclitus, *enantiodromia* meant the reversal of a state into its
   opposite. Jung uses the word in the same sense.

Chapter 10. *Lucius Returns to Himself*

1. Apuleius, *The Golden Ass* (translated by W. Adlington), book XI,
   i, p. 539.
2. I prefer to translate *redde me meo Lucio* literally, as "Render me to
   myself again, Lucius."
3. Apuleius, *The Golden Ass*, book XI, i–ii, pp. 539–543.
4. Ibid.
5. Ibid.
6. On the problem of the fourth, cf. Jung, *Psychology and Religion*,
   paras. 243ff.
7. Paras. 52ff.

8. For a woman, the process would clearly be the reverse, the integration of the animus leading to a feminine image of the Self.
9. Jacobsohn, *Timeless Documents of the Soul.*
10. Apuleius, *The Golden Ass,* book IX, iii–iv, pp. 543–545.
11. In Japan, Amaterasu, the goddess of the sun, is represented by a mirror in Shinto shrines.
12. One can compare these snakes with the *uraei* of the kings and gods of Egypt.
13. Cf. Berthelot, *Collection des Anciens Alchimistes Grecs,* vol. 1, p. 95.
14. Cf. Etienne Perrot, *La Voie de la Transformation d'après C. G. Jung et l'Alchimie,* pp. 191, 215–239.
15. *Der Ochs und sein Hirte,* edited, with commentary, by Daizohkutsu R. Otsu.
16. There are parallels for this. In Africa, for instance, one chases away the demons who cause storms or an eclipse of the sun by making as much of an uproar as possible.
17. Apuleius, *The Golden Ass,* book IX, iv–vi, pp. 545–549.
18. Cf. R. Merkelbach, *Isisfeste in griechisch-römischer Zeit.*

Chapter 11. The Goddess Isis

1. Helmuth Jacobsohn, "Das Gegensatzproblem im altägyptischen Mythos," pp. 171ff.
2. On the problem of the quaternity, see especially Jung, *Psychology and Religion,* paras. 243ff.
3. Cf. A. Noguera, *How African Was Egypt?* passim.
4. Cf. Jung, *Psychology and Religion,* paras. 268ff.
5. Cf. Jung, *Two Essays on Analytical Psychology,* paras. 202ff.
6. Cf. Jung, *Psychological Types,* paras. 814ff.
7. Cf. Jung and Pauli, *The Interpretation of Nature and the Psyche.* Jung's monograph "Synchronicity: An Acausal Connecting Principle" is republished in *The Structure and Dynamics of the Psyche,* paras. 816–968. See also Marie-Louise von Franz, *Number and Time,* especially part 5, pp. 235ff; von Franz, *C. G. Jung: His Myth in Our Time,* chapter 12, passim; and Etienne Perrot, "Le sens du hasard."
8. Something similar is reported in the Acts of the Apostles. In a vision, Philip receives a command to meet a high Ethiopian official in order to baptize him (Acts 8:26–40). Peter is also warned through a vision that he must baptize a Roman centurion and admit non-Jews into the Christian community (Acts 10:1–48, 11:1–18).
9. Apuleius, *The Golden Ass,* book XI, vi, pp. 549–550.

10. *Pastophores* were priests who carried holy objects in the Isis procession.
11. Apuleius, *The Golden Ass*, book XI, xxx, p. 595.
12. Matthew 13:44–46.
13. Cf. Jung, *Two Essays on Analytical Psychology*, para. 227.
14. In antiquity the persona was the actor's mask. Jung uses this term to designate the social role of the individual, who sometimes identifies with it in an exaggerated way.
15. Cf. Jung, *Psychological Types*, passim.
16. Cf. Jan Bergmann, *Ich bin Isis*. See also R. E. Witt, *Isis in the Graeco-Roman World*.
17. Cf. Jacobsohn, "Das Gegensatzproblem im altägyptischen Mythos," passim.
18. Ibid., p. 175.
19. On the individuation process, the concept with which Jung characterizes the realization of the totality of the individual, see Jung's introduction to *Psychology and Alchemy;* Marie-Louise von Franz, "The Individuation Process," pp. 157ff; and Etienne Perrot, *La Voie de la transformation*, part 1, chapters 3 and 4.
20. Jung, *Psychological Types*, paras. 375ff.
21. Published by Günther Röder in *Urkunden zur Religion der alten Aegypter*, pp. 297ff.
22. Cf. von Franz, *Number and Time*, part 4, pp. 171ff.
23. Cf. *Quantum Physics and Parapsychology*, the proceedings of an international conference held in Geneva in 1974.
24. Paras. 410ff.

Chapter 12. Matter and the Feminine

1. Cf. Griffiths, *Apuleius of Madaura*, 207.
2. Jan Bergmann, *Ich bin Isis*, p. 147.
3. For an interpretation of his visions, see Jung, *Alchemical Studies*, paras. 85ff.
4. Cf. Berthelot, *Collection des Anciens Alchemistes Grecs*, vol. 1, pp. 199, 220, 291; "Le livre de Komarios," p. 208.
5. In ancient texts the vessel of the transformation of the substances was compared with the tomb of Osiris. Cf. Berthelot, *Collection des Anciens Alchemistes Grecs*, vol. 1, p. 95.
6. Cf. Griffiths, *Apuleius of Madaura*, pp. 228ff.
7. He has been transformed into Osiris Hydreios.
8. Cf. Jung, *Memories*, pp. 267ff.

9. Cf. Marie-Louise von Franz, *Aurora Consurgens*, passim.

10. Cf. Bernard Maupoil, *Le Géomancie à Ancienne Côte des Esclaves*, pp. 24, 89.

11. Apuleius, *The Golden Ass*, book XI, xiii, p. 561.

12. Cf. Griffiths, *Apuleius of Madaura*, pp. 160ff.

13. Apuleius, *The Golden Ass*, book XI, xix, p. 155.

14. Cf. B. Büchsenschütz, *Traum und Traumdeutung im Altertum.*

15. Cf. Erwin Preusschen, *Mönchtum und Serapiskult.*

16. Latin, *partes illas*—literally, "those parts."

17. Apuleius, *The Golden Ass*, book XI, xx, pp. 571–573.

18. Ibid., pp. 573–575.

19. Apuleius, *The Golden Ass*, book XI, xxiii, p. 581.

20. Mithras, of Iranian origin, is the sun hero who also becomes one with his father, the sun god.

21. Apuleius, *The Golden Ass*, ibid.

22. Apuleius, *The Golden Ass*, book XI, xxiv, pp. 581–582.

23. Cf. Bergmann, *Ich bin Isis*, p. 281, note 2.

24. Apuleius, *The Golden Ass*, book XI, xxvi, p. 587.

25. Cf. Berthelot, *Collection des Anciens Alchemistes Grecs*, vol. 1, p. 118.

26. Apuleius, *The Golden Ass*, book XI, xxvii–xxviii, pp. 587–591.

27. Ibid., xxix, pp. 591–593.

28. Ibid., xxx, p. 593.

29. Ibid., p. 595.

30. This reminds one of Christ's saying, "You are gods" (John 10:34).

31. Cf. Emma Jung and Marie-Louise von Franz, *The Grail Legend.*

32. Acts 9:1–19.

33. Cf. Marie-Louise von Franz, *The Passion of Perpetua.*

34. These ideas which are merely referred to here are developed in von Franz, *C. G. Jung: His Myth in Our Time*, chapter 14.

BIBLIOGRAPHY

Abt, A. *Die Apologie des Apuleius von Madaura und die antike Zauberei*. Giessen, 1968.

Andreae, Jean Valentin. *Les Noces chymiques de Christian Rosencreutz*. Strasburg, 1616. Translated by Bernard Gorceix in *La Bible des Rose-Croix*. Paris: Presses Universitaires de France, 1971.

Andreae, V. *Chemische Hochzeit*. Stuttgart: Neudruck, 1973.

Apuleius of Madaura. *L'Apologie*. Translated by P. Velette. Paris: Belles-Lettres, undated.

———. *Florides*. Translated by P. Valette. Paris: Belles-Lettres, undated.

———. *The Golden Ass: Being the Metamorphoses of Lucius Apuleius*. Translated by W. Adlington, 1566; revised by S. Gaselee. (Loeb Classical Library) Cambridge, Mass.: Harvard University Press, 1915.

———. *The Golden Ass*. Translated by Robert Graves. Edinburgh: Penguin Books, 1903.

———. *Opuscules et Fragments*. Translated by Beaujeu. Paris: Belles-Lettres, undated.

Aurigemma, L. *Le signe zodiacal du scorpion dans les traditions occidentales*. Paris: Mouton, 1976.

Bergmann, Jan. "Ich bin Isis." In: *Studium zum memphitischen Hintergrund der griechischen Isisaretalogien*. Uppsala, 1968.

Berthelot, M. *Collection des Anciens Alchemistes Grecs*. 2 vols. Paris: Steinheil, 1897/98.

Binder, G. R. *Das Märchen von Amor und Psyche.* (Wege der Forschung, vol. 116) Darmstadt, 1968.

Binder, G., and Merkelbach, R. "Amor und Psyche." In: *Wege der Forschung,* vol. 126. Darmstadt, 1968.

Büchsenschütz, B. *Traum und Traumdeutung im Altertum.* Berlin, 1868.

Danckert, W. *Unehrliche Leute: die verfehmten Berufe.* Bern/ Munich: Francke, 1963.

Diels, H. *Doxographi Graeci.* Berlin, 1879.

Eliade, Mircea. *Rites and Symbols of Initiation: The Mysteries of Birth and Rebirth.* Translated by W. R. Trask. New York: Harper & Row, 1965.

Friedländer, Ludwig. "Das Märchen von Amor und Psyche." In Binder and Merkelbach, *Amor und Psyche,* pp. 16ff.

Griffiths, John Gwyn. *Apuleius of Madaura: The Isis Book.* Louvain: Brill, 1975.

Grimm, The Brothers. *The Complete Grimm's Fairy Tales.* New York: Pantheon Books, 1972.

Gubernatis, Angelo de. *Zoological Mythology.* New York: Arno Press, 1978.

Hako, Matti. "Das Wiesel in der europäischen Volksüberlieferung." In: *Folklore Fellow Communications,* vol. 66, No. 167. Helsinki, 1956.

Harrison, Jane. *Themis.* 2nd ed. Cambridge: Cambridge University Press, 1927.

Helm, Rudolf. "Das Märchen von Amor und Psyche." Re-edited. In Binder and Merkelbach, "Amor und Psyche." *Wege der Forschung.* vol. 126. Darmstadt, 1968.

Henrici, Georg. "Zur Geschichte der Psyche." In: *Preussische Jahrbücher,* vol. 10, 1897.

Hepding, H. *Attis, seine Mythen und sein Kult.* Giessen, 1903.

Hillman, James. "The Myth of Analysis." In: *Spring 1972.* Dallas, Tex.: Spring Publications, 1972.

Hoevels, F. E. *Märchen und Magie in den Metamorphosen des Apuleius von Madaura.* Amsterdam: Rodopi, 1979.

Hofmeister, Philippe. *Die heiligen Oele in der morgen- und abendländischen Kirche.* Wurzburg: Augustinus Verlag, 1948.

Hopfner, Theodor. *Griechisch-ägyptischer Offenbarungszauber.* Amsterdam: E. Hakkert, 1974.

———. *Plutarch: über Isis und Osiris.* 2 vols. Darmstadt, 1967.

I Ching, or Book of Changes. Edited by Richard Wilhelm. New York: Pantheon Books (Bollingen Series XIX), 1950.

Irenaeus, Saint. *Contra (or Adversus) haereses libri quinque.* In: *Patrologiae cursus completus.* Edited by Jacques-Paul Migne. Paris, 1844–1866.

Jacobsohn, Helmuth. "The Conversation of the World-Weary Man with His Ba." In: *Timeless Documents of the Soul.* Evanston: Northwestern University Press, 1968.

———. "Das Gegensatzproblem im altägyptischen Mythos." In: *Studium zur analytischen Psychologie C. G. Jungs.* Festschrift for the 80th birthday of C. G. Jung. Zurich: Rascher Verlag, 1955.

Jung, C. G. *Aion.* Vol. 9, part 2 of the *Collected Works.* Translated by R. F. C. Hull. Princeton: Princeton University Press, 1959.

———. "Answer to Job." In: *Psychology and Religion.* Vol. 11 of the *Collected Works,* paras. 553–758.

———. Memories, Dreams, Reflections. New York: Pantheon Books, 1963.

———. *Mysterium Conjunctionis.* Vol. 14 of the *Collected Works.* Translated by R. F. C. Hull. Princeton: Princeton University Press, 1963.

———. "The Philosophical Tree." In: *Alchemical Studies,* paras. 304–482. Vol. 13 of the *Collected Works.* Translated by R. F. C. Hull. Princeton: Princeton University Press, 1968.

———. "Psychological Aspect of the Mother Archetype." In: *The Archetypes and the Collective Unconscious.* Vol. 9, part 1 of the *Collected Works.* Translated by R. F. C. Hull. Princeton: Princeton University Press, 1959.

———. *Psychological Types.* Vol. 6 of the *Collected Works.* Translated by R. F. C. Hull. Princeton: Princeton University Press, 1971.

———. *Psychology and Alchemy.* Vol. 12 of the *Collected Works.* Translated by R. F. C. Hull. Princeton: Princeton University Press, 1953.

————. *Psychology and Religion.* Vol. 11 of the *Collected Works.* Translated by R. F. C. Hull. Princeton: Princeton University Press, 1958.

————. "The Psychology of the Transference." In: *The Practice of Psychotherapy.* Vol. 16 of the *Collected Works.* Translated by R. F. C. Hull. Princeton: Princeton University Press, 1954.

————. "The Relations between the Ego and the Unconscious." In: *Two Essays on Analytical Psychology.* Vol. 7 of the *Collected Works.* Translated by R. F. C. Hull. Princeton: Princeton University Press, 1953.

————. *The Structure and Dynamics of the Psyche.* Vol. 8 of the *Collected Works.* Translated by R. F. C. Hull. Princeton: Princeton University Press, 1960.

————. "Synchronicity: An Acausal Connecting Principle." In: *The Structure and Dynamics of the Psyche* (q.v.).

————. "Woman in Europe." In: *Civilization in Transition.* Vol. 10 of the *Collected Works.* Translated by R. F. C. Hull. Princeton: Princeton University Press, 1964.

Jung, C. G. and Kerényi, Karl. *Essays on a Science of Mythology.* New York: Pantheon Books (Bollingen Series XXII), 1949.

Jung, Emma and von Franz, Marie-Louise. *The Grail Legend.* Translated by Andrea Dykes. New York: G. P. Putnam's Sons for the C. G. Jung Foundation, 1970.

Kerényi, Karl. *Die griechisch-orientalische Romanliteratur in religionsgeshichtlicher Beleuchtung.* Tubingen, 1927.

————. "Urmensch und Mysterien." In: *Eranos Jahrbuch,* Vol. 15. Zurich: Rhein Verlag, 1948.

Lacagnini, Bruno. *Il significato ed il valore del Romanzo di Apuleio.* Pisa, 1927.

Lancel, Serge. "Curiosités et préoccupations spirituelles chez Apulée." In: *Histoire des religions,* vol. 160. Rome, 1961.

Leisegang, Hans. *Die Gnosis.* Leipzig: Krönersche Taschenausgabe, 1924.

Lewis, C. S. *Till We Have Faces.* New York: Harcourt Brace Jovanovich, 1980.

Luck, Georg. *Hexen und Zauberei in der römischen Dichtung.* Zurich: Artemis, 1962.

Maier, Michael. *Atalanta Fugiens.* Latin version first edited by

Oppenheim in 1617; French translation by Etienne Perrot, *Atalante Fugitive*. Paris: Librairie de Medicis, 1969.

Maupoil, Bernard. *Le Géomancie à Ancienne Côte des Esclaves*. Paris: Institut d'Ethnologie, 1943.

Meier, C. A. *Ancient Incubation and Modern Psychotherapy*. Translated by Monica Curtis. Evanston, Ill.: Northwestern University Press, 1967.

Merkelbach, R. *Isisfeste in griechisch-römischer Zeit: Daten und Riten*. (Beiträge zur klassischen Philologie, vol. 5.) Meisenheim: Verlag Hain, 1963.

———. *Roman und Mysterium in der Antike*. Munich/Berlin: Verlag Beck, 1962.

Merkelbach, Reinhold and Binder, G. "Amor und Psyche." *(Wege der Forschung)*, Vol. 26. Darmstadt, 1968.

Neumann, Erich. *Amor and Psyche: The Psychic Development of the Feminine*. Translated by Ralph Mannheim. New York: Harper & Row, 1962.

Nitzsche, Jane C. *The Genius Figure in Antiquity and the Middle Ages*. New York/London: Columbia University Press, 1975.

Noguera, A. *How African Was Egypt?* New York: Vantage Press, 1976.

Otsu, Daizohkutsu R. *Der Ochs und sein Hirte*. Munich: Neske, 1957.

Perrot, Etienne. "Le sens du hasard." *Revue de Psychologie,* no. 93, Oct. 1977. Paris.

———. *La Voie de la Transformation d'après C. G. Jung et l'Alchemie*. Paris, 1975.

Plato. "The Symposium." In: *The Dialogues of Plato*.

Plinius Minor. *Epistulae*. Edited by R. Kukula. Leipzig: Teubner, 1957.

Preisendanz, K. "Le glaive de Dardanos." In: *Papyri Graecae Magicae*.

———. *Papyri Graecae Magicae*. 2 vols. 2nd ed. Stuttgart: Teubner, 1973.

———. "Prière à Eros." In: *Papyri Graecae Magicae*.

Preusschen, Erwin. *Mönchtum und Serapiskult*. 2nd ed. Giessen: Ricker, 1903.

Quantum Physics and Parapsychology. Proceedings of the International Conference, Geneva, 1974. New York: L. Otari, 1975.

Reitzenstein, R. "Das Märchen von Amor und Psyche bei Apuleius." In: Binder and Merkelbach, *Amor und Psyche* (q.v.).

Röder, Günther. *Urkunden zur Religion der alten Aegypter.* Jena: Diedrichs, 1923.

Seltmann, Charles. *The Olympians and Their Guests.* Paris/London: 1952.

Shlam, C. C. Bibliography of Apuleius, in *World,* no. 64, 1971.

Solié, Pierre. *Médicines Initiatiques.* Paris: Editions de l'Epis, 1976.

Svahn, J. *The Tale of Cupid and Psyche.* Lund, 1955.

von Franz, Marie-Louise. *Aurora Consurgens: A Document Attributed to Thomas Aquinas on the Problem of Opposites in Alchemy.* Translated by R. F. C. Hull and A. S. B. Glover. New York: Pantheon Books (Bollingen Series), 1966.

———. *C. G. Jung: His Myth in Our Time.* Translated by William Kennedy. New York: G. P. Putnam's Sons for the C. G. Jung Foundation, 1975.

———. "The Individuation Process." In *Man and His Symbols.* Edited by C. G. Jung. New York: Doubleday, 1964.

———. *Number and Time.* Translated by Andrea Dykes. Evanston: Northwestern University Press, 1974.

———. *The Passion of Perpetua.* Irving, Tex.: Spring Publications, 1980.

———. *Puer Aeternus.* Boston: Sigo Press, 1981.

von Franz, Marie-Louise and Jung, Emma. *The Grail Legend.* Translated by Andrea Dykes. New York: G. P. Putnam's Sons for the C. G. Jung Foundation, 1970.

Witt, R. E. *Isis in the Graeco-Roman World.* London, 1971.

Wyss, Karl. "Die Milch im Kultus der Griechen und Römer. In: *Religionsgeschichtliche Versuche und Vorarbeiten.* vol. 15, no. 2. Giessen: Töpelmann, 1914.

Other C. G. Jung Foundation Books
from Shambhala Publications

Absent Fathers, Lost Sons: The Search for Masculine Identity, by Guy Corneau.

★*The Child*, by Erich Neumann. Foreword by Louis H. Stewart.

Cross-Currents of Jungian Thought: An Annotated Bibliography, by Donald R. Dyer.

★*Depth Psychology and a New Ethic*, by Erich Neumann. Forewords by C. G. Jung, Gerhard Adler, and James Yandell.

Dreams, by Marie-Louise von Franz.

★*From Freud to Jung: A Comparative Study of the Psychology of the Unconscious*, by Liliane Frey-Rohn. Foreword by Robert Hinshaw.

A Guided Tour of the Collected Works of C. G. Jung, by Robert H. Hopcke. Foreword by Aryeh Maidenbaum.

Individuation in Fairy Tales, Revised Edition, by Marie-Louise von Franz.

In Her Image: The Unhealed Daughter's Search for Her Mother, by Kathie Carlson.

★*The Inner Child in Dreams*, by Kathrin Asper.

Knowing Woman: A Feminine Psychology, by Irene Claremont de Castillejo.

Lingering Shadows: Jungians, Freudians, and Anti-Semitism, edited by Aryeh Maidenbaum and Stephen A. Martin.

The Old Wise Woman: A Study of Active Imagination, by Rix Weaver. Introduction by C. A. Meier.

Patterns of Dreaming: Jungian Techniques in Theory and Practice, by James A. Hall, M.D. Foreword by Edward C. Whitmont.

Power and Politics: The Psychology of Soviet-American Partnership, by Jerome S. Bernstein. Forewords by Senator Claiborne Pell and Edward C. Whitmont, M.D.

The Way of All Women, by M. Esther Harding. Introduction by C. G. Jung.

The Wisdom of the Dream: The World of C. G. Jung, by Stephen Segaller and Merrill Berger.

Woman's Mysteries: Ancient and Modern, by M. Esther Harding. Introduction by C. G. Jung.

★Published in association with Daimon Verlag, Einsiedeln, Switzerland.